SOCIAL POLICY, WELFARE STATE,
AND CIVIL SOCIETY IN SWEDEN

VOLUME II

Sven E. O. Hort is Professor in Social Welfare at the College of Social Sciences, Seoul National University, Korea. He is an alumnus of Lund University. In Sweden he taught sociology at Linneaus and Södertörn universities.

Currently he is the chief editor of the Swedish journal *Arkiv. Tidskrift för samhällsanalys* and a deputy editor of *European Societies*. With Stein Kuhnle he is the author of "The Coming of East and South-East Asian Welfare States", *Journal of European Social Policy* (2000).

This work is an updated and enlarged edition in two volumes of Sven Hort's well-known and wide-ranging dissertation *Social Policy and Welfare State in Sweden*, published under the author's birth name Sven E. Olsson in 1990.

The first volume contains the original four essays and covers the formation and evolution of the Swedish welfare state 1884–1988.

In praise of the first edition:

"… takes us beyond simple analyses, emphasizing the deep historical roots of social democracy in Sweden and considering the role of ideas, the organization of politics, and the activities of social classes other than labor in building and securing Swedish social policy. Olsson's book presents a comprehensive overview of the development of the Swedish welfare state and a detailed consideration of several key episodes of welfare-state development."

– *American Journal of Sociology*

"This is a very scholarly and broad ranging analysis of the postwar Swedish welfare state … which is invaluable for comparative policy analysis."

– *Critical Social Policy*

"… essential reading for sociologists and political scientists."

– *Contemporary Sociology*

Sven E O Hort

Social Policy, Welfare State, and Civil Society in Sweden

Volume II

The Lost World of Social Democracy
1988–2015

Third enlarged edition

Arkiv Academic Press

Arkiv Academic Press is an imprint of

Arkiv förlag
MAILING ADDRESS Arkiv förlag, Box 1559, SE-221 01 Lund, Sweden
STREET ADDRESS Lilla Gråbrödersgatan 3 c, Lund
PHONE +46 (0) 46 13 39 20
arkiv@arkiv.nu
www.arkiv.nu

A list of Arkiv Academic Press titles can be found in the last
pages of this book. For up-to-date information on distribution
and available titles, please visit:

www.arkivacademicpress.com

This work is available in the following editions:
HARDCOVER: edition for the international market
PAPERBACK: edition for the international market
both by Arkiv Academic Press
DUTCH BINDING: edition for the Swedish market by Arkiv förlag

Cover design by Kicki Edgren Nyborg

© Sven E O Hort/Arkiv förlag 1990, 1993, 2014
First edition published by Arkiv förlag 1990 as
Social Policy and Welfare State in Sweden
(under the author's birth name Sven E Olsson)
Second enlarged edition 1993

Third enlarged, reset and revised edition in two volumes 2014 as
Social Policy, Welfare State, and Civil Society in Sweden

Volume II: *The Lost World of Social Democracy 1988–2015*
Arkiv Academic Press international paperback edition
For print information, see the back page of this copy
ISBN: 978 91 980854 6 4

For Rebecca

Contents of Volume II

Introduction. Tax-financed Welfare after the Latest Crisis

> At the end of the Short Twentieth Century the
> "Swedish Model" was in retreat even in its own
> country.
>
> Hobsbawn (1994). *The Age of Extremes: A History
> of the World, 1914–1991*, p. 411.

In politics, public discourse, and the social sciences, the recent triumphalism of the bellicose right, a number of scandals in tax-financed welfare programmes in Sweden, and signs of sectarian responses from the respectable left in Scandinavia, make it urgent to ask where the twenty-first century welfare state is headed, and why. Is it headed towards the Nordic model, towards "social Europe", or towards something entirely different that has perhaps not yet surfaced in another part of the world of welfare "as we know it"? In early 2013, a leading light of the global mainstream media, *The Economist*, presented the welfare state of Europe's far north as "the next supermodel". There is every reason to go beyond conventional wisdom and take a fresh look at the conclusions reached almost twenty-five years ago in *Social Policy and Welfare State in Sweden*, in its latest edition *Social Policy, Welfare State, and Civil Society in Sweden* (henceforth the first, foregoing, former, original, or preceding volume or book).

The basic question is: Where is the welfare state situated, right now, as both a worldly practice and a figure of secular thought? Moreover, where is the *model* welfare state standing – in space, the river of time, and cyberspace? Scandinavia of course comes to mind, along with the remarkable comeback of the Nordic model in the last decade. What about the course taken by Sweden, the Swedes, and their society – "the most successful society the world has ever known" according to *The Guardian* and reiterated in the international press in September 2010,

9

as a national election confirmed a somewhat unfamiliar political route already chosen in 2006, before the advent of yet another end of business and economic history?

Writing about Scandinavia, Eli Heckscher (1932) entered a reservation and he methodologically argued that researchers should not unnecessarily preoccupy themselves with "second rank" countries. This seems ironic in that the countries of the far north have been at the forefront of social inquiry. Scientific controversy has arisen between universalistic critics of Dano-, Finno-, Norwego-, or Swedocentrism and those particularists, close to a "family of nations" approach, who simultaneously recognize both substantial intra-Scandinavian differentiation, and the deviations of these second-rank countries from the general patterns of global societal development. Following the latter strategy, the aim here is to investigate the applicability of the *Sonderweg*, or exceptionalism, thesis to a time between two major crises. From the vantage point of a few years into the second decade of the third millennium, and seen not only through the lenses of the particular, but also of comparative welfare state research, we may ask what has happened over the last two decades to social policy and the welfare state. The question especially applies to the Swedish welfare state and practice – and to the adjacent though somewhat larger heuristic or normative Nordic or Scandinavian Model – at home, in the vicinity, and farther abroad. How has *civil society* come to challenge the welfare state? To invoke the ghost of the first book in the series Lund Studies in Social Welfare (Marklund 1988): Has Paradise been regained, finally lost, or is the venerable middle or third, even fourth, road to an earthly land of milk and honey still open?

Though these questions may sound provincial, provocative, perhaps even self-congratulatory, the issues they touch on are global, regional, and national as well as local. They concern human ambitions, desires, and expectations: hopes of living in decency and dignity, hunger for reciprocal human recognition and respect, and the vision of a secular "promised land" or society in which class and status distinctions of all kinds – from age and disability to race and gender – are reduced to a minimum. Taken together, these questions form the fundamental topic to be addressed in this separately published sequel to a series of articles written during the crisis of the welfare state in the 1980s, collected into a single volume over twenty years ago, and presented and defended as a Ph.D. thesis at Stockholm University on 6 June 1990.

In the early 1980s, the OECD had already proposed an alternative to this model welfare state: the (Japanese) welfare society, understood as civil society (Olsson 2013:244; the "original volume", separately reprinted in 2013). In 1990, at the beginning of the *decennium horribile* of the Swedish welfare state, the basic argument against the crisis thesis, or doomsday prophecy – the withering away of the welfare state – stated in the final page of the first book's introduction, was that the social policies in such states had institutionalized and regulated social justice – neither bare security nor pure equality – to such an extent that any attempt to scale down state-organized welfare had to take issue with a pattern of practices and knowledge much larger than the political party, or movement, usually associated with it (Olsson 1990:35). According to received wisdom, the sustainability of the welfare state rested, of course, on sound economic foundations and efficient organizational practices (a performing and regulated accumulation regime), and their legitimacy. Added to such social relationships were political and human social forces capable of creating broad popular support and of articulating the interests of a broad-based coalition – forces inferred by this author to be of utmost significance.

This combination of economics and politics accounts for the welfare state's present global reach (i.e., competitiveness in the realm of an increasingly singular modernity of thought and practices), though relegated as this model is, to a remote and deserted corner of the geophysical globe – a welfare state of the periphery, though not a peripheral welfare state as two colleagues once put it (Alestalo & Flora 1994). Whether these prerequisites remain in the aftermath of the financial meltdown of 2008, the ensuing global instability, as well as the Swedish national elections of September 2006 and 2010, clouded as the most recent election campaign and its outcome was by intolerance, is a matter of inquiry. However, outside the boundaries of its native continent and country, there is definitely hope for a future for this welfare state model, as attested to by growing worldwide interest in the Nordic model. This paradox of rising expectations and hope existing amid currents of pessimism runs through the coming pages. In view of the rapidly approaching 2014 general elections in Sweden, the hints given in this work are subject to change, debate, and reformulation.

For the sake of argument, and to explore the future of the democratic, egalitarian, institutional, solidaristic, and/or universal welfare state, in particular the Scandinavian welfare society, these afterthoughts on a project started in the late 1970s initially take one or two steps backwards. Since the start of the project, the river of time has flowed on and the worlds and peoples of welfare have changed significantly in both composition – form as well as content – and direction. To stress a point made but perhaps insufficiently emphasized in the introduction to the first volume, it would be pedantic to overload these notes with a theoretical apparatus only the most orthodox devotees would be interested in today; the credibility of the language of social science "thin rationality" has gone as have so many other seemingly coherent methodological paradigms. Following a "public sociology" approach (Clawson et al. 2007), the true reconfiguration of this field is both an academic and a social-political dilemma, during this period defined not least by the longest revolution of the second sex in an intransigent civilizing process simultaneously coordinated, over-determined, embedded, and subsumed by class and power competing for immaterial and material resources (Mitchell 1966; also evident in the present author's change of surname; cf. Hort 2013).

Narrowing the perspective somewhat, the social sciences are chained to the contemporary world not least through the big business of peer-reviewed academic publishing, and even their most rigorous and detached sociological practitioners are not unfettered creatures justifiably claiming innocence. Their various branches parcel up social inquiry in such a way as usually to prevent the underlying determinants and dynamics of social formation from coming into full view. The original "Introduction" in the first book touched on the analytical issues involved in comparative welfare state research and hinted at the most obvious theoretical and methodological interdependencies and connections between the four articles included in the first and second editions. The respective starting-points and immediate universes of the four articles were then elaborated upon. However, further exploration of the surrounding scholarly landscape had to wait for the postscript to the second edition of the book (Olsson 1993:349–85). This is why these afterthoughts start where they do, replacing a twenty-year-old and in many respects outdated postscript. Nevertheless, some, but not many, themes from that sequel are repeated in the coming pages. Methodologically, this work is based on its predecessor's approach, here pursued rather flexible (see appendix).

These afterthoughts consist of five main chapters, apart from this introduction, and a few concluding remarks related to the matrix of enquiry, i.e., the initial questions posed in the first paragraph of this essay, the questions guiding four of the five separate chapters (chapters 2–5), and, not least, the questions shaping the original articles of the first book (henceforth chapters I–IV together with their "Introduction").

As a guide to the reader, I note that the following chapters can be read separately, as was the case with the four chapters initially comprising the first volume. Of course, these chapters could be read in their original sequence (see the general introduction to that book), as can the following chapters, particularly chapters 2–4, which are connected by the notions of imagined local or national welfare communities (ILWC or INWC, respectively) and common pool resource (CPR) institutions.

The first chapter, "Mapping Comparative Welfare State Research", on the political sociology of welfare, contextualizes the themes and topics of the other chapters through the lens of global comparison and asks where comparative welfare state research stands at the start of the second decade of the third millennium. The second chapter, "The Social Welfare–Industrial Complex: Social Policy and Programmes, 1990–2014", investigates the social policies and programmes, typical and atypical, of the Swedish welfare state, while the third chapter, "The Lost World of the Social Democratic Welfare Regime Type, 1988–2014", approaches the agents and institutions of this state through broader macro-constellations: demographic, economics, politics and power similar to those treated in section 4 of chapter III in the preceding volume.

Analytically, these afterthoughts enter chapter 2 at the meso-level, chapter 3 looks into the macro-foundations of the welfare state, while chapter 4 operates at the micro-level of modern human society. Chapter 4, "Civil Society: Challenging the Welfare State since the 1990s", delves into civil society, a guiding principle of the original book's first chapter and a nascent subject in Swedish academic discourse, though rapidly growing in terms of output in the last two decades – the key to any critical exploration of the new welfare model. The temporal relationships between the three main motives – social policy, the welfare state, and civil society – are illustrated in figure 1 (see also p. 170).

Any sober analysis of the present situation concludes that the old regime is gone, though not the "tax state", and another not yet solidly established (cf. Lindbom 2011). Once a visionary blueprint for a new society, today this provisional utopia exists only as a reminder of times past and as resistance to an emerging order. Somewhat paradoxically, in Scandinavia the near-universal welfare state has proven sustainable and the crisis-ridden newcomer bears the marks of a vulnerable and precarious entity. In this interregnum, new modes of operation are also emerging, retrogressive as well as experimental. It is from such a platform that laboratory trials are taking place, carried out by more or less careful and discreet actors – blue turncoats as well as red plutocrats, not to mention green idealists, grey realists, active or passive (counter)revolutionaries, and born-again evangelists, to name a few.

Figure 1. Conceptual map: Parallel temporalities of social policy, welfare state and (civil) society

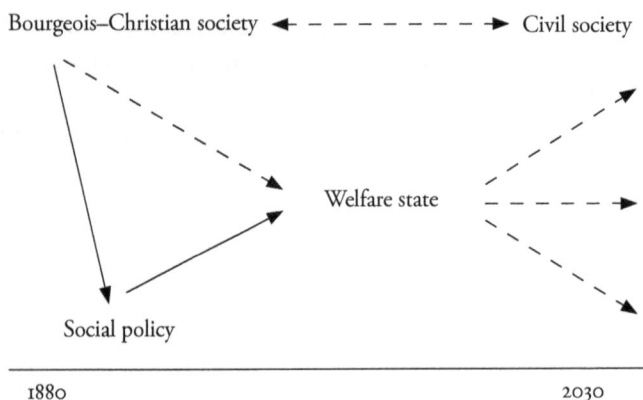

The fifth chapter, "A Republican–Secular Society under the Umbrella of the Nordic Model?", steps out of the local Northern context and focuses on the remarkable global spread of the Nordic model over the last decade. Throughout, the tone and approach in these chapters is one of scepticism with no reference to a not-so-golden past. The golden age is in us, as the late and great Irish-American contrarian Alexander Cockburn reminded us (1995; cf. Bull 1995). To end, I conclude with a few still preliminary observations on the interdependency of the welfare society and the social welfare state between and after two crises, the first being the crisis of the early 1990s, the second relating to the 2008 global/American meltdown and its European aftermath, which in the spring of 2013 has perhaps reached its Eurozone nadir. My aim is to contribute, although modestly, to an emerging Eurasian republic of letters on the future of current social formations in a far older human but nonlinear civilizing process.

1. Mapping Comparative Welfare State Research

> Historically the welfare state is a rather recent but nonetheless extremely influential social invention. It has fundamentally transformed relations between the state and its citizens – both as individuals and members of social groups, that is, classes, generations and sexes.
>
> Stephan Leibfried and Steffen Mau (2008). "Introduction" in *Welfare States: Construction, Deconstruction, Reconstruction*, p. xi.

At the time of the original publication of the first book, two books framed much of the discussion in history and social sciences in the 1990s: Peter Baldwin's magisterial *The Politics of Social Solidarity: Class Bases of the European Welfare States, 1875–1975* (1990), whose interpretation of the Swedish case was discussed in some detail in chapter II in the preeeding volume, and a book by Danish-American sociologist Gösta Esping-Andersen, *The Three Worlds of Welfare Capitalism* (1990), which set the tone for the rest of the decade for the theoretical debate about welfare models or regime types. Esping-Andersen coined the notion of the "social democratic welfare state", whose sociological imagination rested on another concept, decommodification (cf. Olsson 1993). In this project, Sweden was singled out from 18 advanced welfare states as the model regime type, although in slightly less enthusiastic language than in his earlier intra-Scandinavian comparison *Politics Against Markets* (1985). The influential works of Esping-Andersen are part of a common heritage to be included in a wider stream of research into the varieties of capitalism that gained momentum with the end of the cold war, in many respects replacing the societal standoff between capitalism and socialism (Hall & Soskice 2001; see also Esping-Andersen 1996, 2009, et al. 2002). Given the end of socialism and rise of a

Washington D C consensus, perhaps a fourth book ought to be added to this canon, Paul Pierson's *Dismantling the Welfare State* (1994).

This Northern nexus of West versus East is the starting point of *comparative welfare state research* in history and the social sciences, a fairly recent branch of social research focusing on social policy. This project, which has yet to fully encompass the present world beyond the North–West axis, can be divided diachronically into three consecutive periods or generations of research, and synchronically into a diverse set of subcategories depending on, for instance, disciplinary orientation and scholarly creativity (cf. Castles et al. 2010; and Leibfried & Mau 2008). Three "generational shifts" structure these notional and factual considerations concerning the engagement between citizenship, social rights, and the political economy of the welfare state. In this way, the inherent conceptual ambiguity already hinted at in the notion of the welfare state will again be highlighted, this time from the vantage point of the present conjuncture of (creative) reconstruction. Optimism of the intelligence has so far been the hallmark of this research current.

First-generation welfare state studies and their research objects

Once the subjects of kings, queens, cardinals, and archbishops, feudal ladies, and landowning squires, today modern female and male citizens and denizens, belong to fairly well-defined communities under the nation-state umbrella. They are former bondmen and bondwomen made free – free to buy and sell most commodities (including labour power), free at the ballot box, as well as free to organize, mobilize, and voice their concerns through a number of national institutions, including before supposedly independent courts and judges ("the rule of law") – and are even allowed to exit, if not enter, such institutions as legal residents within defined geopolitical boundaries. Mutual dependency and loyalty thus also have their limits, and states are still sovereign and supreme organizations that reflect the distribution of power between and within particular territories, where state machinery exerts coercive control and political authority to extract resources from those living within their boundaries, whether citizens or subjects, rural or urban residents. Welfare intersecting with citizens and denizens is not only equated with individual welfare – human lives of decency and dignity, or their dialectical opposite, as well as more or less formalized and institutionalized citizenship rights or entitlements and their obverse, obligations – but also encapsulates social welfare, the wellbeing of society as a whole and its members, whether citizens or denizens, national or imperial, and the allocation of resources following the social patterning of such societies.

In a state- and nation-building biography, the amalgamation of *welfare* and *state* is of recent origin, suggesting that this sense of welfare is still not as self-evident as is a judicially and territorially defined state and its human members. Philologically the connotations of welfare differ between Europe and the United States of North America, and these two continental significations are in unequal competition in the age of the present Empire. Hence, despite the fact that "to ... promote the general Welfare" is listed in the Preamble of the Constitution as one of the six fundamental purposes of the government of the United States, the connotations of welfare are closely connected to institutionalized help for poor people, and the poor alone as a select target group whether deserving or undeserving (e.g., gendered as "welfare queens"). In Europe, on the other hand, welfare comprises institutionalized support for the population at large or the workforce in a broad sense. Compassionate liberal-conservatives commonly complain that the welfare state punishes the diligent and rewards the idle, while it transforms everyone into subservient taxpayers and dependent clients of government. On the other hand, ideologues of other persuasions, nationalistic and/or "cosmopolitistic", may advocate state intervention to reduce poverty, invoking the common cause and strength of communality and reciprocity between proximate peoples (an understanding recently accorded the status of exact science in the memory of Alfred Nobel; see Ostrom 1990). Welfare exists on a scale between "fare well" and "misfortune" – i.e., fare poorly – tinged with the derogatory "wine and such welfare" (Williams 1976:332).

While the etymology of welfare reflects the quite different paths of human reciprocity and official support in Western Europe and United States – with Imperial Britain or "Ukania" somewhere in between – the continental European welfare state grew out of conscious institutional and political efforts to minimize the ascendancy of the working-class movement, in particular in Germany, where these efforts are referred to as the "social policies/politics of the state" (*Sozialpolitik* and *Sozialstaat*).

In 1870–1871, the victorious nation-building chancellor Otto von Bismarck and his counsellors were able to see the strengths of defeated

France, not only its centralized state but also its mutual or friendly societies (social insurance institutions, in France later *l'etat providence*). For a year or so, Prussia encircled Paris, stole many of its grand projects, made them even more magnificent, and established them as part of the Wilhelmine Second Reich (Clark 2007; cf Englund 2007). A modified, adapted form of this workerist social model – which in Germany was *not* citizenship based – was adopted in neighbouring Scandinavia early on and reached as far as Imperial Japan (if not to occupied Korea). Across the political spectrum from right to left, the proponents of social insurance mustered strength and invoked inspiration. For Bismarck, the organizational features of the French voluntary institutions became role models for top–down compulsory, risk-preventing state agencies. In the European working-class movement, industrial safety institutions – labour inspectorates – and occupational injury insurance came first. Gradually, industrialists also became proponents of joint compulsory schemes rather than individual enterprise welfare – or none at all. From this time onwards, social insurance programmes – industrial injury and sickness insurance as well as old age pensions – emerged across Europe and became a major topic among state administrators and policy-makers in Berlin as well as Vienna, St. Petersburg, Rome, and back again in Paris. In London, state support for unemployment insurance gained prominence through the efforts of William Beveridge, among others. In the far north of Europe, too, particularly in Denmark, this type of institutional set-up emerged and soon expanded, both towards the citizenship approach and into related policy areas such as housing, medical care, and education. Intertwined with the above-mentioned social insurance programmes, the Danish arrangement was later to form the basis of the reputation of the Scandinavian or Nordic welfare model or laboratory (Alestalo et al. forthc.). In the first half of the twentieth century, social insurance institutions spread around the world, at first glance fairly randomly from Australia to Uruguay. By 1921, the International Social Security Association (ISSA) was founded with headquarters in Geneva adjacent to the tripartite International Labour Organization (ILO).

Leaving aside for a moment the truly global ILO-ISSA complex as well as Scandinavia in the search for the lineages of the national universal welfare state, such more or less comprehensive social policies were imported from New Zealand at the periphery and recast at the centre of the British Empire – the Beveridgean welfare state of Thomas

Humphrey Marshall and Richard Titmuss and its citizenship model – at a time when state-organized social protection not only for soldiers but also for mothers and workers was making decisive inroads in North America with FDR's New Deal (Skocpol 1995). In Joseph Schumpeter's words (1943) and conflictual world, capitalism, socialism, and democracy went hand in hand in creative construction. In the USA of the late 1930s, social insurance was renamed social security, a term that has become the trademark of social protection for workers and other employees and their families throughout the non-colonial world in particular. Under the heading of social security, five branches – (1) occupational injury insurance, (2) old age pensions, (3) sickness and maternity benefits, (4) unemployment insurance, and (5) a fairly loose set of family support programmes, including the general child allowance – were lumped together into a more or less coherent universalist whole (SSA 1939 onwards; various editions). These were serialized by social researchers into successive "stages" or sequences of welfare state development, also including more preventive and proactive measures (Flora & Alber 1981). From its inception, the idea of the (national) welfare state has oscillated between a more comprehensive or universal approach, on the one hand, and – to varying degrees – a selective social safety-net approach, on the other, featuring in some cases poor relief (i.e., welfare handouts) and what is called, also in the former First World, by the euphemistic term "anti-poverty programmes".

This artefact was to succeed in the First World of the post-War era more or less in full, as in North-Western Europe, or sometimes only partially, as in the USA, which, pre-Obama, lacked compulsory health insurance, still lacks a universal child allowance programme, and where a 2012 Supreme Court decision sheds light on a class society in which the workers' movement has become a prisoner of the American dream (cf. Davis 1986). Social security also became a distinctive feature of the social system of the second (i.e., communist) world, where the right to a job at least in theory, in particular for men, made unemployment insurance unnecessary (Aidukaite 2004). In the shadow of the Soviet Union, from 1951 onwards, the People's Republic of China also developed a social safety system though with a certain rural poor relief twist: the iron rice bowl. With the advent of the Cold War and competition between the First and Second worlds, the developing Third World became fertile ground for the proponents of social security, although success was often more limited there than in the more developed parts of the world. Outside the core of welfare capitalism and state social-ism, the Indian state of Kerala has often been cited as an early exam-ple of public welfare institution-building (cf. Heller 1997). Later on, a more amicable convergence between these two societal models was conceived, in which economic growth was the ultimate cause of welfare state development, partly explaining the absence of countries such as China and India from the early "industrialization paradigm".

The patterning of the worldwide growth of social insurance or social security institutions became the successful object of Harold Wilensky's pioneering study *The Welfare State and Equality: Structural and Ideo-logical Roots of Public Expenditure* (1975), the foremost example of first-generation welfare state studies. Wilensky, the dean of this paradigm, included the operations of the Washington-based HEW (Department of Health, Education and Welfare of the Federal Administration) in his international dataset, which consisted of 1966 national social and mili-tary expenditure and GDP figures. From the start, therefore, empiri-cal comparative welfare state research has been fairly global in scope, though it never explored the commonalities and details of the more peripheral national welfare state types. *The Welfare State and Equality* spanned all five continents (China being represented by the ROC, i.e., Taiwan) and included data on social spending and social welfare pro-grammes in 64 countries ranging from Australia – with its subjects of the British Queen – to newly independent post-colonial Zambia with its free citizens, a member of the Commonwealth.

In its principal analysis, however, Wilensky's sample was narrowed to focus on the 22 most advanced states. The latter included the core West and North European countries, Israel, Canada and the USA in North America, three Eastern European countries (i.e., Czechoslovakia, GDR, and the USSR), and Australia and New Zealand in the Pacific. Japan was number 23 on the list, intermittently replacing Iceland in the empirical analysis. This work captured the geography of the world's advanced welfare states in 1966. In conceptual terms, Wilensky dis-tinguished between four types of welfare states: democratic (31 coun-tries with India at the end of the premier league; Wilensky 1975:138, table 8), totalitarian (eight countries; the Soviet bloc plus Yugoslavia but not the People's Republic of China), authoritarian oligarchic coun-tries including Taiwan (17 countries), and authoritarian populist states (eight countries). The last two authoritarian types were not really part of his analysis, and very little was said about the differences between the first two apart from their most obvious Cold War aspects. Overall, he stressed the similarity, or convergence, of the core welfare states.

This was the era of the disarmament agreements and of détente between West and East, including the Helsinki human rights settlement (see also Mishra 1976). On the other hand, the countries of the East and West differed in their organization of benefits and services, not to mention levels of spending. In 1966, the United States ranked top in GDP per capita, closely followed by Sweden, Iceland, Switzerland, and Canada, while Upper Volta, Burma, India, Pakistan, and Cameroon were the bottom five of the 64 ranked countries. Regrouped by social security spending as a percentage of GDP, Austria came out on top in 1966 at 21 per cent, followed by the Federal Republic of Germany, France, and the Netherlands, with Italy, Luxemburg, and Sweden sharing the fifth position at 17.5 per cent, while Pakistan (0.6 per cent), Syria (1.0 per cent), Honduras (1.1 per cent), Burma (1.1 per cent), and Iraq (1.2 per cent) made up the bottom group, slightly below India at 1.4 per cent (Wilensky 1975:122–24). It is no coincidence that the sequel, published twenty-seven years later, was entitled *Rich Democracies* (Wilensky 2002). Again, not only the bottom group but also middle-income countries were omitted from the empirical analysis of the (Western) world of welfare. The new world of welfare was fading at a time of immense global restructuring, and the road was blocked to those on their way up. In a remarkable reversal, the research object of this tradition had become inward-looking.

Second-generation welfare state studies and their research objects

The European reaction among comparative welfare state researchers against Wilensky's North American global analysis was intense. Indeed, it was challenged by a considerable number of scholars, in particular from West German and Scandinavian universities and research institutes (i.e., Flora & Heidenheimer 1981), who argued that social security expenditure figures said little about welfare state developments. The decommodification concept, originally launched by Claus Offe (1984), was proposed, indexed, and popularized as an alternative analytical starting-point with Gösta Esping-Andersen's seminal *The Three Worlds of Welfare Capitalism* (1990), a work that in many ways summarized the research following in the wake of Wilensky. This book is the most widely quoted – and read – example of second-generation comparative welfare state research, in which the conventional sample had shrunk to eighteen or fewer Western countries. Japan was included, Israel gone and, most importantly, Eastern European countries, of the totalitarian type, had completely disappeared as had the rest of the world including Deng's China and Gandhi's India. For instance, twelve Western European countries were documented and analysed in Peter Flora's monumental but never-finished *Growth to Limits: The West European Welfare State Since World War II* (1986–1987) and its parallel data handbook *State, Economy and Society in Western Europe 1815–1975* (1983–87). The latter tried to measure nation building and state formation by scrutinizing national administrative statistics from throughout Western Europe and making them truly comparative to an extent never done before, while the analysis of this collection of mass data never came to full fruition. A harbinger was released early on by Flora's close comrade, Jens Alber, in his *Vom Armenhaus zum Wohlfartsstaat* (1982), a book never translated into English though part of the comparative canon.

Whether the welfare state had reached its true potential – decommodification – or its limits in terms of spending and personnel, however, was overshadowed by the reconfiguration of the world outside the research laboratory. Nevertheless, Alber's insistence on a single, though controversial, successful welfare state, Flora's comparative Western European focus extending from North (Scandinavia) to South (Italy), and Esping-Andersen's (and Korpi's) larger Western–Pacific sample must in retrospect be considered a foundation for the shift to the "varieties of capitalism" approach that followed in the wake of first- and second-generation comparative welfare state research. Europe in contrast to the United States, not only as a single market, but as an entity in its own right with the prospect of an ever tighter social union, and later also the possibility of enlargement into the former East, became a major subject of thought at this time. At a time of neoliberal triumph, the social investment state gradually returned by the back door with the end of the Cold War (cf. Morel, Pallier & Palme 2011).

Western mass democracy – in particular, universal suffrage, electoral support and trade union strength – had become a key indicator in selecting research objects, although the decline in social development in Eastern Europe and parts of the Third World should not be forgotten. Instead of convergence, differences among the Western welfare states were emphasized, in particular among those who followed fairly closely in the steps of Esping-Andersen. Set against the Anglo-Saxon liberal male-breadwinner welfare model of the UK and USA, with the latter's tenor of welfare in particular, and thus no (heuristic) model at all, entered two other welfare regimes and their elaborations. On the one hand was the hierarchical and stratified continental or conservative traditional family-oriented welfare state, in West Germany in particular, and, on the other, the archetypical welfare state, the egalitarian and women-friendly Scandinavian or social democratic model with its state-feminist, gender-equality approach (i.e., Liera 1993; Lewis 1992). As already mentioned in the introduction to volume I, and worth emphasising again, Theda Skocpol's contributions to this research current cannot be underestimated. She was an early and sharp critic of the Swedocentrists, and several of her associates also made innovative analyses in the study of social policy and gendered welfare regimes (e.g. Orloff 1999 and Quadagno 1994). It was in this milieu the paradigmatic journal Social Politics appeared in 1994.

Early on a fourth, "lib/lab" model was mooted but never fully materialized (cf. Chung & Muntaner 2007). This was followed by a special Southern European model – a second-class version of the conservative–continental model – and a few years into the 1990s, by a no longer structural or totalitarian but post-socialist model in Baltic, Central, and Eastern Europe (Aidukaite 2009a and b). This model building with 18 cases or fewer ended up in five different model regimes with an "encompassing model" representing the ultimate welfare state. So far the latter is the most elaborate version from the dataset, taking account of welfare coverage, redistribution, and citizenship rights; it was created in Stockholm by Walter Korpi, and the data were collected by him and his many collaborators over more than three decades (Korpi & Palme 2003). In this world of models and regime types, Japan was always an outlier, unique or hybrid, though in many respects close to the German model (Dore 2000; Esping-Andersen 1997). At the start of the epoch of the spectacle, comparative welfare state research turned inwards, towards the North and the Far North, at a time when the outside world was going truly global.

Before turning to third-generation comparative welfare state studies, another growing stream of global social research should briefly be mentioned: the civil society literature. As mentioned, in the wake of Wilensky's work, the OECD initiated a project on welfare states, the growth of the public sector, and social expenditure (OECD 1981). Wilensky himself was a contributor to the OECD volume, which in the end advocated the Japanese welfare society – a blend of occupational and voluntary welfare, in the Titmussian terminology, in which farmers were the only group under the umbrella of state (and ruling party) social protection – as an alternative to the European welfare state. This was at the height of the Japanese miracle, long before its drawn-out regression.

Welfare society can of course also be understood as civil society, which at that time otherwise conceptually came to the fore in Central and Eastern Europe as a critique of the existing Soviet system, and in Latin America as a critique of the military dictatorships. Civil society had, as mentioned in the introduction to and the fourth chapter of the first book, a prehistory dating back to the Scottish enlightenment and continuing into the contemporary "new Scottish enlightenment" (Ascherson 2000; Goody 1998). In the 1980s, this current came to occupy a respected position among those Western social researchers affiliated with or close to both Eastern European dissidents and Latin American critics. The relationship between civil and political society was a key dilemma in this research stream.

This was also the case in Scandinavia, where the notion of civil society developed as part of a critique of existing socialism or "social-democraticism" (or welfare) and of the shortcomings of various failed attempts at radical insurgency in Latin America, finally to reach into an explicitly social-conservative research paradigm. The civil society concept actually came to be part of an international self-critique of the radical reform agenda through a statist strategy most obvious in the works of Cohen and Arato (1992). However, the civil society challenge with its emphasis on voluntarism never reached into the core of comparative welfare state research or, as stated by two Swedish civil society researchers, Jeppsson Grassman and Svedberg (2007:145), "it is striking how systematically the voluntary and informal sectors have been overlooked or ignored when analyzing welfare". While the civil society literature often borrowed from and explicitly referred to second-generation comparative welfare state research, the opposite was seldom the case. In addition, in the most recent handbook of comparative welfare state research the absence of any engagement with the civil society literature is striking; there is not even an entry for civil society in the index (Castles et al. 2010). Moreover, this handbook does not even hint at the possibility of various imagined – welfare – communities.

Varieties of third-generation welfare state studies: globality and sustainability

Since the early 1990s, the geography of comparative welfare state research has changed dramatically. Globalization, and in particular global formal democratization if not global citizenship, has put its mark on social research in this field of inquiry as it has tried to escape from the prison-house of the three (North-Western/Pacific) worlds and back to the world beyond such conceptual limits. An inward-looking research community turned outward towards the details and patterns of the more peripheral national welfare states. Outside this community, capitalism with a neoliberal face had caught the imagination of the elite professions with the advent of the Reagan and Thatcher regimes, and as institutional public practice it was further advanced, particularly in the Third World, from the late 1970s, most notably in East and South-East Asia (Chang et al. 2012, Woo 2007, Therborn & Khondker 2006, Anderson 1998).

Later, it was not only that the welfare systems of the former Second World were challenged by this ideological and social force; it should also be remembered that welfare states such as Finland and Sweden were on the brink of fiscal collapse in the early 1990s. This was the *decennium horribile* of the post-war advanced welfare state when, even in Europe, existing welfare systems were pruned and privatized (Schubert et al. 2009, Gilbert 2002). At the end of the Cold War, the *sustainability* of the welfare state was an issue that attracted growing attention from social scientists as well as contemporary politicians and pundits, whether on the left or right. While much of the discussion naturally took place in the West – in the USA, federal welfare "as we know it" was dissolved – it is also pertinent to recall the IMF's and World Bank's structural adjustment programmes in the Third World and their intentional downsizing of the public sector, including education and health programmes, not to mention infant social security schemes (Gough et al. 2004; see also Deacon et al. 1997 and Ahmad et al. 1991). The debate gained momentum with the collapse of the Second World and the eastward enlargement of the European Union (Offe 2009). For instance, in neighbouring Latvia – previously one of the Baltic republics of the USSR – social administrators or welfare engineers from Sweden were able to test a new, market-friendly and slimmed-down defined-contribution pension system under the auspices of the World Bank before it was implemented at home.

Academic economists in particular, but also some political scientists and sociologists, held that the idea of the welfare state became too costly and inflexible when the global race to the bottom began in earnest after the fall of the Berlin Wall (Alber & Standing 2000). New regime types, such as the insecurity and poverty regimes, reappeared and posed questions about the possibility of growth without welfare (cf. Breman 2007). Out of this conundrum came, on the one hand, the post-socialist welfare regime type closely resembling the Southern European model of the previous decade and, on the other hand, the concept of the developmental welfare state in East Asia with its new broad-based, "productivist" social programmes such as health and old age pension insurance (Kwon & Kim 2012; Abrahamson 2011; Kuhnle 2011; Kwon 2005). Most of this "comparative turn" was captured by the social science research community included in Leibfried and Mau's three-volume work *Welfare States: Construction, Deconstruction, Reconstruction* (2008) – a thorough summation of a research industry that exploded after 1990 – or in third-generation comparative welfare state research transcending the 64/22-nation world of 1966 to encompass almost half of the 192 United Nations member states at the dawn of the third millennium, in which most of the above-mentioned social researchers appear (ranging from Alber to Wilensky; Breman, Chang, Kim, Kwon, and Muntaner being the exceptions), writing on the new worlds of welfare and insecurity.

The present period is still too recent to permit any definite judgments. In Europe, it is the relationship between the national welfare states and the Social Union that has attracted the attention of comparatists (Falkner 2010; see also Ferrera 2009). Following the fairly recent period of the politics of retrenchment and permanent austerity – deconstruction or the initial phase of the global neoliberal regime – the most recent discussions of the sustainability of the welfare state and the contemporary dilemmas facing various social actors in this arena are framed as "reconstruction" (in contrast to the initial construction). Controversy over indicators faded, as did the exclusive focus on de/recommodifying regime types, giving way to a multiplicity of analytical approaches to the necessity and possibility of a new welfare state differing from the insecurity/poverty regime. At a time when neoliberal assumptions were being overturned, a new question emerged with the demise of Lehman Brothers. If "how sustainable is the welfare state" was the question of Leibfried and Mau (2008, p. xii) we are now allowed to ask: Is the new global political economy – the still fairly loose and incomplete integration and reconfiguration of the First, Second, and Third worlds – sustainable without either some kind of "global welfare programmes" or institutionalized, encompassing national social welfare states?

Of course, the matter of Greece and the sustainability of the PIIGS (i.e., Portugal, Ireland, Italy, Greece, and Spain), 2010–2012, comes to mind. Haggard and Kaufmann's *Development, Democracy and Welfare States: Latin America, East Asia and Eastern Europe* (2008) signals the advent of a preoccupation with such questions in the three worlds of welfare outside the old centre, though the treatment is still constrained, being a mirror-image of its analytical prototype, *The Three Worlds of Welfare Capitalism* (Esping-Andersen 1990). Recently, another avenue has been proposed by scholars focusing on the relationships between corruption, inequality, social trust, and the welfare state (Rothstein 2011; cf also Charron et al. 2013, Halleröd et al. 2013, Klitgaard 2012, Rothstein & Uslander 2005). How powerful this avenue may turn out to be is still an open question, this research still being in its infancy. So far only Western Europe and a few other advanced countries have developed more or less sufficient systems of impartial social protection and child-, family-, and work-friendly welfare policies, although significant steps have been taken in such countries and territories as South Korea and Taiwan (Ringen et al. 2011; Wong 2004; Son 2002; Hort & Kuhnle 2000). Some Latin American countries are other cases in point (Barrientos & Santibanez 2009; see also Huber, Mustillo & Stephens 2008, Draibe & Riesco 2007, and Huber & Stephens 2005). However, South Africa is a country where segregated subjects are on their way to being emancipated into citizens by a Leninist-led national movement in power pursuing more or less neoliberal welfare policies far from the early twentieth century ambitions of the international working-class movement (cf. Olivier & Kuhnle 2008). Where the other BASIC/BRIC/BIC countries (i.e., Brazil, India, China, and ex- or including Russia and South Africa) or more recently the CIVETS countries (i.e., Columbia, Indonesia, Vietnam, Egypt, Turkey, and, again, South Africa; there are other combinations including, e.g., Mexico) are heading is of considerable interest to this research current (cf. Carrillo Garcia 2012).

These issues will be revisited in chapter 5 at the end of these after-thoughts. In the meantime (see chapters 2–4), the focus will be on one of the model welfare states of the far north of Europe – Sweden – set within a Eurasian and global sociological context of organizational macro-systems and cautiously civilizing but commodified, embedded, recalcitrant, stratified and, we may perhaps add with Leibfried and Mau, sustainable processes.

2. The Social Welfare–Industrial Complex: Social Policy and Programmes 1990–2014

> The Nordic countries reduced the income replacement provided by various social insurance programs and also cut spending on public services in the early 1990s, but reforms of the welfare state were far more circumscribed than the deregulatory reforms ... Budgetary pressures rather than market-liberal ideas clearly constituted the primary motivation behind these reforms, and spending cuts were restored as economic growth picked up in the second half of the 1990s.
>
> Jonas Pontusson (2011). "Once again a Model", p. 106.

Introduction: the sustainability of the welfare state

Is the welfare state sustainable? Has the welfare state survived in Sweden? The answers to these questions, as several observers have concluded since the late 1990s, are undoubtedly "yes" (for an early verdict, see Kuhnle 2000; see also Lindbom & Rothstein 2005). Furthermore, the previous chapter ended with Leibfried and Mau's (2008) assertion that the sustainability of the welfare state is the most salient feature of the contemporary comparative research canon. Moreover, the reappearance of the Nordic model on the international scene is another obvious indicator of this phenomenon, which will be revisited in chapter 5 below. However, the domestic answer may be qualified in various ways, as the Swedish State Welfare Commission – under the leadership of Joakim Palme and with significant contributions from his equally qualified colleagues – did a decade ago; the Commission was primarily interested in policy outcomes, although it did follow conventional delimitations of policy areas.

Full employment, one of the cornerstones of the model, was not restored from mass-unemployment during the course of the decade. Also, the active labor market policy, which is often associated with the full-employment strategy, could not accommodate the rapid increase in unemployment. When it comes to social policy, the large number of changes that made provisions less generous is perhaps the most characterising feature of the 1990s. Yet it would be misleading to conclude that the model has been abandoned. Universal social services and benefits, as well as earnings-related social insurances, are still dominating the system. However, a number of decisions, as well as non-decisions, might trigger more systematic change in the longer run by changing the interest formation around social policy institutions. It might be that non-decisions that are most important in a model-perspective. As ceilings in most systems are not changed, and real wages increase, this means that an increasing number of citizens have earnings above the ceilings. This in turn might in the long run transform the earnings-related system into a flat-rate one, presumably shifting the responsibility of insurance to private schemes ... the sustainability of the particularities of the Swedish model of welfare remains an open question. (Palme et al. 2002:15–16)

Following another decade of austerity, during which cutbacks, deregulation, recalibration, and retrenchment have not been entirely absent, more such measures were to be added than the Commission could have predicted at the time. However, the focus here is on the policy input side. One way to make the picture more diverse, yet somewhat more complete, is to look at all or most of the policies, programmes, and schemes of the welfare state (defined here as the input side) before turning to the policy outcome and redistributive output. The most recent international overview of the entire body of welfare state research singled out twelve policy areas and four policy outcomes for scrutiny (Castles et al. 2010, whose definition of input slightly differs from the one established here). This chapter has merged most of these areas into cruder entities, largely following the central–local intra-state dialectic and its historical roots in Sweden. These are: selective active employment programmes including support for farmers, income maintenance including passive unemployment support (i.e., social security), needs-based human investment programmes ranging from education to terminal care, and the ways and means of financing this social welfare–industrial complex. Most likely, only a meteorite impact could seriously alter this globally admired system before the election year of 2014.

First, I offer an introductory note on the human communities that constitute this multitude or benefits, benefactors, beneficiaries, and services.

The imagined communities of the social welfare–industrial complex

The social programmes and policies analyzed in this chapter constitute the core of what is hereafter termed the social welfare–industrial complex (SWIC colloquialy) of the *imagined national welfare community (or INWC)* of Sweden. These programmes bind and bond beneficiaries, citizens, clients, denizens, taxpayers, wage-earners, workers, and voters with the well-known institutional set-up of the welfare state, comprising, for example, the Employment Service (once AMS, now Af) or the (Social) Insurance Office (Fk, according to Swedish abbreviations). Other institutions that have joined this complex within the last few years are the Pension Authority and a network of authorities and enforced voluntarism associated with the political–agribusiness complex, which has often been forgotten in the social policy literature. Such pooled resources and programmes serve to deepen and strengthen social relationships. In addition, advanced societies as manmade artefacts existing under historically given conditions are characterized by robust horizontal human relationships, despite abiding and durable social or vertical inequality between members of different social classes and categories in the contemporary post-peasant/proletarian era (cf. Tilly 1998). The boundaries are elastic, even inclusive and plastic some would argue; however, the INWC is usually limited to one national community, even though the farmlands of European Union (EU) rurality have been Europeanized and imagined because the members never personally know or meet most of their fellow cultivators. In the mind of each beneficiary, citizen, client, denizen, taxpayer, and voter is the image of a sovereign governable communion of belonging.

In short, this is the wamparish interpretation of a thirty-year-old analytical tool for grasping nationhood and nationality, used here to illuminate the mechanisms underlying welfare and the society–state relationship in Sweden (Anderson 2006; see also Nairn 2003). Moreover, it is through the existence of an additional number of imagined *local* welfare communities (or ILWCs) – another wamparish interpretation, this time of the original ideas of human bonding through common pool resource (CPR) institutions (Ostrom 1990) – that many of the social programmes examined here are reified to community residents, or denizens. The boundaries between ILWC and INWC are porous, and even more so are those between ILWC and CPR, as their memberships are constantly overlapping (cf. also Streeck & Schmitter 1985). All over the country, denizens are categorized as adolescents, adopted (children), adults, bi-, homo-, hetero-, or trans-sexuals, business(wo)men, children, disabled, dying, elderly, employable, employees, employers, self-employed, farmers, women, library visitors, men, students, or youths; in the prenatal clinic, the delivery ward, the child welfare clinic, the foster home, the nursery or preschool, the leisure home, the public library, the school, the university, the hospital, various rehabilitation centres, etc., until they reach terminal care and the graveyard, where they are visited by family and friends. Through the everyday life experience of such institutions, as well as certain national services such as the Employment Service and the Insurance Office, community members recognize the imagined as real, not apparitions.

These institutions are also part of what one may refer to as a social welfare narrative. When these institutions do not work according to established customs and norms – when they offend human dignity – they are often criticized, not least in the media ("welfare scandals"), which provides evidence for administrative or legislative changes (recent cases in Sweden are those of Lex Maria, Lex Sara, and several others). With some obvious exceptions, these social welfare institutions have usually been initiated, organized, and financed by local government, whether regional or municipal. These well-documented common pool programmes and policies shape and sustain the distinctiveness of the belief in and practices of a common people able to transform their secular society, social state, and even "model" (cf. Unger 1997). Moreover, there are symbols that express this imaginary society, from flags to currencies, overlooking local symbols. While the Swedish flag is a somewhat controversial ceremonial treasure except at sports events, the dead people on contemporary banknotes are not. Currency serves as a constant, if latent, reminder of common identity. In using these coins and notes as a consumer, pensioner, rentier, taxpayer, tenant, or wage-earner, one participates with others in a common venture, developing a sense of trust in both the endeavour and one's fellow participants. In Sweden, the bank note pictures of revered figures such as Nobel Prize Laureate Selma Lagerlöf and internationally acclaimed scholar and scientist Carl von Linnaeus epitomize progenitors of an imagined distant past and contribute to orderly exchange (cf. Elgenius 2011). When in 2010 a well-known Swedish feminist burned bank notes at the Almedalen Week political forum protesting the male–female wage gap, it was considered deeply insulting by respectable public opinion.

The zone of engagement between the national and the local is the crucial nexus in the Swedish IN/LWC–CPR case. It is also the argument advanced in this chapter and developed in chapter 4. In this context, a welfare market society of customers, evaluators, inspectors, and service providers is emerging. Admittedly, a contradiction is involved in this complex between the state as traditionally viewed and the CPRs, a contradiction that can only be resolved at the theoretical level when consumers and producers are also taken into account (cf. Lundquist 2011). In the meantime, a simplified model (see figure 2) shows the communities meeting the complex, or CPRs. Within these parameters, the dialectics of decentralization and privatization, discussed in chapter IV in volume I, are transcended; later, I will return to this issue in chapter 4 through discussing an extended version of this model (see p. 145).

Figure 2. The social welfare industrial complex:
IN/LWCs meet the CPRs in 1980/90s

SCALES OF GOVERNANCE AND GOVERNMENT		Common pool resource institutions	
		Top-down	Bottom-up
Imagined welfare communities	Supra-national	European law and directives	Subsidiarity
	National	Macroeconomic steering	Deregulation
	Local	Privatization	Decentralization

The Swedish social welfare–industrial complex comprises money and people, and as of 2013, more than 50 per cent of the country's GDP consisted of public expenditure, one of the highest figures in the OECD area and the subject of a study of internal variation in chapter 3 in this volume. In total, roughly a million people living in Sweden (27 per cent of the labour force) are employed by public CPRs, mostly in local government. These people make up more than 60 per cent of the total public workforce in the municipalities. Most of them work for the public social welfare–industrial complex, which can also be measured by tax-financed social expenditure, both central and local for education, health, income maintenance, and social services, whether these services are delivered by private or public providers. It is still difficult to determine the exact extent of publicly funded private delivery of welfare services. If the measure used is public social expenditure (i.e., central and local outlays for education, health, income maintenance, and social services), it is necessary to observe that such money contributes not only to public employment, but also increasingly to what is classified as private employment (Statskontoret 2011a). Compared with the late 1980s (see chapters III and IV in the preceeding book), the version of the Swedish Welfare Model that has emerged since 2000 is a slimmed-down one. In particular, it was in the mid-1990s that social expenditure and employment in public welfare services was pruned, while the growth of tax-financed private employment truly began at the beginning of the last decade of the old century, rising from around 10,000–20,000 in 1990 to more than 130,000 in 2012 with the take-off at the end (SCB 2012).

This chapter outlines and scrutinizes the blurred but growing public–private mix of the social welfare–industrial complex through the various programmes that constitute it. If not otherwise stated, the cited facts and figures are from official sources plus some ongoing surveys, sponsored by national research funders, conducted for instance by the SOM Institute in Göteborg, Statistics Sweden and other central state agencies, as well as the National Association of Municipalities and County Councils (see also "Sweden" in Flora 1987, volume IV). Most documents are available on the websites of the relevant central state agencies or local authorities, where counterarguments and counterfacts to those presented here can be found. Taken together, this differs from the usual approach, as fairly abstract aspects and dimensions (such as universality) are usually at the forefront. The first topic for discussion is agricultural policy as a social policy programme, followed by more traditional welfare state policies and programmes, such as: employment programmes; income support (operated by the central state); education, health, and social services under the auspices of local government; and, finally, the financing of all these programmes through tax policy along with associated politics. The chapter will also touch on the strange disappearance of housing policy, which has been replaced as a public concern by homelessness and, more recently, housing shortages in the most expansive and expensive metropolitan areas. Combining these various components serves to establish the link to overall macroeconomic policy or steering, which in Sweden has long been closely coordinated with social welfare policy, including the active or (following Myrdal) "productivist" labour market policy, which was recently renamed the "social investment approach/paradigm" (cf. Morel, Pallier & Palme 2011). Of course, this coherent or inclusive CPR approach is in stark contrast to the typical Anglo-American academic and social scientific division between macroeconomic, welfare, and tax policies that was most recently reiterated by Peter Baldwin (2009) in his thought-provoking compendium of 212 comparative New–Old World charts and graphs (cf. Olofsson 2012).

Agricultural subsidies: the European salvage

In the most recent political dynamics in the imagined national Swedish welfare community, the rural-agrarian Centre Party was transformed into an organ for urban forest owners and landowners (known as "Stureplanscentern" after a square in the financial centre of Stockholm), becoming the backbone of the ruling "Blue Labour" Alliance for Sweden after 2002. This reconfiguration necessitates a brief addendum regarding the almost Bismarckian selective social policy represented by agricultural policy, which also includes the non-arable areas under the auspices of deregulated forestry and the animal welfare administration, as well as indigenous-community welfare, which is partly self-regulated by the Sami community and its representative association (cf. Green 2009 and Lawrence 2009; see also Mörkenstam 1999, Kvist 1995 and Olsson & Lewis 1995). More than a focus on the rights of indigenous peoples, however, it is the transcendence of another imaginary, that requires an impasse on these social programmes: the byzantine European social model (cf. Schmitter 2012; also Supiot 2012). In the introduction to the foregoing book, apart from the conventional welfare state policy areas, "significant public regulations and subsidies in such areas as agriculture" (p. 26) were highlighted along with the other social policy programmes. The reason, of course, was a series of historical compromises between the political representatives of the popular social movements of peasants and workers, which formed the basis of the institutional model that had come to characterize the Swedish system until the late 1980s and even into the mid-1990s. Such programmes were usually glossed over in the conventional social policy literature of the 1980s (for an exception, see Rothstein 1992).

At the end of the 1980s, politicians and professionals in the Ministry of Finance made concerted efforts – not least through the Expert Group on Public Finance – to short-circuit the type of support that had hitherto successfully sustained both the livelihood of a diminishing number of Swedish farmers and its vibrant research and teaching branch at Ultuna and Alnarp. At that time, there was a plethora of benefits, both in-kind and cash, usually jointly administered by the organized farm interests and the central state (Wetterberg 1994 and 1988; see also Molander 1989). Consumer prices were negotiated annually between the agribusiness associations and the state, the latter including voices from the main trade unions, representing an imagined national community of everyday food shoppers and urban gourmets or, more philosophically, the general will. The proposed re-regulation of agriculture – in no sense environmentalist – became a bone of contention between the above-mentioned representatives of the urban majority and the rural minority. The new Green Party was on the advance, propelled by a new agenda of welfare change, and the agrarian Centre Party proceeded to retreat.

However, devoted civil servants from the Treasury had penetrated far into the inner circles of the Ministry of Agriculture and new policies and, for a short while, programmes came into operation, transforming farmlands into golf courses and cash subsidies into tax deductions. While some (semi-metropolitan) landowners benefited, others, particularly those working the land and raising livestock, protested vehemently (Lindberg 2008, 2007). Conflicts with vested interests gained momentum, and it was not until Sweden had entered the EU with its far more farmer-friendly, generous, and retrograde Common Agricultural Policy (CAP) that these issues were resolved – at least for the time being. The EU entry thus facilitated the crucial, but to date not particularly well-documented, historical compromise of the mid-1990s when a diminished Centre Party for a few years again backed a Social Democratic government, to rescue and sustain the once world-famous social democratic welfare state regime type. I will return to this issue at the end of this chapter when discussing the financing of social policy (which is developed further in chapter 3).

Full (un)employment:
the institutional downscaling of NLMB

As of early 2013, the unemployment rate in Sweden is hovering around 8 per cent. Of a labour force of over four million, 75 per cent of people aged 16–64 years are gainfully employed (66 per cent for the 15–74-year age group). Approximately one million people of working age are outside the labour force, in addition to some 300,000 unemployed and a similar number covered by "active measures". Added to these are 250,000 registered jobseekers (as of June 2013), some 500,000 people not covered by unemployment insurance (including two-thirds of the registered unemployed), and 25 per cent of the 16–24-year age group "on the dole", of which half were more or less active students. Consequently, full employment is almost as far away as it was during the worst years of the great recession of the 1990s, though towards the end of that period (1994) the lowest employment rate, measured as the number of gainfully employed, was 71 per cent.

Full employment is still the official aim of the active labour market policy, which had previously been described as a civilized version of workfare. Workfare was once a jewel in the crown of the Swedish welfare system, albeit since the 1990s at a different rate of accepted unemployment and since 2007 under the auspices of a reduced, recalibrated central welfare administration (the Employment Service, or Af). Internationally, the Swedish Welfare State and the adjacent Nordic Welfare Model were established as distinct entities, based on the active labour market policy. For several decades, this was considered an exceptionally successful labour market policy (Kenworthy 2010). However, Anglo-Saxon anti-welfare state rhetoric also undermined this market interventionist model, as Keynesianism in general fell out of favour in the late 1970s – despite *The Economist* (1991) coming to its rescue when the model first became an object of deconstruction and reconsideration. Before the 1990s, unemployment never exceeded 4 per cent and, even during economic downturns, active job-creation measures reached a maximum of 3 per cent of the workforce. Since that time, much has changed in terms of numbers and percentages. The deindustrialization of more or less remote areas is another highly visible concern compared with the time when in the North, the AMS (the Swedish initialism for the once-omnipotent National Labour Market Board) proclaimed that "all must [go] south" (*"alla måste söderut"*).

Until the 1990s, Sweden managed to avoid open unemployment of continental dimensions, although there were considerable regional variations, which particularly hit the sparsely-populated areas in the northern and the interior south-eastern parts of the country. The southern parts, where almost nine-tenths of the population resides, were hit by deindustrialization, but unemployment was less severe and commuting was a more realistic alternative for jobseekers at the time. From this time onwards, the difference between labour market insiders and outsiders grew, which put pressure on work activation or social inclusion programmes (Holmqvist 2010). Increasing numbers of working-age people had to rely on meagre public cash benefits instead of earnings from gainful employment. This even affected the younger cohorts of the upper classes, as sensitively portrayed by film director Johan Klang in a 2007 movie with the telling title *Darling* (see also Holmberg 2005).

The last two decades have witnessed the ups and downs of business cycles and related policy intervention. Unemployment insurance (a passive measure discussed in the following section) remains secondary to active labour market measures in Sweden. Furthermore, the idea is that full regular employment will secure the tax base of the Swedish welfare state by turning outsiders, particularly the young and newly arrived, into insiders on the labour market. More recently, however, the Employment Service has been criticized as ineffective, not only by Swedish Business but also by trade unions. This agency continues to offer a variety of programmes to compensate for job loss and to prepare for future employment, although the quality of its present measures is more questionable than ever. Depending on the business cycle, 1–3 per cent of the workforce was served by this type of programme, even though such training and retraining programmes were discredited in the 1990s.

Since this time, however, a 2 per cent higher unemployment level – 4 per cent as a starter and, in recent years, perhaps 6 per cent or more – has been formally tolerated by various governments. For most of the period, the unemployment rate has actually been higher than that, with long-term and youth unemployment being of special concern. Combating unemployment has been a major national policy goal throughout the last two decades, despite obvious obstacles. With the advent of the 2006 "Blue Labour" Alliance for Sweden government, the highly regarded work-first principle has put new emphasis on low-wage job creation. The Employment Service and related agencies have been given the task of implementing this policy when markets fail, although deregulation has followed in the wake of the global success of "new public management" when, for instance, coaching and staffing companies have flourished and replaced traditional measures such as vocational training and retraining programmes. However, the educational wing of the old National Labour Market Board, responsible for organizing labour market training and retraining courses throughout the country, was split off in 1986. It became a state agency of its own, and later a state company, although it has operated as a specialized sub-contractor to AMS, the Employment Service. When a market for vocational training was created in the 1990s, this company had to compete with private firms on an educational quasi-market for contracts with AMS, even though it usually remained the preferred choice. This company has repeatedly been offered for sale, but the new government has not yet taken any action. In the last decade, moreover, a new national authority under the Ministry of Education has been assigned the task of improving vocational training. However, the pressure to supply skills to a growing number of jobseekers along with an immature bidding system for such courses has resulted in growing quality concerns.

Work-to-welfare (i.e., the obligation and right to become a wage-earner and thus a taxpayer), also known as work activation, remains the hallmark of the Employment Service, which operates throughout the country via a network of local employment exchange offices, though it has closed local offices in certain areas and neighbourhoods worst hit by unemployment. In a similar vein, other national agencies are involved in other growth-promoting activities and local public authorities are no less active in pursuing social inclusion through employment promotion. Since the late 1990s, adult education has been prioritized in an attempt to halve unemployment, while recent and not-so-recent immigrants have been encouraged to improve their Swedish language skills and to start businesses. The latter is easier said than done, and lessons learned from the deep recession of the 1990s have affected current initiatives to combat racial discrimination, poverty, residential segregation, social exclusion, and unemployment (Schierup et al. 2006; see also Castles & Schierup 2010 and Mulinari & Neergaard 2005). For instance, there has been strong public concern about the fate of children of first-generation immigrants and their opportunities for social mobility via higher education, which has impinged on the numerical growth of higher education in the last decade. Since the mid-1990s, new colleges supplying tertiary mass education have expanded and been built in segregated suburban areas dominated by immigrant populations.

In contrast to the 1990s, trends have turned upwards in the last decade; with minor fluctuations over the years the employment rate went up, while the youth unemployment rate remains high. For instance, most young immigrants live in the large cities, where residential segregation has been considered a social problem as it has increased in certain suburban areas. In 2000, a six-year joint central–local urban policy programme known as the Metropolitan Development Initiative, which had considerable central state funding, was initiated with the stated double aim of promoting economic growth and "breaking" socioeconomic, ethnic, and discriminatory practices. Unlike in many other countries where urban development programmes comprised physical and socioeconomic measures, the major foci of the Metropolitan initiative in Sweden were labour market, educational, cultural, anti-crime, and health-related interventions. Only to a minor extent did this programme involve the physical regeneration of targeted exposed areas of supposedly residential and ethno–national segregation in selected urban neighbourhoods where unemployment had hit hard during the deep recession of the 1990s (Andersson 2006). The ability of this programme to achieve its targets was limited, primarily because the central state, through lack of communication between, for instance, its Employment and (Social) Insurance offices, was unable to coordinate its activities at the grassroots level. Therefore, usually the municipalities, but in some cases particular central state agencies (ranging from the police to the local employment agencies, varying between the 24 selected metropolitan residential areas), took command, along with community, civil society, and ethnic–national organizations and, in a few neighbourhoods, individual firms. Since 2006, no central seed money has been available, although non-funded policies are still in place. Nonetheless, the central state managed to some extent to sell this initiative on the international policy market, particularly in the EU, as a fairly lively development environment blossomed.

New semi-professional groups emerged, creating a kind of social integration sector involving many high-profile activists from the diverse Swedish multi-ethnic community employed both privately and publicly, as foreign-born immigrants and their native-born children left the ranks of social assistance recipients for paid work (cf. Stigendal 2012;

also Kings 2011 and 2010; Hertting & Wedung 2009; Hajighasemi et al. 2006; Hosseini-Kaladjahi 2002). Moreover, the central state expanded the number of municipalities involved from seven in the three metropolitan areas to well above 20 city governments throughout the country (Statskontoret 2010). In higher education, recently arrived adults increasingly became involved in new programmes such as "Immigrant Academies" to improve employability and lift educated newcomers out of social exclusion. Of particular importance was municipal language education aimed at unskilled and illiterate refugees and asylum seekers (Högskoleverket 2006). Again, the work-first principle gained the upper hand and passive measures declined in significance. Despite being financed through the central Migration Agency, programmes for migrant asylum-seekers have in most respects become a municipal concern. This has been especially noticeable since 2006, with the end of MDI and the advent of another "new" urban development policy and its focus on certain residential areas in 20 more "big towns" after the change of government.

Since the great recession of the 1990s, the municipalities have been heavily involved in labour market training programmes for those whom the state authority considers unemployable or not yet employable. In particular, newly arrived non-Swedish men with resident permits dominate such municipal programmes (female labour force participation is much lower in this group, being below 50 per cent in 2012). Consequently, there is still some concern regarding ghettoization, the creation of "permanent refugee camps", with an informal grey- or black-market untaxed economy of "outsiders" and a new intersectional mix of class, gender, and ethnic cleavages in certain suburban areas in metropolitan centres (cf. Brännström 2005). The civilized version of workfare may have become slightly less civilized with tightening benefit criteria and an increased requirement to take up wage labour at whatever pay is offered. As trade unions still have an impact on pay levels, this means that grey- or black-market labour seems to have grown, although no reliable records are available. Trade union activists in the transport sector complain, however, that some religious-right churches have imported labour from EU countries such as Romania, and provided jobs paying far below the tariffs and without paying social contributions. A government initiative to make certain services (e.g., domestic services) tax deductible has to some extent helped whitewash such jobs (see also Platzer 2006).

In any assessment of the period under review, it is necessary to combine long- and short-term perspectives. In the Swedish case, only a decade-long view would suggest anything other than a positive outlook for the future. In hindsight, the upward trend in most economic indicators during the first decade of the new millennium – until the autumn of 2008 and returning to the upward trend in 2010, down again in 2012 – stands in sharp contrast to the crash and deep recession of the preceding decade, while simultaneously being consistent with medium-term post-war prospects. Of course, the most recent downturn, the effects of which are still being felt among unemployed youth, is another thorn in the side of active labour market policy. Having said that, the low-interest-rate life is fine for those whom the commercial banks consider creditworthy "homeowners" or for debt-ridden borrowers (cf. Dienst 2011; also Blackburn 2006).

Income maintenance:
social insurance schemes as a public safety net

In terms of public budgets, social insurance is the main component of central state social welfare spending and the main object of the research into retrenchment that has followed in the wake of Paul Pierson's pathbreaking *Dismantling the Welfare State* (1994). In focus in the income maintenance category are pensions, sickness (including occupational injury) benefits, family cash support (i.e., paternal insurance and the general child allowance), and unemployment insurance (which is on the fringe of the state system, but financed from public coffers and is considered a passive measure). Naturally, the public purse also pays for the above-mentioned active labour market programmes, which, compared with the huge cost of pensions, are not particularly impressive. This is not to say that senior citizens have been neglected with the focus on employment, as they were with the exception of one brief line in the first statement of the new 2006 government: "The pension reform agreed between the Alliance parties and the Social Democratic party is important for Sweden and will remain in place" (Swedish Government 2006, p. 5). The income maintenance system was built up to complement and, for people aged 60–65 years and above, to partly sustain centrally negotiated reimbursements from wage labour, via the social insurance system of occupation injury, pensions, sickness, and unemployment benefits. It also safeguards against certain social "risks" by means of investments, both flat-rate and income-tested (which should not be confused with means-tested), ranging from children and pregnant women to elderly voters. This system can be interpreted as the equivalent of a guaranteed basic income of an imagined welfare community of nine million people, or seven million adults with voting rights (that is, Sweden) with a (means)-tested component (i.e., social assistance) at the local community/government level. However, this kind of basic income was far from the dreams of the social engineers of the 1980s, who were attracted to this provocative enlargement of welfare that was constantly rejected by the domestic rational humanitarians (cf. Jansson 2003; see also Kildal 2000 and Zetterberg 1967). In Sweden, social benefits are still fairly generous and taxes are comparatively high. This situation has not altered greatly over the last 20 years. Cutbacks have occurred in parts of the various schemes throughout the period under review, however, and the income guarantee for the unemployed or those on the fringe of the labour market is neither generous nor basic anymore.

In the 1990s, the most important institutional and legislative change in the field of income support turned out to be the construction of a new pension scheme. It merged the older duality of universal pay-as-you-go basic and general supplementary earnings-related benefits (the work record being fairly generously defined) into a unified life-long contribution-defined earnings- and capital-return-related benefit scheme that offered a minimum guaranteed component to those who have lived in Sweden for more than 40 years (Hinrichs & Lynch 2010; see also Ståhlberg 2009 and 1997). After a protracted ideological war in the 1980s, a painful bi-partisan process started during the crisis years of the early 1990s. The process had the backing of the four parties in power at the time and was finally accepted by the Social Democrats after two years of internal battles following the party's return to power in 1994. Two minor political parties that were close to the Social Democrats, but of lesser significance in the mid-1990s, were the Green and Left parties. While neither party ever formally accepted this compromise, this had no impact on the outcome of the five-party talks or on the implementation process (Loxbo 2007; see also Immergut et al. 2005; Lundberg 2003 and Lundberg & Åmark 2001).

From a state budgetary perspective, cost containment has been quite successful since the introduction of the new system, which for another fifteen years still harbours the old, or vice versa. Technically, an artificial "demogrant" (see the following paragraph) is also part of the new system to counteract systemic cost pressures due to changes in population composition. The pension system, which is the most important part of the income maintenance system, covers everyone aged over 61 years who has a residence record of 40 years or more in the country (before 1993, the period was only five years). However, the recent tightening of rules is not the only change. In the future, Sweden will have two public pension systems that are currently administered by a new central state agency: the Pension Authority. Those born before 1937 will receive a pension according to the rules governing the old system, while benefits for those born between 1937 and 1954 will be paid out of a mix of the old and new systems. The first pensions fully following the rules of the new system will not be paid out until 2020.

The future aside, the old public pay-as-you-go system was considered too costly by the great majority of the organized political and social forces, if not always by their members (Hort 2004b). As noted above, the old system started being phased out in 2000, and in 2012, most retirees were receiving a pension benefit determined according to the mixed system. Moreover, complementary pension schemes that promoted early retirement have partly been scrapped. The main aims are to reduce state pension expenditure, increase work incentives, and make the new system more actuarial and less redistributional. Still, the state-budget-financed minimum benefits will guarantee a basic income for everybody at old age with low or no earnings over their lifetime. However, the intention is that most income earners at retirement should receive a pension benefit that corresponds to work and earnings records. It is hoped that this will encourage able-bodied people to postpone their retirement until age 70 or even later. In the new system, wage-earners and their employers each pay a contribution (altogether 18.5 per cent of the wage) to the state insurance fund, which operates on a pay-as-you-go basis. Depending on how much is paid in, an indexed (according to earnings, not consumer prices) and demographically weighted cash benefit will be paid out. With increasing longevity, the demographic component makes pension payouts lower. Furthermore, 2.5 per cent of the individual contribution is set aside for a premium reserve scheme, which enables individual investments in market funds operated by private investors (e.g., merchant banks and insurance companies). Payouts from such private financial funds are expected to top up the indexed earnings-related pension benefit, although most income in the new private system currently seems to end up in the pockets of the actors in this vibrant investment scheme. To date, no major differences from the old system have been evident, although there were some minor benefit reductions in 2010 due to the 2008 financial meltdown. However, the impact of the new system on the standard of living of retirees is only gradually being felt, and perhaps the full effects of the new system will never materialize.

The second largest of the social insurance provisions is the sickness insurance system, which covers the entire workforce and offers daily cash benefits for the temporarily ill. Since the 1990s, the work injury compensation system, which operates under the same umbrella, has been in constant flux (cf. Kangas 2010; Freeman & Rothgang 2010). This part of the income maintenance system has increasingly become the most controversial part of the welfare state, even according to public administration actors themselves (cf. Olofsdotter Stensöta 2009). In the 1990s, for instance, the National Audit Office felt that its programmes were easily abused and that the national social insurance agency had been naïve in handling roughly a third of total public expenditures. In practice, during the first two weeks of employee illness, the employer is obliged to make daily sickness insurance payments. After this period, the central state Insurance Office takes over, although the employer is obliged to contribute to employee rehabilitation. This is only one of many reforms since the 1990s designed to encourage early return to wage labour. However, the sickness insurance system also includes compensation for long-term illness, participation in labour market rehabilitation programmes, and benefits payable to expectant mothers who are unable to work during pregnancy. The general replacement rate is 80 per cent of earned income (since 2008 only for the first three months), with a wage ceiling, but most wage earners are reimbursed closer to their actual salary following agreements between the branch associations on the labour market. Hence, the public system is coordinated with negotiated occupational benefit schemes to prevent overcompensation (above 100 per cent). Linked to the sickness cash benefit system is a "temporary" disability benefit, which has replaced the former disability (partly unemployment) pension system. The replacement rate in the new disability system is lower, at 65 per cent, than that of either the former disability pension system or the new sickness benefit system, which encourages the bureaucratic transfer of hard-to-rehabilitate beneficiaries from the more generous system to the less generous one.

Although still low, the outright rejection rate for potential claimants has increased as medical doctors have faced bureaucratic scrutiny from the National Audit Office (Hultgren 2011, 2007; cf. also Lindqvist & Lundälv 2012). Since the mid-1990s, the growing numbers of people relying on sickness and disability benefits have caused alarm, and since the early 2000s, a number of changes in the system have created heated controversies. Policy changes and organizational adaptation have exposed sickness insurance to severe popular criticism and heated media debate (Johnson 2010). The level of social trust in this public authority has diminished significantly and it is debatable whether this agency is still part of the imagined national welfare community; instead, it probably contributes negatively to the common pool resource institutions (Frykman et al. 2009). After the general election of 2010, the responsible central government minister was sacked and replaced by a veteran of the welfare wars of the 1990s who most recently had been a municipal councillor on the outskirts of metropolitan Stockholm and was once ousted by the present PM as chair of the national Moderate Youth Association. The new minister immediately had to demonstrate his political skills. Without a firm majority in parliament, the national government, in particular, the Ministry of Health and Social Affairs, has had to take into account the positions of a split but majoritarian opposition that has been responsive to vehement public criticisms.

However, criticism of the social insurance administration has not, to the same extent, spilled over to another part of this income maintenance system, i.e., parental insurance and similar family cash benefits, despite the increasing surveillance of this system's beneficiaries through compulsory bureaucratic monitoring (removed in 2013) by the child day-care centres. In the past two decades, several social welfare reforms have been introduced with a view to giving women and men the opportunity to combine work with parental responsibilities. Apart from the active labour market policy, child- and family-friendly programmes are the most distinctive features of the present image of the Nordic model (Lundqvist 2011; Melby et al. 2010; Berven 2004; Hobson 2002; also Bradshaw & Finch 2010). In Sweden, parents are entitled to an earnings-related parental leave benefit for 480 days during a child's first years, to be divided between the parents (60 days are non-transferable between the parents). Since the mid-1990s, the intention has been to enable a special "daddy period" during early childhood, which otherwise remains a period of female responsibility in practice. In addition, all fathers are entitled to a ten-day leave of absence when a child is born, recently in practice extended to a month. This benefit, along with 390 of the above-mentioned 480 days, is compensated at 80 per cent of previous earnings, with the remaining days at a lower flat rate. Either parent or another insured person may also take temporary parental leave with compensation for loss of income (again 80 per cent) when a child is sick (up to 120 days per year per child) until the child is eight years old. Single parents are allowed to take the full parental leave themselves. To make it easier for parents to combine work and family life, parents of children under the age of eight years are also entitled to reduce their working day by two hours, with a corresponding non-compensated reduction in pay. Other family benefits in the Swedish welfare system include a flat-rate universal child allowance (up to the age of 16 years), complementary study allowances for those aged between 16 and 19 or 20 years in secondary schools (i.e., the extended general child allowance and, for those aged 19 years and over, the activity benefit), and a housing allowance for low-income earners with children. Single parents may receive advance payments, the weak link in the system, which in principle are recovered from the non-custodial parent (usually the father). The Swedish family welfare system also includes some special benefits for orphans and disabled children (see also volume I).

Family life and paid work are not easily reconcilable, but the intention has been to design child support in accordance with the active labour market programmes and the risk of unemployment in order to improve household sustainability and the life chances of the younger generation in particular (Kravchenko 2008; Ström 2002). Therefore, trade union funds that reimburse unemployed members of the labour force are organized by voluntary unemployment benefit societies, but financed mainly by contributions from employers. Benefits are taxed and, to become eligible, an employee must have been a member of such a society for twelve consecutive months and have had a regular job for a similar length of time but spread out over a longer period. Rules are set by the state and also include a waiting period before a benefit is paid out (Bendz 2004). A major changed occurred in 2007 when the membership fee was no longer tax deductible; furthermore, the benefit societies in most cases were forced to increase the fee. Taken together, these changes led to half a million members leaving, signalling a decline in this CPR institution. Simultaneously, the new government announced a compulsory system whose implementation remains in doubt (cf. Littorin 2010).

This is the most significant "welfare recalibration" after the change of government in 2006, and the outcry from the trade unions was immediate. In 2010, Sjöberg, Palme, and Carroll concluded:

> Due to the fact that statistics productions lag behind a number of years, we have as yet no comprehensive picture beyond 2005. Yet available information allows us to detect a number of interesting changes after 2005, even if these changes do not transform the general picture. We find, for example, that Sweden introduced a number of changes in its unemployment insurance programme following the election of a centre–right government in 2006. The changes include downward adjustments of benefit level, cutbacks in benefit duration and increased contributions from the insured individuals. These changes may be seen as expressions of political preferences, but their explicit aims were to increase labor supply in a booming economy. As economic prospects change, policy-makers respond. (Sjöberg, Palme, and Carroll 2010:433)

Moreover, a study from Uppsala University in late 2010 concluded that the present Swedish unemployment insurance (UI) system was "second to worst" among those of fourteen European countries (Lindgren 2010). The replacement level is considerably lower than in the daily sickness benefit and the wage ceiling is much lower, with four out of five people receiving less than 80 per cent of actual earnings, if they are covered at all. The design of the system reflects the historically close relationship between the benefit societies and the blue-collar trade union movement. The intention is to compensate for short-term unemployment and encourage a smooth transition to new regular employment. The long-term unemployed may receive a public job offer to qualify for continuing membership in the unemployment funds, as well as again becoming a taxpayer and thus being eligible for a further period of compensation. There is currently no end to this type of continuing compensation except ordinary retirement, but the above-mentioned 2007 reform did mean that large numbers left the system as fees increased, particularly in funds that cover the highest rates of unemployment. Moreover, fees were no longer tax deductible. For those who do not qualify, there is still a temporary flat-rate benefit; in most cases, however, these recipients have to rely on means-tested municipal social assistance. Municipalities therefore have every reason to make an unemployed person employable. For labour market insiders – i.e., the taxpayers of the workforce in the strict sense – the social insurance system combines with the residual social assistance to form a work-incentivizing version of a basic income system. To conclude,

UI has been partly dismantled and partly recalibrated, in the words of Pierson (1994), which makes the municipalities, and traditional family and friendship networks, the lenders of last resort.

Social assistance remains outside the framework of social insurance and is a cash programme handled by local authorities under national framework legislation (Bahle et al. 2010; Johansson 2001). For the working poor, it is a last resort, while it also sometimes covers the basic needs of the non-working poor and the destitute (when the latter do not turn to charities or outright begging). This is also the welfare system that has to deal with emerging and still controversial child poverty. The ups and downs of social assistance still largely reflect economic conditions, and the system has been relied upon more in times of hardship than during boom years. Increasingly, it has had to take care of all those who become uninsured or otherwise fall through the gaps in the social safety net. The great majority of its recipients are not the same in 2010 as in 1990, but the stigma associated with social assistance remains. Social assistance had to take its share of the burden during the long recession of the 1990s, although no lasting "culture of dependency" arose according to welfare and poverty researchers (Bergmark och Bäckman 2004; Salonen 1994). As part of overall social expenditures, it has been marginal throughout the period, while it has been frequently held up as an indicator of the "flight from universalism" or the dismantling of the universal welfare state (Sunesson et al. 1998).

Less heard of in the last decade, its role as a sensitive social barometer has been frequently cited in the apparently resurgent poverty research, in contrast to welfare research, not least in connection with child poverty among single-parent families (O'Brien & Salonen 2010). Social assistance is likely to continue to shape futures of permanent austerity in local communities, as well as inform national public and social scientific debate about welfare-to-work, workfare, and other more or less open methods of cooperation, coordination, cohesion, consent, and even coercion. So too the social security system: At the time this manuscript was submitted to the publisher, a report to the State Social Insurance Commission concluded that the Swedish system had fallen from its top-ranking position, and become a fairly ordinary European welfare system (Ferrarini et al. 2012). Nevertheless, in a radio commentary on this report, the Commission's secretary, a former sociologist turned "super-policyprofessional" (Garsten, Rothstein & Svallfors 2011), immediately declared that the Swedish system was "robust".

Needs-based in-kind welfare services: the deregulation and recalibration of health, education, and personal social services, including disability and old age

People meet the state. As stressed in chapter IV in the original volume, the welfare state consists of more than just the "jewels in the crown" combined with aspects of "pure" social security or income maintenance. Social welfare policy includes policies on families, disability, children, old age care, gender equality, migration, health, education, urban and regional affairs, among others, under the auspices of the professional social services (cf. Andersson 2013). Together, these policies are part of the social service state frequently referred to in the international literature (cf. Anttonen & Sipilä 1996; Sipilä 1997; also Olofsson 2010) and analyzed in the comparative contributions on health, long-term care, disability, social assistance, and education in the *Oxford Handbook* (Castles et al. 2010). Classifications aside, most of these policy areas are fairly loosely defined, subject to change over time, and even partly over-lapping. Their main shared characteristic is that, in most cases, they are not handled directly by the central state but under the auspices of local government; in Sweden, this means the approximately 290 munici-palities and 20 county councils or, more recently and only in a few geographical areas, regions operated by elected party representatives. There are also joint ventures between and within these levels of govern-ment, and operated by professionals. Doctors, nurses, and teachers are most typical welfare professions. In terms of social expenditure, local and regional government is as costly as social insurance, but is financed predominantly through direct income taxes. Between one-quarter and one-third of municipal and county outlays are financed through the national inter-governmental transfer system, whereas wealthier coun-ties and municipalities contribute to equalizing the services provided, regardless of the structure of the tax base. In 2012, roughly 30 per cent of Sweden's GDP was consumed by local welfare expenditure – today a war chest of considerable importance.

From a life-cycle perspective, a cradle-to-grave approach is charac-teristic of the Swedish welfare system. Strictly speaking, the welfare sys-tem starts before the cradle is set in motion, with sexual health guidance and birth-control centres (e.g., free abortion is available through strong adherence to a secular pro-choice approach) as well as maternity clinics offering parental education and regular check-ups of expectant mothers, which are free of charge throughout pregnancy. This is not to say that these are giveaways – as competing political parties all claim at election time – rather, they are paid for by the taxpayers-cum-voters. Free, if not compulsory, parental education is also widespread and organized by county council outlets. Child delivery and midwife services are also free. Throughout the country, local child clinics provide vaccinations, health check-ups and consultations, as well as certain types of treatment to all children below school age. Health services are also available for school-age children. Apart from regular school nurses and doctors, publicly employed district nurses provide medical treatment as well as advice and support, in schools, at their own surgeries, and on home visits. All medical treatment, including dental care, is free of charge for children and young people under the age of 20 years. The county councils may also provide dental care. At such clinics, paying adults can also receive dental treatment. Otherwise, it is private dentists who provide most services on the dental market. Demand is only partly (and rather poorly) tax subsidized, and the public support system – dental insurance – has been remarkably less stable than other parts of the welfare system. Therefore, going to other EU member states for dental check-ups has become an alternative, particularly for those living near the Swedish ports of the Baltic Sea in the vicinity of Estonia and Poland, where the fees for dental treatment are considerably lower.

All adults have the right to choose not only their dentist, but also their own general medical practitioner, though the sparsely populated areas in the Swedish north and interior have limited choice in this regard. This is not new, but the situation has not improved in recent years as cost containment has caused severe organizational problems. Nonetheless, national legislation now obliges county councils to organize primary care clinics staffed by a variety of medical professionals, including doctors and nurses. These clinics treat diseases and injuries that do not require advanced or expensive medical technology and hospitalization. In addition to public services, private doctors also provide publicly funded, highly subsidized primary care. Each county council sets its own fee for outpatient care. County councils also run hospitals offering advanced, high-technology medical care, either alone or in cooperation with each other. Hospitals are still heavily subsidized out of general income taxation, but a user fee is always charged. Recently, some county councils have started to contract out their hospital services. This is clearly an area currently in organizational flux (cf. Selberg

2010; Hasselbladh et al. 2008; also Österlee & Rothgang 2010). Following legislative changes at the national level in the 1990s, private initiatives gained ground, although they remained largely financed by public funds. Outpatient clinics were either sold or contracted out by county councils, first by local authorities where the political majority was non-Social Democratic, but later as part of bipartisan agreements all over the country. Since the mid-1990s, and particularly after the shift to a right-centre national government in 2006, major hospitals have also been privatized, but this remains a bone of contention between the right and left in Sweden.

Competition and private alternatives have increased in the Swedish health sector over the last decade. New private hospitals have opened and private insurance companies have offered ways to bypass the queues in the subsidized system. Pharmaceuticals are still sold by a state-owned company at regulated prices, but in 2010 this sector was opened up to competition from selected private firms (see chapter 4 on for-profits in civil society). Prescribed drugs costing above a certain limit are subsidized by the sickness insurance system (see above). This means that all residents of Sweden, regardless of citizenship, are entitled to use Swedish health services at subsidized prices, as are visitors from EU member states who need emergency attention and from other countries with which Sweden has special agreements (e.g., Iceland, Norway and Switzerland). Health expenditures, which rose from 3 per cent to 9 per cent of GDP between 1960 and 1980, remained at the higher level throughout the 1980s, and then fell back slightly; cost containment, however, remains a major priority. Still, the health system is essentially public, though supremely marketized, and private practitioners are funded mainly by public sources under the auspices of the audit state.

Since the turn of the century, Sweden has become a frontrunner in turning primary and secondary education ("basic education") towards marketization (Björklund et al. 2005). For more than a century, basic education was a mixed central–local government system similar to that in other Nordic countries. Since the early 1990s, most of the system has operated under municipal auspices and generally been funded out of local income tax. The privatization trend has been notable (see chapter 4), and the public education system has user fees for pre-schools, child day-care, and after-school activities, although most costs are funded through the municipal budget. In the 1990s, the much newer pre-school system was merged with the older primary and secondary schools into a unified school system. Every child above one year of age has the right to a place in a pre-school or child day-care centre, and from the age of seven years is obliged to attend primary and secondary basic education. Compulsory schooling lasts for nine years (although in practice it is closer to 12 years, with a few dropouts before secondary education); it is free of charge and guided by national legislation (cf. Busemeyer & Nikolai 2010). However, frequent changes in the system have caused alarm, as comparative PISA figures cast Swedish students in an unfavourable light, and the incoming 2006 government emphasized the urgency of educational reform, not least of teacher's education. The layout of the most recent system of change has met growing criticizims as quality has not improved.

The basic school system is still financed and organized by local government with an obligation to serve local students. In many cities and local communities, there are also private schools financed out of the public purse through vouchers. As a result, schools have started competing for students and parents have become consumers of private or public branded schools, the system having become more fragmented, less transparent and subject to closer scrutiny from central state inspectors (Gustavsson 2010). The implementation of the new system has been full of stumbling blocks for instance challenging the capacity of the municipalities to provide schooling in case of private bankruptcy (see also chapter 3–5). Special grants, reminiscent of the traditional social welfare approach, are still provided by several municipalities to schools in certain areas (mainly suburban) with poor school results in order to promote advanced studies and prevent dropout (Lindström 2006). In recent years, central state grants have also been provided to certain schools with the highest-achieving students in subjects such as math and science. Tertiary education is still the prerogative of the central state, academic education has no tuition fees, and a mixed system of grants and repayable loans is available for students to cover basic amenities. A quasi-market for universities has been created in which higher-learning institutions compete for resources based on their scores on the international peer-reviewed publishing market. Over the last decade, this has led to growth in certain areas, particularly medical and technical research, which were deliberately promoted by the 2006 government.

While the medical health and educational systems have long been heavily regulated and coordinated from top to bottom by politicians and academic professionals, laypeople and local government have traditionally had more leeway in organizing care for the elderly and disabled. This leeway has increased since the mid-1990s, when county councils were required by law to hand over some of the medical care responsibilities for elderly and disabled people. More recently, however, the national government has tried to tighten up the system, partly due to awareness of the problem of "cherry picking" and various scandals in both private and public institutional care of the elderly and disabled. With an ageing population, an increase in female labour force participation, and an emphasis on the ideas of "normalization" (or de-institutionalization) and independent living, services to the elderly and disabled have become much more of a public concern, for both relatives and the authorities (Lagergren & Batljan 2000). Local governments are responsible for domestic care of elderly and disabled people, although such services, such as nursing homes, can be contracted out to private providers. Some municipalities have introduced choice through vouchers, while others have tried to outsource the delivery of such services to private providers (Statskontoret 2012a). Furthermore, the municipalities are also obliged to pay for patients whose hospital treatment (under the aegis of county councils or private subcontractors) has finished but who must remain in hospital because the municipality cannot offer them a place in a nursing home offering round-the-clock care. In an effort to reconcile conflicts below the national level and resolve tension between counties and municipalities, the national associations of municipalities and county councils merged in 2007, creating a united and tendentiously powerful local government public welfare lobby organization of two vocal former associations.

In a similar vein, local authorities are also responsible for living arrangements, employment, and support services for people suffering from long-term mental illness (cf. Hollander 1995). Municipalities charge individuals using these services out of their individual social insurance income, but most of the cost is financed out of the common pooled budget, including those services provided by the county councils or regions. The municipalities also financially support volunteer-provided services for vulnerable individuals who are in need or at risk, services such as preventive health care, family therapy and counselling, alcohol and drug treatment, shelter for the homeless, and protection for women and children threatened by domestic violence (cf. Cocozza & Hort 2011; Pringle 2009). In recent decades, the municipalities have also become responsible for the integration of newcomers to Sweden (i.e., refugees or other migrants), although the central state has intervened on occasion and currently plays a larger role in this policy area (Sarstrand Marekovic 2011 and 2010). Some of these services are provided by voluntary welfare organizations – secular philanthropic as well as religious charities – partly with the support of tax money (see chapter 4).

Overall, local government is the backbone of social service provision. As noted, the municipalities are the largest employers in Sweden, with 768,000 people on their payrolls as of 2009. Most of these employees work either in schools or as care workers. County councils are the second-largest employers, with 230,000 employees in the medical/health sector. As mentioned, the municipalities are also the owners of the public housing companies, which offer rental apartments to almost one-fifth of the Swedish population (the topic of a special section). Housing more or less disappeared as a policy area in the early 1990s, and there have been conflicts at the national level – the INWC – regarding the possibility of transferring public housing to private actors at the ILWC level. The central state has tried to "strike back" at the independence gained by local government during the early post-war decades of welfare state construction through audits, inspections, and evaluations. The deconstruction, as well as the reconstruction, of the welfare state is a controversial affair that involves many civil society and political actors.

Housing: the disappearance of a policy area

As in most other Western countries, most Swedes have had homes of their own throughout the modern era. As urbanization spread, the role of public housing increased in Sweden, as described in chapter III in volume I (see also Fahey & Norris 2010). As of 2010, the role of private housing had increased at the expense of public housing for two decades. Public housing subsidies became fairly controversial starting in the early 1980s, and a decade later, universal housing policy more or less came to an end (Davidson 1994; c.f. Bengtsson 2009;). The central state Ministry of Housing ceased to exist in late 1991 with the advent of the centre-right government (comprising the Moderate, Liberal, Christian Democrat and Centre parties), while in parliament, the Standing Housing Committee continued its meetings for a decade. In this policy arena, downgraded central state agencies moved most of their operations from the capital region to fairly remote cities (e.g., Gävle and Karlskrona) after the closure of military outposts there. At the local government level, municipal building societies remained in business, but few new dwellings were erected in the 1990s. Since the 2000s, the exception has been rapid growth in areas such as university towns (e.g., Växjö) and around big cities. Throughout the period, the privatization of existing housing stock became the main mode of operation in several leading-edge municipalities (Carson 2005). This was encouraged by central government, which favoured owner-occupied apartment buildings and an enlarged housing market – a market that soon exploded (see also Hort 1997). An unintended consequence of the abolition of housing policy was that young people, particularly university students, facing rising housing costs remained living with their parents; naturally, this pattern was confined to the larger university towns and cities before the young people either became tenants or, if better off, borrowers from the major banks, often with parental support (Kings & Kravchenko 2012).

Otherwise, municipal housing companies have remained major actors on the housing market, though not generally as joint policy actors at the national level (SABO, the national association of municipal housing companies, is a shadow of its former self). Housing is still considered a welfare component, not least at the micro-level of society – in the ILWCs – where the threat of eviction and homelessness may force the social authorities to intervene to protect children and adults (Eriksson et al. 2010). Since the 1990s, these companies' role as financiers of the municipalities has increased in importance, although there is a yield cap closely monitored by the tenant associations. Financially, these companies have often been incorporated into larger municipal companies (e.g., in the areas of culture, energy, sports, and water), which has created an arena partly beyond local public control and has obstructed operational transparency, even facilitating corrupt practices, as were uncovered in Göteborg in 2010. As of 2012, the municipal housing stock still amounted to almost a fifth of the total, down from well above one-quarter at its height in the 1980s. The variation in this proportion between municipalities is considerable and has increased over the period. A major challenge to these companies is investments in the renovation and upgrading of the large housing estates built in the late 1960s and early 1970s. In most municipalities, it is the buildings from earlier in the post-war period that have been attended to, while private investors and building companies have been the major actors behind the recent increase in the number of owner-occupied dwellings in expanding metropolitan areas (Hedin et al. 2012).

The latter also applies to the increase in apartment accommodations designed for and most often owned by senior citizens. In the 1970s, almost all forms of institutional residences were under constant attack. Since that time, new national policies have been under continuous development, stressing independent living and enabling older and disabled people to live on their own with a high quality of life (Edebalk 2011). Senior citizens should be able to grow old securely, be treated with respect, retain their independence, be able to lead active lives, and exert influence on society and their everyday lives. An accessible society, reasonably priced housing, transport services, and various home-help services are examples of important ways to realize such a public programme. One of the most important principles of Swedish policy for the elderly is that public resources should be framed so that older people can continue to live in their own homes for as long as possible, even when they need extensive medical and social care. For those who for some reason cannot live at home, private or public short-stay housing is available for rehabilitation, for instance, after hospitalization. For those permanently unable to live at home, group housing and nursing homes are available, though shortages are typical in growing metropolitan regions. Thus, these noble goals are far from reached. It is also in these settings that the above-mentioned corruption scandals involving tax-financed welfare services have occurred, which has caused much public alarm and placed private firms in particular under close public scrutiny. At the time of writing, Carema Care – the name of one of these subcontracting companies – has become synonymous with old age care malpractice all over Sweden.

Accordingly, another municipal obligation is to support private housing for the elderly and improve general housing conditions for this group, under the careful watch of the five national associations of pensioners and the associations of the disabled. Mandated by national legislation, the municipalities provide grants for certain measures to enable disabled and elderly people to use their homes more efficiently, and to make needed changes to their homes so that they can continue living in them. Home-care services, whether privately or publicly delivered, are offered around the clock, which means that even individuals with extensive health-care needs can remain in their own homes. Elderly people are increasingly living at home towards the end of their lives, and even the severely ill receive medical and social care in their homes. Common adaptations include removing thresholds and rebuilding bathrooms. There is no cap on such costs – though they are closely monitored by local social authorities – and grants cover the entire reconstruction cost, regardless of the applicant's income. But administrative, bureaucratic and legal skills – unevenly distributed in the population at large – are required to get access to such support. Moreover, elderly and disabled people can obtain personal safety alarms connected to a local service unit. Those who cannot use regular public transport are entitled to transportation services, usually via taxi, but sometimes special vehicles are available. Users who need to travel outside the range of the local transportation services, for instance, for family reasons, can be approved for national transportation assistance by the (Social) Insurance Office. In 2011, well over 90 per cent of elderly people (i.e., aged 65 years and over) lived at home, either with or, in most cases, without public home-care services. Nowadays, housing conditions for the elderly do not differ significantly from those of the population at large and the general standard of housing is often high, though poverty among the elder remains behind closed doors. In recent decades, private and public housing and construction companies have invested in high-quality independent assisted-living facilities intended and adapted for senior couples and singles aged 50 years and over. With growing affluence among the elderly, this has also become an attractive alternative for many non-seniors with an eye to the future. Likewise, those who have been tenants in attractive areas, particularly in metropolitan regions, have usually benefited from the sell-off of public housing. So have those who used to pay property tax, which was abolished in 2008 and subsequently replaced with a flat-rate fee in 290 of the imagined local welfare communities – that is, the municipalities.

Taxation and the financing of the social welfare–industrial complex

If changes in housing policy are the most obvious sign of the beginning of the end of the social democratic welfare state, taxation and tax policy are where the long road to its decline started. Any investigation of the financing of a large welfare state (resource extraction into a common pool) requires more than just figures, whether regarding money or people. The fiscal crisis of the state instigated a management crisis in which the state's capacities to simultaneously levy taxes and provide welfare became much more intertwined than during the build-up of the welfare state (Obinger & Wagschal 2010; see also Steinmo 2010 and Martin, Mehrotra & Passad 2009). Since the crisis of the welfare state appeared on the global arena – or, more precisely, one decade after the dismantling of the welfare state was added to the domestic agenda – the sustainability of the common pool has been thoroughly demonstrated in Sweden, albeit at a different level of quality and distributional fairness than previously.

In 2011, compared to the 1980s (see chapters III and IV in the foregoing volume) the mode of overall financing is largely unchanged: one-third comes from direct income taxes paid to local authorities and two-thirds comes from two types of indirect taxes paid to central government (i.e., VAT and payroll taxes or delayed pay-out of wages, including employee social contributions reintroduced in the 1990s). This financing pattern exists despite a major overhaul of the system in 1990 and the abolition of the controversial property tax in 2007 (Skatteverket 2011). During a period of global turmoil or permanent welfare austerity, the welfare state has proven robust, if not unscathed, as demonstrated in the preceding sections. Tax evasion is a minor issue that became less common after the 1990 tax reform, and the Tax Authority is held in high esteem, versus, for example, the (Social) Insurance Office. Paying taxes has become a fundamental citizen obligation, a prerequisite for becoming a decent community member and deserving recipient of still fairly generous benefits. This idea has been hammered into the belief system of the great majority of the population by various friends of the universal model (or in the words of one Singaporean, "to become rich is great but to pay taxes is glorious", *Financial Times*, 21 October 2011), which has perhaps been facilitated by the absence of any major tax increases between 1990 and 2006. In fact, the trend during this period has in fact been one of modest tax decreases.

However, examination of the present type of state welfare financing – which survived the crisis of the early 1990s – calls for a somewhat longer timeframe than does examination of previous policy eras, as such examination must take account of the most recent economic, institutional, and political developments, as considered in chapter 3. It is not so much the instruments and measures that require special attention as the policy formation. However, a few instruments and measures do stand out, such as reducing the top marginal tax rate, abolishing the property tax, and, most recently, providing tax "deductions" for everyone who has a job (in contrast, particularly, to pensioners with occupational, private, and/or social insurance income). None of these instruments or techniques has had a particular impact on the overall financing of the welfare state, but taken together they have definitely helped frame the issues involved, whether these have been formulated in the language of academic economics, efficiency, and incentives, or in terms of political rhetoric, social justice, or solidarity. The emergence and development of the tax state is part and parcel of the transformation of the welfare state – its deconstruction and reconstruction – and of the conflicts that penetrate and surround the various levels of the imagined welfare community.

While 1981 is not a crucial year in the development of social policy, it is of the utmost importance in the history of Swedish taxation and represents the beginning of the end of a long and bitter struggle between and within the right, centre, and left. This was the year of the "wonderful night", in the words of the incoming (1982) Minister of Finance (cf. Feldt 1992). It was the year when the opposition Social Democrats shrewdly managed to bring down the third 1976–1982 non-Social Democratic government, leaving the agrarian Centre Party in command of a minority fourth coalition, with the Liberal Party as junior partner. The largest centre-right party at that time, the neoliberal conservative-leaning (later old) Moderates, left the coalition because of a bipartisan agreement on a first cap on marginal tax rates. So much for the "stability of governments" – as referred to 25 years later in another incoming right-centre government declaration (Swedish Government 2006). Lower taxes were central to the platform of the (old) Moderate Party, which at that time included young neoliberal Swedish "Reaganites" (or "Thatcherites"), and the 2002 election result was a wake-up call for them. Again and again, tax proposals have been the weakness of this party, threatening the financing of the universal welfare state, even in the eyes of competing parties neighbouring it on the ideological spectrum. Only when it has managed to set aside such proposals has a true, "responsible" alternative to the Social Democrats, the traditional national party, seen the light of day. For the (new) Moderates, this was a necessary compromise. In the eyes of their foes, it was a hidden road to overthrowing the old social contract and implementing an explicitly neoliberal welfare regime.

Through the 1981 agreement, the Social Democrats set the stage for an attempt at a consensual major tax reform process that was undertaken in the mid-1980s but ultimately backed only by the Liberal Party. The 1990 tax reform became a success story, not least in international policy diffusion circles. Domestically, competition among the centre-right parties again took its toll. However, as the Liberals became a governing coalition party in 1991, under a Moderate PM, they pushed through the changes that had already been decided on by the rest of the incoming coalition, that is, the Moderates (i.e., conservatives), the Centre Party, and the new Christian Democrats. Of course, the new government was much more open than was its predecessor to private entrepreneurs competing for tax money by operating traditional municipal welfare services, such as schools, preschools, and home help services for children and the elderly. Moreover, professional economists, inspired by the new academic mood, advocated what in more traditional circles were considered more than modest changes in an esteemed model and practice. The controversy that followed, not least of which was the threatened creation of a women's party in the 1994 election, impeded the neoliberal takeover of tax-financed public services and social benefits.

In the late 1960s, as pointed out early on by Wilensky (1975), Sweden became a leading spender on social services and income maintenance programmes (Castles 2010). To finance such benefits in kind and cash, the welfare state raised money through various levies on goods, services, and income. Direct tax on income, indirect tax on goods (especially the VAT), and a payroll tax on top of income paid by the employer (i.e., employer "social contributions") came to finance the Swedish welfare system. As mentioned, the weakness of the system was the income tax system and its marginal tax rates. In 1990, a ceiling was introduced of 50 per cent of earnings for the top bracket on the progressive income scale. Instead of further taxes on direct income, the tax base was enlarged by imposing VAT on services that had previously been non-taxed or taxed below the general levy of 20–25 per cent. For most people, therefore, direct taxes became similar to the flat municipal or ILWC income tax depending on legal domicile, garnering around SEK 30 of every SEK 100 earned. Only some 15 per cent of taxpayers paid the extra tax – still progressive – to central INWC coffers. Not least among the remaining controversies was the property tax. Somewhat later, the payroll tax reached its ceiling in an attempt to limit unit labour costs, and employee social contributions were reintroduced, which increased direct taxation while maintaining, or even slightly reducing, the overall tax level.

However, soon after the implementation of the 1990 tax system, the financing of the welfare state almost collapsed as the general economy went into a deep recession (defined as negative economic growth over three consecutive years, i.e., 1991–1993). The public purse was forced to raise money, particularly through borrowing on the national and international money markets. Several commercial banks went bankrupt and a State Emergency Fund had to be created to clean up the mess. The solvency of the state also came into question. Day by day, as underlined in the major business newspaper *Dagens Industri*, the public debt grew alarmingly, and interest paid on the debt was a major budget item throughout the 1990s. This situation was aggravated by the fact that, starting in 1991, the national party, the Social Democrats, had been out of office for the first time in nine years and only the second time in 59 years. In late 1992, there was a rapprochement and an accord between government and opposition when the Central Bank's interest rates twice reached unprecedented levels and the krona went into free-fall. The accord had a temporary impact, but few of its measures came to immediate fruition, so the financial market did not trust the governing capacity of the newcomers (the same four parties that have formed the government since 2006).

In 1994, the Social Democratic Party returned to power with an explicit plan to put the house back in order, through welfare benefit reductions, scrutinizing local government finance, and a few more taxes. It did so despite internal grumblings, especially from its key partner, the trade union movement, regarding these retrenchment policies. Unemployment and sickness benefits again became the targets. There were fewer complaints this time when taxes were raised. The party kept its promise, although this required negotiating a deal with one of its historical political partners – the Centre Party, formerly the Farmers' League, which was still often a partner at the local authority electoral level. Together, these parties also levied an extra tax on top incomes, known as the temporary austerity tax (which is still in force as of 2013), thereby raising the top marginal tax rates well above the 50 per cent threshold for those who paid direct income tax to the central state agreed upon by the Social Democratic and Liberal parties with the institution of the 1990 tax system though not reaching the astonishing Astrid Lindgren Pomperipossa levels of the mid-1970s (cf. Petersson & Wetterberg 2012).

For the 10 years between 1996 and 2006, the Swedish Social Democratic cabinet was for the first time chaired by a former Minister of Finance. He had only held that position for two years (1994–1996), but these were perhaps the most crucial years of the financial reconstruction of the welfare state, when an informal Social Democratic–Centre Party coalition took shape in the corridors of the Ministry of Finance. The cabinet was also the first to have a Social Democratic PM who had been mayor of an industrial municipality at a certain physical as well as mental distance from the capital and from the traditional governing circles within the party and movement, though with a long history in its youth organization. The Centre Party's support for the coalition came from a close-knit group around the party leader and from the chair of parliament's Standing Committee on Taxation. Centre Party support also came at a time when Sweden was entering the EU, making CAP, and not a tightened Swedish agricultural policy, the main financier of the party faithful (cf. Swedish Government 1996). To parts of the old political establishment, however, the new-style national government of the new EU member state seemed like a typical Swedish local authority transferring its sovereignty to outer space. The Minister of Finance's Wall Street debut in 1994 was mythologized, as interest rates on Swedish bonds stabilized. Moreover, the new PM later outlined his welfare philosophy in a book with the telling title *A Man in Debt is Never Free* (Persson 1997).

A prudent budget policy continued, although expenditure pressure increased after the 1998 election when the tough welfare state finance reconstruction period ended with the demise of the informal Social Democrat–Centre Party coalition. Despite declining support in the election, not only for the Centre Party but also for the Social Democrats, the PM managed to renew his mandate by gaining the informal backing of the Green and Left parties. With a little help from the following economic upturn – the appearance and celebration of the new IT Economy at the turn of the millennium before this bubble burst – the cabinet, which initially had limited funds, also managed to buy off its varying demands, the most expensive of which was probably the new northern Bothnia railroad. However, the government was also haunted by its closest friends: the blue-collar Swedish Trade Union

Confederation, often in tandem with their white-collar colleagues and competitors. Expenditure pressures continued to an even greater extent after the 2002 election victory, when the necessary informal support in parliament was maintained in an election in which the (old) Moderates again reiterated their traditional tax proposals. This caused widespread concern and unease among their socio-demographically and ideologically neighbouring competitors-cum-collaborators over the sustainability of universal welfare.

Since the late 1990s, public income and outlays have basically matched each other and social expenditure has been fairly tightly controlled. Since the early years of the new millennium, but before the large-scale 2008 financial meltdown, there was even a budget surplus. The debt itself, both principal and interest, has been largely repaid. Under the Social Democrats, public responsibilities were more or less frozen, not least welfare, which was not allowed to expand and was devolved to the local authority level ("recalibration") to be executed under tight central control. As the overall economy has grown throughout the last decade, this has not meant a similar growth of public tasks or of the social welfare–industrial complex. Instead, the Social Democrats, in power with the reluctant support of the Greens and in particular the Left Party, tried to achieve a balance between minor increases in social benefits and reduced income taxes – a strategy once known in the welfare discourse as "private wealth, public squalor". Furthermore, in Sweden, as in most developed Western countries, marketization and privatization have reached into most corners of the artefact known as society, or INWC. This development has occurred despite sometimes considerable opposition and resistance, in particular from various welfare protest movements, ad-hoc groups, and the trade union movement, most noticeably at the municipal or ILWC level. However, it was only when established academic accountants and researchers started to mildly question the benefits of welfare recalibration that such voices began to be heard (see also chapter 4, end section).

Conclusions: from permanent austerity to volatile globality?

The civilized version of workfare-to-welfare survived the crisis of 1981–1983, but the early 1990s saw the near bankruptcy of the welfare state with shrinking employment levels and permanent austerity, first in the private and later also the public sector. Simultaneously, the centre-right parties returned to power. This time, the three parties that had tried to govern in the late 1970s, together with a new neo-social conservative Christian Democratic Party as a fourth partner (which entered parliament in 1991 together with the populist New Democratic Party, while the Green Party followed their first spell in parliament by leaving for one term). Now, these four parties attempted to deal with open unemployment, which was at double-digit levels, as well as a major migration influx from war-torn areas in the Balkans. For the first time, replacement levels were cut back in major social welfare programmes, such as the general child allowance, sickness insurance, and parental insurance. These cuts were first instituted by the ruling Social Democrats in cooperation with the Liberals, and later jointly by the incoming government and the Social Democratic opposition to halt the 1992 currency crisis. In comparative terms, however, these cutbacks led to benefits remaining at a high level (often 80 per cent, but sometimes as low as 65 per cent of earned income). On its own, the centre-right government stuck to the old welfare contract and even expanded the system for certain groups (e.g., through disability reform). This was probably the last government to have a significant head at the Ministry of Health and Social Affairs, at the same time the vice-premier and leader of the Liberal People's Party.

Paradoxically, the survival of the social welfare–industrial complex occurred simultaneously with the near bankruptcy of its financing. Likewise, gender equality policy took a new twist through a proposal by the Liberal Minister of Social Affairs to introduce a special "daddy's month" into the parental insurance programme. The minister had to pay for this reform by allowing the Christian Democrats to introduce a "protectionist" care allowance for "non-productive" stay-at-home mothers (Björk 2004). The mishandling of the public debt and state budget took a toll on the parties of the non-Social Democratic government of 1991–1994. Four months before the 1994 general elections, the leader of the agrarian Centre Party – but not the other Party members in his cabinet – left to prepare for a new deal with the Social Democrats whereby austerity and survival were combined, leading to "hibernation" or even "volatile sustainability".

Between two crises – the crisis of the early 1990s and the most recent Western financial meltdown of 2008 – the Swedish welfare state hibernated. In the aftermath of the latter crisis, from a larger perspective the continuing Eurozone crisis, the full effects of deregulation and recalibration are evident in Sweden. Chapter IV in the preceeding volume – "The Dialectics of Decentralization and Privatization" – argues that these "dialectics" are still with us. To repeat what was written some 20 years ago: "If one were to believe Georg Friedrich Hegel, the dialectics between decentralization and privatization may give rise to a synthesis on a new and higher order of social welfare" (Olsson 1990:288). If this was the thesis, there may have also been an antithesis or "lower order": the survival strategy of the late 1990s and first half of the first decade of the new millennium. Without invoking further Hegelianism, of which post-modern social sciences are full (cf. Stephanson 2010), behind the strategy were actors other than Minerva's owl. The argument here is that with the advent of the "Blue Labour" Alliance for Sweden in 2006, this interdependency has taken a new turn – or synthesis.

From the vantage point of history, however, the founding moment for the remaking of the welfare state was the chaos of the early 1990s when a blend of social liberals and neoliberals, including some social conservatives, set a new course for the social order known as Sweden. The national party and other traditional movements and parties behind the old regime adjusted and adapted to this course when they returned to the helm in the mid-1990s. They tested the limits of "formula three", the decentralization strategy of the previous decades, during a decade under a prudent fiscal regime and since 2006 in the (Nordic) "context of a new era" (Schubert et al. 2009:428). At the helm was a rhetorically transformed and programmatically united right-of-centre political alliance, a subject to which we will return in the following chapter.

3. The Lost World of the Social Democratic Welfare Regime Type, 1988–2014

> And after all the State is no dead body but consists of living people whose ideals and whose work are living.
>
> Tage Erlander (in Björnsson 2012:55).

Introduction: from welfare administration to market administration?

If the welfare complex – that is, the totality of social policies and programmes – still exists, what has happened to its state and to its dominant national popular social mass movements? We are actually talking about a social democratic regime type, after all, even though decommodification has lost out to recalibration, recommodification, and retrenchment. The Social Democrats, however, were never the only actor in this world of movements, though a large and often decisive component of this environment, while others were key allies in extensive lay coalitions. With the previous chapter having inspected the individual social policies and programmes of the Swedish welfare state, including its financing over the last two decades, it is time to move to another level of analysis and ask: Where do the institutions of the welfare state and its underlying parameters stand in the present situation? If most of these policies and programmes have survived, what about the demographic, economic, organizational, and political correlates that have influenced the making and remaking of the institutions of the Swedish welfare state in recent years? This chapter focuses particularly on the discussion of the macro-correlates and causes explored in chapter III of the previous book in which demographics, economics, politics were singled out for further inquiry, and again taken up, albeit in a slightly different mode, in the concluding part of that book (chapter IV), which added a discussion of power and scarcity.

The aim of this chapter is to overcome the well-known methodological formalism of Swedish sociology (cf. Gouldner 1973:310–3) as well as the limits of Rokkan's schema inherent in chapter III in the preceding book (cf. Rokkan 1999; also Karvonen & Kuhnle 2001). With a little help from a, though limited, plurinational and eclectic reading of the macro-historical sociology of culture (from aesthetics and arts to religion and urbanity), economy, and politics – informed as these subdivisions are by a focus on states rather than firms, not states as firms, in the current international research community – this chapter also aims to shed new light on the imagined national welfare community (Kaspersen 2008 for a related example; see also Engelstad & Kalleberg 1999). Another input, of course, has come from within comparative welfare state research: What mechanisms make a model welfare state tick, and what mechanisms enable various "vested interests" to exert a certain control or influence over processes both inside and outside national welfare states? Is there still an irrigation system cultivated by local modern tax farmers rather than a leaky bucket nourishing overseas tax haven nouveau riches, whether blue, green, or red? These questions reach back to a perennial debate in the social and economic sciences about the relationships between the adherents of creative destruction and critics of destructive creation: the welfare state, democratic societies, and capitalist industrial organization, all three within a reconfigured, maybe embedded, civilizing process.

This chapter explores the special socioeconomic relationships between the three fundamentals of contemporary social formations: the territory, the throne, and the tribe; that is, the nation-state as an expressive totality in an archipelago of nearby and distant organizational relatives (cf. Scott 2009; also Slezkine 2005). In particular, this chapter scrutinizes the central state institutions and their relationships with some of the other "realms of society" (cf. Zetterberg 2009/2010). This especially includes demographics and economics, but also the national popular political party, the Social Democratic Party, and its surrounding institutional and social forces in society and state. The chapter begins with a few archaeological remarks, before moving on to a discussion of demographics and then economics, which is chronologically divided into three brief eras: of uncertainty or deconstruction (even industrial decline), recovery (a renewed economy under "volatile stability"), and permanent austerity and reconstruction (sustainability, globality or a return of "competence"). The next parts of this chapter discuss the demise of institutional set-up, the early post-war welfare state bureaucracies being subordinated to intra-state inspectorates, and the previously dominant national movements and parties, followed by some, still preliminary, concluding remarks.

The secular social state in a world of tribal nations of extended clans and families

States consist of institutions, peoples, resources, and territories, and are embedded in social power relationships that can be economic, ideological, military, or political (Mann 1993). On one hand, these relationships can be with other organizations at the same level, either other territorial states or inter-state conventions or meta-organizations such as the EU, Geneva Convention, ILO, IMF, NATO, UN, or WTO, including courts such as the ICJ and ICTY. On the other hand, the relationships can be reflexive; in a similar vein expressing the competing, coordinating, and mobilizing interdependency between social actors and associations ranging from clans, churches, and firms to movements, networks, and parties. States are extraordinary territorial meta-organizations – Leviathans – which have intrigued the practitioners of political philosophy and sociology through their multiple combinations, even outside the four-fold box of, in particular, strong/weak national popular governments and hard/soft central bureaucracies including ideological state apparatuses (cf. Bötker 2007). The role of local government tends to disappear in such larger accounts, though. As indicated in chapter 2, the modern republic is still fundamentally based on a polymorphous national community with a blend of horizontal and vertical sub-communities.

At the millennium shift in the Swedish case, when most residents born abroad were speaking either Arabic, Bosnian–Croatian–Serbian (BCS), Farsi, or Spanish, a proud minister of education, the Swedish-only speaking (Mienkieli) Thomas Waaranperä, persuaded parliament to recognize a few "post-colonial Others". In linguistic terms, these included the historical and contemporary Finns (the only group of any numerical significance) the travelling Gypsies or Romani, the Eastern European Jews (Yiddisch), his own Tornedalen Mienkieli, and the adjoining Sami of the mountainous far north (Lapponia). Nor was it deemed necessary to include neighbouring Danes, Norwegians, and Swedish-speaking Finns as friendly but distinct Scandinavian brothers and sisters when residing in Sweden.

Apart from the separation of church and state, to be emphasized in chapter 4, the modern republican state also saw the rise of differentiated social classes and fragmented professional enclosures (Brante 2005). Nevertheless, the nation states that emerged from the great revolutions against empires, even the negative ones, and the new world order these brought about, have had one common denominator, namely the nation and its institutions as the embodiment of the extended clan, kinship, tribe, or people (Carsten 2004; cf. also Therborn 2004). Regardless of what conventional theory suggests, human subjectivity has entered the scene cautiously and recently and is still in its infancy within defined territorial boundaries. Nationness and majoritarian residential belonging remain the modern configuration of cultural, economic, military, and political state power, and tribal nationalism is its overarching ideology, regardless of the cultural–republican values the state has emulated and the minoritarian causes that have prevailed. Above the level of nationhood, starting with the Coal and Steel Agreement and the Treaty of Rome in the 1950s and without historical precedent, a new community has over the decades created a famously complex institutional framework of byzantine complexity within an ever larger union of member states, prospects, and "wannabes" (Anderson 2009). Below the level of nationhood, however, another set of communities has emerged in Scandinavia over the centuries. In the nineteenth and twentieth centuries, these were propelled by more or less republican–secular social popular mass movements, which emphasizes that the polities of the Far North stand in marked contrast to the Hobbesian "war of all against all", nineteenth century Norway being an egalitarian frontrunner in Europe.

It was in this global context that the historical kingdoms of Denmark–Norway and Sweden gradually began their transformations, moving from the pre-modern world of warfare into the modern world of welfare, starting in 1809 with the military secession of Sweden's eastern half – most of what is now Finland – and ending in 1905/1918 with the peaceful break-up of the less-than-hundred-year-old monarchical union with Norway in the west, and the violent birth of the republic of Finland in the east. Parliamentary power and universal suffrage date to the end of World War I when the Kaiser and the Czar were ousted in neighbouring Germany and Russia, respectively, although the demise of the Lutheran state church and the military, and the institutional shift towards an impartial bureaucracy had started earlier (see chapter I in the first book). During the twentieth century, the popular movements of the social classes shaped the formation of a dual, central and local, almost tripartite (parliamentary party) state, despite its still being a monarchy with a royal head of state inscribed in the 1974 Constitution (which replaced the 1809 Instrument of Government). This state included the dominant social organizations in agriculture and rural areas, as well as the main associations of industrial and urban business and labour, housing, and consumer markets, the latter multiplying with the growth of modern organizational society (see chapter III in the original volume; cf. also Modéer 2009).

However, unlike in the Soviet Union, it was not the Social Democratic Party but the associated movements – and their counterpart the Employers Association (nowadays Swedish Business) – that tried to attain a veto on the executive. For many years, if not decades, the VU or "standing committee" of the Social Democratic Party acted like a Swedish politburo, while the farmers and financiers of the welfare state usually remained firmly backstage. Similar patterns developed all over Sweden, beginning in the big cities, where the urban liberals and conservatives replaced the representatives of the agrarian Centre Party during the long period they governed jointly with the Social Democrats in the county councils and municipalities. A member state of the European Union (EU) since 1995, the secular social state of Sweden came of age at the turn of the millennium with the end of the state church. As of 2006, the Social Democratic Party had held national power for 69 of the 86 years since 1920 (65 of 74 since 1932); soon after, historical class compromises were reached that set the stage for the coming decades. As indicated, below the level of nationality and nationness, there was a disparate community of communities in Sweden, which still exists. Therefore, in this sequel I have not hesitated to reintroduce a distinction between national and local imagined welfare communities, despite the apparent objection of the concept's originator (see chapter 2 above and Hort 2009a and b).

Urban demographics: class intersectionality, ethno-stereotypes, and social generations

Sweden's population is rapidly approaching 10 million. Roughly two million Swedes have passed away during the last 20 years, and a slightly higher number has been born. Better individual health due to growing prosperity and higher standards of living, partly attributable to welfare state benefits and services, has contributed to significantly increased life expectancy figures (Åkerman & Springfeldt 1995). In 2012, the average Swedish life span was 83 years for women and 79 years for men, compared with 81 and 76, respectively, in 1990. Working-class men and women still die younger than do those who have spent their lives in jobs such as office work, and men who have spent their lives in manual jobs die much earlier than do others, particularly if they have divorced (cf. Linderborg 2007). Although unequal age-group distributions generally change quite slowly in society, most people experience them as they pass through the course of their lives. People may move from one social stratum to another, down or up in existing social hierarchies, either within individual lifetimes or, slightly less obviously, from one generation to another. Therefore, a social generation may be seen as a birth cohort sharing certain chronological and spatial characteristics and experiences that make up the historical conditions for the cultural background of the lives of all those belonging to a particular age group, whether baby-boomers or Generation X, Y, Z. However, neither the young nor the elderly have yet become a historical subject in the sense of a social force, despite the appearance of the youth, or the "aged" or "grey" communities. Nonetheless, their presence has been continuously on the rise in society at large. This means that there are obvious asymmetrical relationships between young and old that go beyond biological asymmetries as part of the social stratification of contemporary differentiated societies (cf. Delcroix 2000).

In addition, the generational mobility of recent decades has transcended domestic and social barriers and boundaries, as well as national ones. This includes elderly immigrants, many of whom arrived after their labour immigrant or asylum-seeking children, as well as many of those working in the care sector as nurses, home helpers, janitors, medical doctors, and so on. These occupations, with the exception of medical doctors, are all in the service sector and in many respects represent the bulk of the "new" working class in Sweden. In 2012, that leaves a potential gender-neutral workforce for the labour market and welfare state of roughly five million professional taxpayers to support the young, old, and disabled with no major change in proportions between the categories, apart from a small but gradual increase in the retired elderly. Thus, mortality and fertility rates generally match each other over the period. The net immigration increase is the reason for the population increase from 8.5 million in 1990 to well above 9.6 million in 2012 (SCB 2012). Another partly overlapping category that has grown constantly for the last five decades consists of considerably younger residents who have at least one parent born abroad. This represents a major demographic transformation of what has historically been a fairly homogeneous clan society: ethnicity and nationality are no longer almost identical. In Sweden, migration is no longer translated as life-long emigration (although the latter still belongs to the national memory), but immigration, making population change a fundamental multi-dimensional and intersectional macro-constellation of the contemporary welfare society and state (cf. Olofsson & Thomell 2012). Following post-colonial doxa, it is the new Swedes, previously considered immigrants or foreigners, that constitute this "other category" changing rapidly in "otherness ranking" from Finns – non-Swedish-speaking citizens of Finland but including the constant Other, the Romani – in the 1960s, through Kurds in the 1980s, to generalized Iraqi or Somalian Muslims of late, the latter according to some experts in this field actually replacing the Romani as the distinct, significant Other (cf. Goody 2004). All Swedish ethno-nationalities differ in some respects, whether chronological, cultural, economic, political, spatial, or symbolic. While some are closer to Foucauldian normality, other such social categories and groupings form a much more deviant habitus-combination than do others, even though most of them, particularly children born in Sweden to parents born elsewhere, share an ambiguous belonging to a social generation or two of the recently arrived: daughters and sons of labour immigrants, asylum seekers, chain migrants, political refugees, etc.

Still, in 2013, some residents perceive themselves as more Swedish than others who also were born and reside there. Surprisingly, such feelings have changed little since the late 1980s, when over 80 per cent of the population belonged to the state church and over one million Swedes were card-carrying members of the national political party, the Social Democrats, affiliated through trade union membership, even though the stereotypical biases associated with more recent churches, communities, and parties have been exposed and mediated by transformative intersectional stratification. In 2012, more than two million people (23 per cent of the Swedish population) were over 60 years old and roughly 1.5 million were over 65, which makes aging a key theme in any projection of the future generational structure of society. The difference between the number of women and men has decreased over the last two decades, partly overshadowing previous class distinctions and perceptions. Hence, more fragmented interest formation may also mobilize voters and affect decisive events, as in the broad-based pro-welfare feminist lobbying before the 1994 national election, which again displayed some strength in 2005 but faded afterwards. Behind the achievements of job creation for women in the welfare sector, a certain demographic component became evident at this crucial time. Soon after the outbreak of the 1990s crisis, fertility rates decreased dramatically and the fear of a decline in the number of native-born children caused some alarm and mobilization. Again child- and family-friendly welfare policies became intertwined with more general women's issues, promoting a positive stance towards central state intervention in demographic issues. Though no longer framed as population policy, the effect of the late-century crisis was in some ways similar to the emerging policy efforts of the 1930s. With an upward trend in births since the turn of the millennium, and another baby boom a decade later, children and parenthood still constitute a discursive demographic factor, though in no sense a collective identity issue, spatially divisive where being ghettoized.

After 20 years of continuous population growth in a sparsely populated territory that has ample capacity to contain and sustain all those who want to settle there, a recent survey indicated that Sweden would be the country of choice of some seven million people around the world – which may upset only the demagogue or specialist. Primary among the noteworthy demographic factors, however, is urbanization, followed by aging, gender, and multiculturalism, with perhaps shifts in generational composition in fifth place. Over the last two decades, the three metropolitan regions and a few educational centres outside them have grown at the expense of the rest of the country. In the south, Malmö and western Scania – Lund and Helsingborg in particular – are becoming increasingly integrated with both Copenhagen and Zealand in Denmark. Building physical bridges, and tunnels, may also affect future social relationships. In the near future, these relationships will even extend towards Hamburg and Berlin, and the region's Swedish hinterland in the north-east including commercial Kalmar, military Karlskrona, and ecclesiastical Växjö as obvious peripheral city outposts, or suburbs (Hort 2010). In the south-west, Göteborg (the second largest city in Sweden) is the hub, with former industrial towns nearby (e.g., Borås and Uddevalla), in the proximity of Norwegian commerce growing and extending southwards from Oslo. Soon there will be a fairly densely populated west Nordic corridor between two Nordic capitals – Oslo and Copenhagen – and the two southern Swedish city regions, also including Halmstad, Gnosjö, Jönköping, and Strömstad. This development may tip the national balance of Scandinavia even farther to the south-west. A northern German(ic) province is in the making, from the south also comes a political reaction against this ongoing social transformation (cf. Glans 1986).

In the Baltic east, however, it is difficult to draw a sharp boundary between Greater Stockholm and the Lake Mälaren region, including the university town of Uppsala, where commuting between centre and periphery is on the increase. Moreover, a fourth, smaller metropolitan region in south-eastern Sweden is emerging, linking the twin cities of Linköping and Norrköping. Taken together, these three or four regions comprise almost half of the Swedish population, and the population of metropolitan Stockholm alone has increased by half a million between 1990 and 2012, demographic projections going through the roof (Lindh 2013). Approximately one million people reside north of the Dalecarlia River, a huge sparsely populated area with Kiruna, Luleå, Sundsvall, Umeå and Östersund as gravitational centres, its southernmost portion bordering on the Stockholm metropolitan area. A recent economic boom in the mining areas has coincided with population stagnation, even decline. These metropolitan growth regions are the parts of the country where the former homogeneity of the Swedish nation-as-people has most strikingly shifted towards an emerging pluri-national or identity-adapted transnational demographic heterogeneity. This is also where the social divisions between rich and poor tend to be most apparent – a familiar scenario in other north-western European cities (Franzén 2009). Gentrified downtown Stockholm and some of its wealthy suburbs – Bromma, Danderyd, Enskede, Lidingö, Nälsta, Saltsjöbaden, and Telefonplan – are, or have recently been, special cases in terms of whiteness.

Demographics matter in any investigation of welfare (Lindh, Malmberg & Palme 2005; see also Sommestad 1998). However, in an institutional-yet-sociological analysis of population, growth or non-growth, including trends and national totals, are intimately intertwined with categories such as class, gender, ethnicity or race, sexuality, region, generation, and even their intersectional moral–spiritual dimensions such as religion, prestige, status, and other systems of belief and recognition. Sweden remains a gendered welfare society in which social divisions, prestige, and status are present, although not always particularly obvious, with the partial exception of the contrasting cases of certain extreme suburban neighbourhoods. The significance of historically organized social collectives cannot be underestimated, even though some of them have clearly lost strength and their traditional historical contours, while others have advanced. Accordingly, theories based on working-class mobilization – which had a strong institutional backing in Swedish academia – are in particular need of renewed critical scrutiny, without dismissing anything for purely ideological reasons (Olsen 2002; O'Connor & Olsen 1998).

The other side of the coin, of course, is the continuing predominance of big business and its trappings in academia, the professions, business, public and social media, society, and the state – i.e., regarding power and knowledge. While either a middle class or an underclass can become a politainment stereotype, any serious examination of the underlying structure will reveal a fairly stable and, therefore, traditional configuration of inertia, regardless of what social stratification model is chosen. It would be simplistic to translate this proposition into a crude class struggle approach, as class movements have been at the helm of politics for most of the period under consideration and have a history far longer than that (cf. Therborn 2012). This has produced its own elites, with the growth of a political labour market that covers the full agenda-setting spectrum and consists of elected full- and part-time politicians as well as professional advisors, editorialists, lobbyists, ombudsmen, op-ed-page editors, pundits, speechwriters, spin doctors, and other courtiers (Garsten, Rothstein & Svallfors 2011). During the two decades under review, politics and entertainment have intermingled in Almedalen, Visby, on the island of Gotland, where the week-long summer camp of the politainment establishment has become big tourism business and an international role model. This was once the site of the start of the political season, when Olof Palme delivered his annual summer speech, and where the labour movement held an economic–political seminar with fewer than a hundred participants. Today, eight parties in parliament evenly share the week's evenings (adding one extra for the latest arrival), and the number of visitors to several hundred seminars totals tens of thousands. A new generation of political entrepreneurs has definitely taken command.

Moreover, the reproduction of the dual, even tripartite, character of the Swedish political class has, on one hand, been elucidated through the continuity of the old regime of the landed aristocracy and financial–industrial bourgeoisie – for example, the royal financier Wallenberg marrying into the nobility as well as what remains of the other "fifteen families" – intertwined with certain fortresses within the old state apparatus, such as the military, which was an important buyer of technological equipment from firms run by the former, which makes it Western and commercial, but also traditionalist in its outlook (Olsson 2013). On the other hand is the ascendancy of another administrative elite around the institutions of the popular social movements and the welfare state, the national party, the "agropolbusiness" complex, and even the trade union movement, in which family bonds and legacies have, in recent decades, tended to improve the chances of their offspring making careers in society at large, but particularly in these institutions and associations (Isaksson 2006; see also Östberg 2009). The symbolic capitals of the two or three ("nouveaux rich" not fully considered in this paragraph; cf. Guillou 2004) may merge or meet institutionally here and there, such as at the Uppsala Military School of Translation, which has produced a welfare recalibration cadre of considerable power and strength and, moreover, has now been open to women for a decade (Orton & Sundqvist 2011; see also Derluguian 2005). Furthermore, the latest royal wedding painstakingly highlighted to the left republican egalitarians the existence of the first elite joining the second/third probably out of pure love. Whatever the case, there remains a considerable gap between these two or three elite circles or sections of the upper classes, which creates new combinations of social conflicts as well as mobility, making relational shifts from one "iron triangle" to another a sensitive positional issue for the future. Nevertheless, the new "red" welfare barons and entrepreneurs have adjusted to the situation and perhaps played according to the rules.

During the decades when roughly one out of five Swedes left for a better life abroad, these prospects were highlighted by the remittances that crossed the North Atlantic. Although the human numbers involved have always been comparatively small, the emphasis on size is relevant to the Swedish and other Nordic cases, where a relatively vast and resource-rich territory was exploited by export-oriented private enterprise and the material surplus has been divided comparatively evenly since the breakthrough of twentieth-century social mobilization and organization. At the start of the new millennium, when inflow had long replaced outflow as the dominant mode of migration, a focus on social exclusion and growing income disparities, particularly in ethno–nationally seg-regated metropolitan areas, was accompanied by a contested awareness among the professional elites of the need to exploit the capacity of all newcomers to the country and eventually involve them in reproducing the affluence of Sweden Incorporated. The following sections, includ-ing three economic subsections, focus on negotiations over the social contract during this period, a drawn-out process of destructive (de)con-struction, sustainable hibernation, and volatile reconstruction.

The political economy of the mature welfare state

The Swedish economy as an institutionalized systemic configura-tion and its various cycles, even conjunctures, are to a certain extent embedded in a particular nation-state and society, with its attendant demographics coupled to (re)negotiated norms, produced and repro-duced practices, and invented and reinvented traditions or cultural mores even during the third industrial revolution (cf. Erixon 2011; also Lindvall 2004; Brenner 1998; Benner 1997). Simultaneously, as a mar-ket it is subject to external and internal competitive and coordinating possibilities and pressures, regulated as it is by international conven-tions and standards since the 1990s, in the Swedish case, especially by the EU and the World Trade Organization (WTO), and also, with regard to human migration and movement, the rest of the UN sys-tem (e.g., UNHCR). In terms of size, the Swedish economy is ranked twenty-second on the World Bank's 2012 list, immediately behind Bel-gium (which has a slightly larger population) and Switzerland (with a slightly smaller population). This suggests that Sweden's economy is of a similar size to the formal economies of other types of European wel-fare regimes. Taken together, however, the four main Nordic economies (i.e., Denmark, Finland, Norway, and Sweden) would place this region among the dozen or so largest economies in the world or within the G20 range, similar to that of Korea, now "Asia's new giant".

In Sweden's case, the crude economic growth figures from late 2011 could be described as "tigerlike", reaching almost 7 per cent for a quarter or two – a figure not seen since the early 1960s and dramatically different from those of the early 1990s – before dipping considerably in the first quarters of 2012. The road to recovery from the great recession of the early 1990s, when GDP dropped for three consecutive years (1991–1993), to the happy days of the most recent year considered here has been fairly bumpy, ultimately reflecting the effects that the 2007 credit crunch and the collapse of Lehman Brothers (on 15 September 2008) had on domestic affairs. Over the last two decades, Sweden's position in the OECD league (purchasing-power-adjusted GDP per capita) has varied between eighth and fourteenth, within a narrow range of countries at a fairly similar level, i.e., Austria, Belgium, Denmark, Finland, (also within this range Australia, Canada, France, Germany as well as Iceland, Japan, and the United Kingdom), while Sweden was held up at the end of the period as a model for others to follow.

In view of recent events, therefore, three distinct sub-periods will be singled out for further scrutiny of the political economy of the welfare state. These are the periods of (1) deconstruction and uncertainty, (2) gradual but unstable recovery, and (3) competence and reconstruction.

*

At some rare moments a nation pauses to reflect on its future. Such moments usually occur in periods of decline and crisis. The ability of a nation to reconsider past decisions and rejuvenate itself is then put to the test. Today Sweden is experiencing its most serious crisis since the 1930s. How Sweden works to overcome the crisis will mark the country for decades to come. The form the solution will take is still an open question. (Lindbeck et al. 1994:1)

1988–1996: The period of deconstruction and uncertainty

In hindsight, there are several harbingers of the shift from a welfare to a market orientation. These include the break-up of the early postwar way of running public affairs, including financial deregulation, the advent of a Swedish neoliberalism "with a human face" after the collapse of the Social Democratic government in 1990 and 1991, and, a year or so later, the near-collapse of welfare state financing, the devaluation of the krona, and consecutive budget deficits caused by an ever-growing public debt. Although the Social Democrats remained in charge for another three-year term, two events signalled the beginning of the end of the old five-party structure and the short twentieth-century national regime type. The first of these was the 1985 entrance into parliament of the leader of the Christian Democratic Party on a Centre Party slate, and the second was the breakthrough of the Green Party in the general election of 1988 – winning 5.5 per cent of the vote and 20 members of Parliament, representing young urban middle-class supporters of the environment and animal welfare. More than 20 years after the ensuing election, it is easy to forget that the Green Party was rejected by the electorate just three years after its first entrance into parliament, only to return in 1994 after three years in the national political wilderness (see also chapter 4 below).

Immediately after the 1988 election, the above-mentioned tax deal with the Liberals was worked out in detail and walked through parliament (see chapter 2). However, a few months after this deal, and less than two years after the 1988 election, the Social Democratic government collapsed under intra-movement pressure: the national trade unions had initially supported a strenuously achieved unity between unions and the Social Democrats, but within hours found themselves unable to support an austerity package including a strike ban as well as economic austerity measures such as a freeze on wages, prices, and income tax. The cabinet handed in their resignations, and, within the labour movement, struggle continued over social and economic policies between the "renewalists", the "Treasury right", or even "Feldt's guerrillas" (nick-named after the ambitious and controversial Minister of Finance) and a broad but diffuse traditionalist centre-left under the firm leadership of the PM (Palme's successor), the former party secretary, the Trade Union Confederation chair, and their close colleagues. However, parliamentary opposition was unable to step in and take the helm as it lacked a clear-cut majority. Instead, the former PM and leader of the Social Democratic party came back as PM, although severely weakened by the departure of his Minister of Finance, who became a high-profile victim of the first political (counter)offensive by the traditionalist political current or faction. However, the Minister of Finance's under-secretary of state, the architect behind the tax deal with the Liberal Party, the chief-of-staff of the "guerillas", and an Uppsala Military School of Translation cadre, remained in charge and was upgraded to the position of cabinet member within the Treasury (in 1996 to become senior Minister of Finance), even though the returning PM in February

1990 chose one of his own close confidants, a former Director-General of the National Labour Market Board, as senior minister at the Treasury (for a different tale, see Eklund & Sjödin 1990).

In Sweden, state fiscal crisis was an almost unknown phenomenon until the 1990s, although the late 1970s did see a significant budget deficit and an increase in public debt. Cost containment was a dominant feature of Swedish social policy in the 1980s (see chapter IV in the foregoing volume). Fiscal prudence characterized much of the 1980s, and a growing Social Democratic faction, centred around the Minister of Finance, became worried by weakening productivity and a perceived lack of efficiency in the public sector. A minor civil war, nicknamed the "War of the Roses", broke out in the labour movement, focusing on issues such as job creation and the financing of the national and local welfare state. Fiscal decentralization increased the responsibilities of local government, which came under strong pressure to set delicate priorities while upholding national standards. Paradoxically, I would argue that this also strengthened the internal morale of local administrators and decision-makers. In some sectors, such as health care and care of the elderly, cost containment was achieved relatively successfully, and benchmarking and "best practices" – learning from others – among and between local authorities gradually emerged. In other areas, such as central state sickness and occupational injury insurance and housing policy, the drive for efficiency was clearly less successful. Accordingly, by the end of the 1980s, the national government had run into severe difficulties financing the welfare state. While the macroeconomic problem of the late 1980s was an overheated economy – unemployment below 2 per cent and a labour shortage – by 1990 the situation had changed and the government had to face recessionary signs.

After the dramatic regrouping of Social Democratic leadership in January 1990, a new accord was reached with the Liberals that included cutbacks in daily sickness benefits – the first time a Swedish Social Democratic government had ever reduced cash benefits. Housing subsidies were scrapped, which meant that a major component of traditional welfare state policies had been abandoned without further consideration. Later that year, in a last-ditch effort by the Social Democrats to save the fixed currency before the general election, the upper echelons of the labour-friendly government announced that fighting inflation had become the government's top priority, at the expense of the traditional full employment target. In a similar vein, an application for membership in the EU was submitted, which would improve the country's ability to implement coherent macroeconomic policy, helping it finance the welfare state. EU membership suddenly became a joint political elite project to promote economic growth while simultaneously protecting costly but generous social programmes. Consequently, it was a weak government that faced the electorate in 1991 and was defeated by the voters.

However, the new minority centre-right government of 1991 – with the tacit but seldom firm support of the populist New Democrats – did not have the same legitimacy as did the previous one in terms of being a guardian of the welfare state, and it ran into severe difficulties as the recession continued and state revenues lagged behind public expenditures. Initially, the new government implemented some bold freedom-of-choice changes following its "New Start for Sweden" programme (see chapter 2). However, the public debt increased considerably and when the long recession started in the early 1990s, the weakness of financial liberalization and of the tax reform became obvious. The tax reform was quickly described as under-financed, and this was underscored by a few visible concessions by the new government to wealthy taxpayers. The government did not take any similarly bold initiatives to raise public revenues, but instead relied on deficit spending rather than major cutbacks in public expenditure. However, social expenditure did not grow disproportionately, as cost control was achieved in traditional budget items; the changes to sickness insurance in early 1990 actually contributed to a surplus in this branch of social insurance and the minor item of worker's compensation was more or less eliminated. At the same time, the cost of unemployment became highly obvious in the form of growth in unemployment insurance expenditures.

In this way, the government increased public borrowing by the day and accumulated a significant public debt. Interest payments on public debt eventually became a significant budget item, making the national currency an easy target for international currency speculators. At a time when the British pound and the Finnish mark were being devalued, the Swedish krona suffered the same fate after a series of spectacular increases in the Bank of Sweden's lending rates, and two formal agreements with an opposition that still had de facto veto power over all crucial public matters. In addition, the central professional administration weakened by the day as the problems escalated – if we are to believe the words of a number of demoralized central state civil servants of the time. It was in this context that the Uppsala cadres – many of whom were also trained at the private Stockholm School of Business where the new centre-right Minister of Finance, a Liberal party MP, had been a professor – stepped up their efforts and from within the Ministry injected new energy into the central state apparatus.

Thus, in the lead-up to the 1994 general election, and in sharp contrast to mainstream "rational choice" election competition theories, the Social Democrats not only advocated cutbacks in welfare benefits to come to terms with the ballooning budget deficit, but also tax hikes. These election promises were promptly delivered, although the Social Democrats initially found it difficult to find dependable support in parliament. After several months of wheeling and dealing with the Liberals to the right, the Greens in the middle, and the Left Party probably to the left, the Social Democrats were finally able to reach an accord with their traditional twentieth-century partner, the still agrarian but now tiny Centre Party (cf. Palme & Vennemo 1998). Although this accord has now been forgotten on both sides, in retrospect it proved decisive for the long-term viability of the welfare state. Although the legitimacy of the welfare state was never in question among the great majority of the population, the fact that two main players at the top level took full responsibility for restoring its main social programmes to a sound fiscal basis defused the explicit neoliberal critique (cf. Nordlund 2003). Furthermore, the growth of the public deficit, including the growth of unemployment insurance benefit costs, was brought under control.

*

In Sweden of the 1990s, the liberal political project has gained a much stronger audience than was expected only a few years ago. (Berner 1996:192)

1996–2006/8: The period of (gradual but fragile) recovery

Well before the global turmoil in the wake of the Asian–Russian financial crisis of 1997–1998, Swedish macroeconomic fundamentals had embarked on a gradual but unstable recovery. The toll the economic recession had taken on society in previous years became a lingering liability for years to come. This period saw a great transformation of working life in Sweden (cf. Kjellberg 2011; see also Bergman & Wigblad 1999). Entire sectors of manufacturing disappeared and more than half a million jobs, most of them in the private sector, were lost. Car companies such as Volvo and Saab became shadows of their former selves under foreign ownership, although parts of them survived successfully as Swedish-owned corporations, producing heavy trucks and defence equipment, respectively. With a solid backing in parliament, the 1994–2006 government acted both cautiously and firmly to prevent collapse, navigating troubled waters to avoid further setbacks (Andersson, J. 2003). However, the disappearance of industries or their sale to foreign investors and the problems generated by the recession of the 1990s made many wage-earning taxpayers redundant, which put tremendous pressure on the pillars of the welfare state. Although many of the newly redundant continued paying tax as unemployment assistance recipients, they paid less in tax and had less money to spend in consumer markets. Those who became social assistance beneficiaries paid no taxes in this capacity and, in most cases, had even less to make ends meet and keep the wheel of consumption turning. However, the growth of the budget deficit had stopped well before the 1998 election, as most social benefits had been reduced at the beginning of the election period but partly restored by the end, benefit rules had been made stricter, and taxes had increased (cf. Lindbom 2007). At the end of the decade, there was even a fairly substantial surplus in public revenues. The public debt remained considerable, and although it was within the limits of European Monetary Union membership (which itself was postponed to the distant future), it was considered a potential liability in any future recession. The possibility of another fiscal crisis in the Swedish welfare state loomed large and was difficult to exclude, even though the spectre of state bankruptcy gradually faded as global demand for traditional Swedish export products increased.

In general terms, unemployment followed a pattern of ups and downs after the sharp increase in the first three years of the 1990s, followed by relative stability and then a clear decline after 1997; unemployment temporarily bottomed before the 2002 election, before increasing somewhat afterwards. A somewhat different pattern applied to incomes, which fell until 1995, but clearly recovered for full-time wage-earners after that. The number of social allowance recipients rose rapidly in the first four years of the decade and then more moderately until 1997, followed by a marked drop. Amid this overall development, however, there have been some marked exceptions to the general rule:

unemployment among single women with children continued to rise when it fell for other groups, child poverty returned as a public issue, while income inequality grew throughout the period, this tendency being accentuated as general income levels recovered. Moreover, the average duration of social assistance did not decrease when the number of recipients fell.

Therefore, between the first and third sub-periods, a major restructuring of the formal economy occurred, with the ICT boom at the turn of the millennium as the first spectacular sign of a "new economy", although this was soon overshadowed by the "old economy" after the stock market crash of late 2000. In the epoch of the spectacle, a brand new social generation had put its mark on Swedish society albeit only for a few years. While mergers in the private banking sector were typical of the early 1990s, and some signs of foreign competition became evident, the dominance of the "big four" banks in the early 2010s is most striking. The Swedish private industrial economy is still based on forestry and manufacturing, including pharmaceuticals and telecommunications, with a remarkable comeback for mining taking place in northern Sweden a few years into the new millennium. Continuity, change, and shifts within the various sectors form the dominant pattern by which new products and enterprises have sprung up while others have faded. Over several decades, an extensive private service sector emerged that, in recent times, has reached into education, health, and personal social services – this is the welfare-state market or freedom-of-choice society.

From the late 1990s until the summer of 2008, most economic indicators improved slightly, with minor ups and downs over the years. Employment improved considerably, although flexible or insecure jobs became part of the pattern to an extent not seen before, and unskilled young people had difficulties establishing themselves on the labour market (Grönlund 2004; Nordenmark 2004). Gender differences diminished, real wages increased, and inflation was kept under control by a Bank of Sweden at arms' length from parliament. Unemployment dropped, including long-term unemployment, but not youth unemployment, which remained a problem for concerned national policymakers as well as municipal politicians and administrators. Income inequality, as measured by the Gini coefficient, increased, while homelessness and residential segregation became slightly more pronounced.

*

The Social Democrats' glory days are long gone and look increasingly unlikely to return. Swedes are less enamoured by the welfare state than they once were. Concerns about jobs and immigration are now more to the fore than equality. And voters seem to put a premium on competence. This election may suggest that the Moderates, not the Social Democrats, have become the natural party of government in Sweden. (*The Economist*, 18 September 2010)

2006/8–2014: The period of competence and reconstruction – a new kind of test case?

Periodizing the beginning of "last month" as part of contemporaneity explicitly elicits the moving target of the conjuncture following the 2006 Swedish election and the 2007 global credit crunch. Whether the autumn of 2006 or of 2008 is taken as the starting point of this period does not matter, as both choices make sense. Here, a twin peak – or deep – solution has been applied to a preliminary answer provided in the autumn of 2010 and afterwards. In October 2006, after 12 years of Social Democratic rule, a new government took over: the four-party Alliance under the leadership of the Moderate Party. Since late 2006, Sweden has again been a social and political experiment, testing its traditional adherence to a civilized version of workfare and social integration, this time in the hands of its domestic "New" or "Blue Labour" – the Moderates or Conservatives – with its "Alliance" government of Liberals, Christian Democrats, and Centre as junior partners. A few days before election day, the incoming PM declared to the *International Herald Tribune* that "What we are doing is taking responsibility for the Nordic Welfare State, but putting it in the context of a new era" (12 September 2006). The Alliance's successful macroeconomic programme was a refreshed work-first one aimed at those people who were eager to work but were outside the labour market, and critical of the welfare system's supposed generosity towards those receiving sickness benefits or relying on other lenient social programmes.

In advance of the election, the Alliance presented itself as espousing a more traditional work-to-welfare platform than were the ruling Social Demecrats and sought a majority on its own. This was the second time since 1991 (the third since 1976) that this coalition had the opportunity to put its stamp on what is perhaps the most famous global welfare model to date. In 1991, the once explicitly neoliberal Moderates and the then-explicitly social liberal Liberals came to power promising a "New Start for Sweden". They managed, albeit somewhat reluctantly, to rally the other two parties, in particular the Centre Party, behind this alternative to the traditional rulers of Sweden. This was also the year in which a right-wing populist party, the New Democrats, entered Swedish parliament for the first time, with some 30 MPs, only to fall apart in the years that followed. Moreover, outside government in the public sphere, think tanks close to these parties, but also close to the interest organizations of business and industry, presented an alternative social model under the slogan of "civil society" (Zetterberg 1995). However, this government and its professional administration had to oversee the worst economic recession since the 1930s. Its three-year performance was put to the electorate and, after the 1994 general elections, the twentieth-century national party of Sweden, the Social Democrats, returned to the helm to resolve the crisis that had been created. After 2006, the reverse occurred: in the narrative of defeat, the new public institutions of the welfare state became weapons of mass deception, or the revenge of civil (welfare) society.

The narrative of victory stresses national responsibility and overlooks the new government's initial period of mediocre performance ("incompetence"). In late 2006, the inexperienced PM seemed indecisive and almost immediately had to sack two female members of his first cabinet, one having paid no payroll tax when employing domestic servants and the other not paying the obligatory annual TV licence fee (though a male cheater survived as Minister of Migration). A year after the election that brought a non-Social Democratic PM to power for the first time in twelve years, the typical public opinion curves – the mid-term support for the governing parties had deeply declined – made the leading national politainer forget that these figures are usually anti-cyclical. It was the handling of the worst Western financial crisis to date, in the aftermath of the bankruptcy of Lehman Brothers (on September 15, or "9.15") that caused the *Financial Times* to crown Sweden's Minister of Finance as the European primus inter pares in December 2011.

In September 2010, regular general elections were again held in Sweden and macroeconomic steering and full employment were again regarded as the most pressing issues by the voters who approved the four-party Alliance government at the expense of a hastily assembled red-green-red three-party alternative – a second-rate version of the so far successful "Blue Labour" Alliance for Sweden. Moreover, (im)migration was lurking in the wings and feelings on the issue were strong enough to mobilize support for another new party, the Sweden Democrats. Of particular interest is that the opposition Social Democrats did not even attempt to capitalize on its "competence" or its achievements of the previous 12 years in government; namely, a solid public purse, a war chest even an unexperienced PM could make good use of after achieving power, and a currency that was not (yet) under attack by international speculators. Perhaps it was because of this missed opportunity in the aftermath of 9.15 that the Social Democrats became associated with non-working "welfare beneficiaries" and various "save the auto industry" attempts instead of its traditional approval of structural change at a time when the Minister of Industry and the Centre Party leader held back at such crisis-mitigating initiatives. According to the World Economic Forum's competitiveness index, which covers some 130 countries, in 2012 the Swedish economy was among the global top five, and in terms of "technological readiness" (i.e., the ability of businesses and households to adopt new technologies), Sweden has, together with neighbouring Finland, been ranked as a global leader for most of the 2000s, Denmark and Norway close behind.

More generally, both within and outside Europe, Sweden's "social model" has again ended up in the spotlight, particularly after the EU member states in the winter of 2008–2009 and afterwards more or less failed to come up with a satisfactory joint response to the economic turmoil. Instead of globalization and "Europeanization" (i.e., the market state), there may be a trend towards "deglobalization" or – in "Euro-lingo" – subsidiarity, i.e., more or less independent actions taken by able-bodied national governments to protect their own state interests and prevent social unrest among their banks, citizens, and electorate. The question is whether the welfare state is still a "shock absorber" in times of crisis, producing social cohesion, or whether its robustness and sustainability will again come under review. In any case, there is great uncertainty everywhere in the Eurozone, particularly in the western portion, about the future, including the future of its welfare states (cf. Roche 2010; Favell & Guiraudon 2011). These are some of the contours of the lost world of the Social Democratic model that will be developed further in the next sections, first as a state, then as party and movement.

The central welfare state
as a meta-institution and policy arena

As of 2012, any previous overview of the most important welfare agencies in Sweden (such as the one from the mid-1980s on p. 112–113 of the
original book; table 2) must be thoroughly revised and reconsidered.
Those welfare agencies and boards that constituted the social welfare–
industrial complex at the time were all under the auspices of the central
government and parliament. The relationship between local authorities
and civil society will be the subject of chapter 4, while the sections that
follow address institutional design, national parliamentary politics, and
political power. In the foreground is the welfare state as an institution
of institutions, or a "meta-organization" attempting to unite various
policy arenas under a joint public agenda in an increasingly regional or
European, even semi-global (i.e., OECD), context (Ahrne 2006).

The central state that intervened in the economy after the 9.15 collapse of toxic assets was a self-assured welfare state that, after more than
a decade of prudent fiscal policy and monetary steering, had its house
in order. It had a public debt financed at a reasonable interest rate,
which kept interest payments as a budget item under control, and at
the start of the crisis it had a considerable budget surplus. Fifteen years
after the collapse of the Swedish krona, macroeconomic planning was
no longer a prerogative of the third party of the traditional apparatus
(the National Labour Market Board), but almost solely in the hands of
the Ministry of Finance (the Swedish Treasury) and a Central Bank that
had been at arm's length from elected laypeople since the mid-1990s.
Hence, in 2010, it was an administration that was able to stand up to
other institutions and organizational arenas and a regime type in which
the state guaranteed a certain basic level of welfare as well as function-
ing markets. It provided somewhat circumscribed support to voluntary
associations in civil society as well as to families and households (the
rule of law in a cohesive society with more or less active members), to
ensure the wellbeing of citizens or particular groups of citizens, residents, and social classes or strata.

This move beyond focusing solely on the state is important, given all
the possible combinations of approaches to and organizations of welfare
provision ("mix") and the ways that responsibility for different elements
can be assigned to different parts of this societal configuration. However,
it is through collective action and decision-making that such delegation

becomes both appropriate and legitimate. Agriculture as a policy arena was a case in point, and favourable opportunities were created early on for an agro–political welfare business complex. Work in this area laid the groundwork for the later regulation of other markets and remains a bone of contention, albeit at the supranational EU or global level. Compared with 1990, therefore, a significant shift has occurred as one policy arena has replaced another as the top public policy priority, whereby an institutional transformation has also taken place within the welfare state. The powerful National Labour Market Board (AMS) – formally under the auspices of the Ministry of Labour (later the Ministry of Industry and then back to the Ministry of Labour since 2006) – was previously the main business cycle regulator, in close cooperation with the Ministry of Finance and, more recently, the Central Bank as well. As a bureaucratic agency with an independent self-confident ethos, the Board occupied a specific position in twentieth-century Swedish administrative history (Rothstein 1996; Pontusson & Swenson 1993). Moreover, its employees were predominantly recruited directly from the inner workings of the labour market – from the trade unions and, to some extent, also from the Employers' Association – and brought up with interventionist zeal within the expanding institution.

Though no longer corporatist in the old sense, as the employers left the Board in the 1980s, it was still an agency with considerable impact on Swedish society and the everyday life of the citizenry. This was despite the fact that the Bank of Sweden was significantly upgraded starting in the 1990s, when low inflation became the primary policy goal at the expense of full employment (Bergström & Rothstein 1999). Furthermore, in the first decade of the twenty-first century, inspired by new public audit and management ideas, the Labour Market Board was reorganized and renamed in line with the local offices as the Employment Service (Af), which signalled the decline of its importance in Swedish society and political life (Lindvret 2006). Still, its inner recruitment pattern has remained fairly non-bureaucratic and close to the actual status of labour market activity; "job coaches" are nowadays typical positions within its ranks, though usually on temporary contracts. In recent years, immigrants well-known to the ethnic and local communities have been recruited by Af to coach other job-seeking immigrants, meaning they have become employees either of this once prestigious public agency or of subcontracting private employment firms (Hajighasemi et al. 2006; Schierenbeck 2003).

Active labour market policy remains an important policy arena and full employment remains a significant policy goal, though it has been downgraded within overall macroeconomic policy and it is probably fair to say that the Employment Service is a shadow of its former self. The work-first principle is still much talked about and adhered to, particularly in contrast to cash benefits, but as a policy goal, full employment has been relegated to the second, or even third, position since the 1990s, replaced as top priority by price stability (though not of real estate) and low inflation. Monetary, fiscal, and competition policy – handled by the Ministry of Finance, the Central Bank, the Tax Agency, and the Competition Agency – have taken command to an extent unheard of during the build-up of the welfare state. Since the 1990s, no Minister of Finance has been directly recruited from the rank-and-file. Consequently, the welfare ministries such as Labour, Social Affairs, and Health have become less significant as portfolios within the cabinet; the Ministry of Housing even disappeared for almost 20 years, before reappearing at the margin in late 2010. In the Sweden of the early twenty-first century, this is how institutions "think" about their proper role in the running of the welfare apparatus, not least in the inner core of the Ministry of Finance and the PM's office (cf. Douglas 1986). Moreover, by 2010, the total number of people employed at the central ministerial level, the Office of Government, had increased from more than 2,000 to almost 5,000 over the previous twenty years, excluding those who worked for various central state agencies and their (now parallel) successors mentioned in table 2. It is still open to debate whether this should be interpreted as signalling an increase in state capacity (Tarschys 2010).

Since 1990, the role of monetary policy and the importance of fighting inflation have attracted the most attention. Starting in the 1980s, and markedly so since the early 1990s, the Central Bank, like those in many other countries, has become a powerhouse on its own, partly decoupled from politics and other governmental agencies (cf. Uusitalo 1984). In Sweden, the Central Bank and its governor were always under the auspices of parliament, although since the democratic breakthrough, it increasingly became a branch of the Ministry of Finance, overseeing the build-up of the welfare state by steering the money supply and fostering price stability. The Central Bank's governing council was usually chaired by the Under-secretary of State within the Ministry of Finance and acted in close cooperation with that ministry. Since the 1970s, with rising inflation, the steering capacity of the Bank (including its governor and council of elected politicians) has come under scrutiny, but it had to wait until four major devaluations and the dramatic failure of a fixed exchange rate to see a new institutional set-up. Simultaneously with the deregulation of credits in the late 1980s, in a first step, the authority of the governing council of the Bank was explicitly supposed to be at arm's length from the Ministry, although no specific monetary targets were written into the new Central Bank Act. In a second move, and in accordance with Sweden's membership in the EU in the 1900s, another law explicitly gave the Bank responsibility for price stability, while remaining accountable to parliament, but with an independent mandate to an executive board of six non-political governors (i.e., academics and bankers) selected on the basis of professional economic merits. Gone was the earlier decision-making board of elected politicians setting interest rates in close cooperation with the Ministry. The independent Central Bank of Sweden must also be added to the list of institutions that belong to national the welfare state – and "inspectorate state" – landscape, not least in times of crisis (*Penning- och valutapolitik* 2010; see also Wetterberg 2009; Molin & Ingves 2008). Moreover, since the crisis of the 1990s, the adjacent National Debt Office and the Finance Inspectorate (both are central state agencies directly under the Ministry of Finance), together with the Central Bank, must be considered a reconfigured cluster of institutions that aim to minimize, if not prevent, the effects of unrestrained global banking, with its modus operandi of organizing much of the population as borrowers (or private welfare beneficiaries/debtors), on the advanced national welfare state, its spending as well as tax-collecting capacity.

Referring to the overview of welfare boards (see table 2 on pp. 112–113 in the first volume), the frequent name changes and the relationships between these boards and central government ministries merit attention twenty years later. As mentioned in chapter 2, the National Social Insurance Board, for instance, has been given the existing name of its local offices and is now called simply the (Social) Insurance Office, while the National Labour Market Board in a similar vein is nowadays officially called the Employment Service, or closer to everyday Swenglish, the "Employment exchange". Recently, both have declined considerably in citizen approval, indicating a loss of social trust in the core institutions of the central welfare state (Statskontoret 2012b). However, most of the welfare boards mentioned in table 2 are still in operation, although their fields of operation may have changed somewhat or been carved up in new and different ways (e.g. Eglinski 1992). Furthermore, over the last decade, most of these boards have, between them and the administrative headquarters of the cabinet, gained a number of parallel central state inspectorates that oversee the daily operations and workings of these central state agencies. The advent of an "inspectorate state" – staffed by superhuman beings formally under the elected government but with a broad mandate to monitor the operations of other central state agencies and of local government – is probably the most significant feature of the present state of the central state; this inspectorate state comprises independent auditing, evaluation, and supervision agencies (cf. Stats-kontoret 2013 and 2011a–c). Coupled to such agencies are the ideologi-cal state apparatuses, the Competition Agency being first among equals (Riksrevisionen 2011).

The evaluation, propagation, and supervision of the efficient use of public resources – i.e., new public management – supply the offi-cial motivation for the establishment of these dual-command central state agencies, such as the Central Board of Education and the School Inspectorate (the latter being an evaluation agency). In those cases in which local government is in charge of large policy areas, political aes-thetics require softer designations. Nevertheless, similar types of con-trol, evaluation, and inspection agencies have been set up, although the Constitution of Sweden does not permit their too close involve-ment in the daily work of professionals employed under the auspices of elected local politicians. Instead, such central state agencies have been given such names as Care Analysis (operating in health and personal social services) or Cultural Analysis (operating in tax-financed leisure activities from the fine arts to sports). In addition, the Growth Agency has a parallel central state-evaluating agency, Growth Analysis, which is also under the leadership of a director-general, a fairly prestigious position in public administration with its own fairly secretive private association. In addition, as of 2012, the 1968 National Board of Health and Welfare is on its way towards partition in a similar vein. More important, perhaps, is the fact that parliament (after a public scandal, or minor attempt at a coup d'état by a civil servant later elevated to the EU level where she helped bring down the Edith Cresson Commission; before her fall out with the then Minister of Finance and the succeed-ing temporary fall from grace, she was the undisputed role-model for a distinguished cohort of female civil servants – akin to the abovemen-tioned Uppsala male translation cadres – within the powerful Budget

Figure 3. The Inspectorate State. The recalibration and reconfiguration
of the Ideological Central State Apparatuses in Sweden in the first decades of the 21st century

ICSAs

The Central Bank of Sweden

Office of the Prime Minister

Ministry of Finance/Budget Directorate

Coalition Government Coordination Office

Ministries of Education, Health, Labor, Welfare, etc.

National Agency for Public Management

National Audit Office

Finance Inspectorate   The Tax Authority

National Debt Office

National Financial Management Authority

Schools Inspectorate

Social Insurance Inspectorate

Care Analysis, Cultural Analysis, Unemployment Insurance Inspectorate, etc.

Competition Agency

National Agency for Education

Insurance Office

National Board of Helath and Welfare (split-up in 2013)

Employment Service ("Exchange")

Abolished agencies after 2007: Animal Welfare Agency, National Board of Integration, National Institute for Working Life

Changing pattern of central level public sector landscape. Comparable table 2 in vol. I, pp. 112–113. Tentative scheme: Agriculture and some EU-related national agencies not included. The notion of Ideological State Apparatus has been further developed among others by Anderson (2001), who stresses its "organic formula" and supplementary ideological/popular component.

Directorate of the MoF, cf. Lindh & Dahlin 2011) took control of the general accounting and audit agency in the early 2000s, which also contributed to increased government efforts to reinstall similar – independent – public administrative agencies close to the ministries.

Of special importance to the idea of an imagined welfare community is the institutional design and turnaround in social insurance. Policy changes, as well as organizational adaptation, have exposed sickness insurance in particular to severe popular criticism, media debate, and political turmoil (cf. Johnson 2009). The level of social trust in this public authority has diminished significantly and it is debatable whether this agency is still part of the national welfare community. Gone are the old semi-public regional institutions overseen by men and women representing various political strands. Before 2004, this field was under the umbrella of 24 decentralized and fairly independent regional Insurance Offices that were actually closer to the imagined local welfare community; they were not formally state agencies, though they had a national superintendent agency, the National Social Insurance Board under the Ministry of Social Affairs. Since 2005, however, this field has been recalibrated, recentralized and re-regulated – the old organizational mix having been replaced by a new central agency, the central state Insurance Office – under intense public criticism. Since 2008, a new, separate and independent central state agency, the Social Insurance Inspectorate, has overseen the workings of the Insurance Office under the auspices of the Ministry of Social Affairs. This has effectively meant the establishment of an almost Soviet-like intra-departmental central state organization (comprising a political commissioner and a professional field commander) to prevent excessive consumption of this type of welfare benefit, which survived the October 2010 sacking of the first Social Insurance Minister of the 2006 cabinet.

Furthermore, Sweden applied for membership in the EU in 1990, and in late 1994 a close-run referendum approved the contract negotiated between Sweden and the EU whereby Sweden, which was crisis-ridden at the time, immediately became a net financier of EU affairs and budget. There was however more than economics into this enlargement of the imagined community (cf. Mathieu 1999). This referendum, which geographically divided the country almost exactly along the lines of the 1922 abolition referendum, created a gulf between the political class and much of the electorate most obvious in elections to the EU Parliament (into which the Swedish Pirate Party entered in 2009).

Within the EU, Sweden immediately became an important advocate of Eastern enlargement, particularly of the Baltic republics which acceded to the EU in 2004, while remaining outside the Eurozone (initiated in 2000), a decision confirmed in a national referendum in 2003. Fifteen years later, the benefits of EU membership for the welfare state and the Swedish model have occasionally been questioned. The free movement of goods, capital, and people has not been unreservedly welcomed, as incidents such as the conflict with Latvia over labour market regulation have made clear. Moreover, national laws have been amended, such as pension rights based on 40 years of residence instead of five, and central state institutions have been redesigned and recalibrated, most clearly in agriculture and in joint efforts to control migration, in Sweden through the Migration Authority (new name since p. 112–113 in the first volume). Apart from the direct election to the EU Parliament, it is still national agencies that implement joint EU directives and decisions made by the EU court. Sweden's social and structural funds are a partial exception, as they are administered by Swedish authorities but financed out of Brussels and, as has repeatedly been demonstrated, are well suited for the type of local partnerships analyzed in chapter 4. Otherwise, the complexity of the EU has probably surprised both friends and foes, and the Euro-scepticism evident at the time of the first membership discussions in the early 1990s still differentiates Swedes from most other peoples of the EU. Part of the imaginary when money pours in from Brussels, EU membership is definitely not part of it when rules infringe on how things used to be and work.

Moreover, with increasing EU cooperation, particularly after the Schengen Agreement came into effect in 2001, the previously fairly generous refugee policy has become increasingly restrictive, with border authorities and regulations coming to the fore. Most recently, new requirements regarding both work and housing for next-of-kin reunification have been implemented in Sweden, in line with European standards and enforced by the Migration Authority in close cooperation with the police authorities. Still, there are differences between "Social Europe" and "the Nordic model". Economic growth and its associated institutional set-up are possible with a number of immigration regimes and welfare state configurations, which vary in scope and generosity, including the characteristics of the Far North. In the early 2000s, a new central state agency, the National Board of Integration, which aimed to increase social and system integration, started operations. However, it was dissolved abruptly in 2006 by the incoming government in an attempt to subsume its welfare activities under the reinforced work-first principle; its director-general, though, was elevated to the cabinet, becoming Minister of the Environment for some years.

The end of the national movement-state: class and gender, minus ethnicity and race

The 302 days of turbulent new leadership lasting most of 2011, when the national party, for the time being by far the largest in opposition, was headed by an inexperienced former backbencher from the south-eastern peripheral municipality of Oskarshamn, was a nightmare for Social Democratic officialdom throughout the country (cf. Loberg 2012 for an eye-witness account from the periphery). The party's approval ratings dropped by the day, and in early 2012, the recently elected party chair, together with his Shadow Minister of Finance and female parliamentary group leader, gave in to media harassment and party head-quarters infighting. In late January 2012, it took less than a week before the (male) chair of the Metalworkers' Federation stepped in to take command, along with a new party leadership team selected from more traditional power circles within the imagined national welfare community, including the central state Tax Authority, and approval ratings rapidly moved back towards normality.

For most of the twentieth century, the Social Democrats had been at the helm of Swedish society and state. However, they were never able to act alone, but were always called to task and constantly had to adapt and reformulate their goals, tactics, and strategies to changing conditions and macro-constellations (Dannefjord 2009; cf. Olofsson 1996). Always in close cooperation with the blue-collar trade union movement and other kindred associations such as consumer and housing co-ops and at arm's length from white-collar unions, the Social Democrats came to be viewed as the national party in the international literature, eventually becoming almost synonymous with the regime type that the labour movement had helped create. However, the class coalition of movements and parties that helped create the welfare state through most of the twentieth century had its locus in the centre of society – the imagined national welfare community – and consisted of farmers, revivalists, teetotallers, and workers from civil society also in the local welfare communities. Concurrent with a time of strong economic take-off, which involved powerful big business organizations, the political and ideological power relationships changed, replacing the old regime centring on the monarch and the Lutheran state church with new and innovative social constellations that represented the world to come. Instead of North American emigration, the likelihood of farm organizers, trade union leaders, and movement and party agitators becoming outcasts or blacklisted diminished, and prospects at home brightened, with sobriety initially paving the way.

Behind each sober man was at least one woman and often several children, gathered around the templar lodge and later also the rural community centre, including the municipal library, the "people's palace" or community centre, and its adjacent amusement park in the imagined local welfare community. For decades, this was a world dominated by men, though with a social structure and an environment of sobriety differing from that of the Anglo-Saxon pub-world or continental working-class masculinity, enabling women to contribute significantly to movements and society. The latter is attested to by the three Annas – Branting, Lindhagen, and Sterky – who, together with Kata Dahlström, were prime early exemplars similar to the female humanitarians elevated in chapter I in this sequel's preceding book (see also Carlsson Wetterberg 2010; Dalström 1987). The Swedish pattern of patriarchal social relationships was also being challenged from both within and without by the '60s generation, at a time when the older national women's organizations, including that of the Social Democrats, seriously considered paying housewives as a means to come to terms with the duality of care and career. Though propped up by generous state grants since the 1960s, the once all-embracing youth movements of the political parties had become entrenched by this time, as both female and male activists found outlets outside the confines of traditional politics (cf. Lundqvist 2001).

Since the 1940s, the Social Democrats have been this movement/coalition's primus inter pares all across Sweden. After the temporary break-up and reuniting of the Liberal Party, however, the popular social mass movements as well as the political parties immediately to their right – i.e., the agrarian Centre and the Liberal parties – fundamentally supported the social welfare state project, although they sometimes challenged the Social Democratic primacy. This created a broad-based covenant supporting the Social Democratic Party, underlying its policies and programmes once the historical compromises had been reached. In the wings were two other political actors that had to adjust to the project of this power centre. To the right, the Conservatives had a social respectability (and a closeness to the Employer's Association) that the Communists to the left (with their closeness to the international power of the Second World) never acquired, although they briefly came close after the Siege of Stalingrad. The Communists were always a junior partner within the labour movement, on the fringe of it from 1948 but in from the cold since the 1960s (see chapter II in volume I). This was the five-party system that lasted until 1988, in which the agrarian Centre and Social Democratic parties had held a firm majority since the mid-1930s, although they were at loggerheads for a while in the 1970s. In parliament, the teetotallers constituted a majority among the MPs well into the 1970s, although sobriety had diminished in the general population. The labour movement was seldom alone, and was periodically in power with the Farmer's League/Centre party, although it dominated in many parts of the country, particularly in its gradually growing urban settings. The rural popular movements were almost as large as the urban ones dominated by the Social Democrats in cities and towns, but their demise came earlier and is more pronounced today as a parliamentary party on the edge of the four-percent threshold. Nevertheless, in a surprising return in the mid-1970s, the Centre Party came to foreshadow the new "Green" movement and reached out to almost one-fourth of the national electorate. In 1980, this national movement reached its peak with the popular referendum on nuclear phase-out (to occur by 2010).

It was not until the late 1970s that partisan politics came to dominate in the municipalities and county councils. Nevertheless, cross-party coalition governments were usual until the late 1990s in these imagined local welfare communities (ILWCs)/common pool resources institutions (CPRs). The Social Democrats had the upper hand in most industrial and urban localities, while the Centre Party dominated the rural areas. The Liberal strongholds were either in a few urban settings or in certain parts of the countryside where the old free churches had a say in local public affairs. Only in fairly atypical municipalities – such as ecclesiastical–military centres or extremely upper-class ones, such as Djursholm or Saltsjöbaden – did the Conservatives manage to keep pace with the new social forces. The City of Stockholm was another exception, where for most of the period the agrarian Centre activists were almost extinct, and the long decline of the Social

Democrats presaged their national demise. Although there were a few decades of record city growth under self-confident and leftist Social Democratic leadership, shared on and off with the Liberals in particular, in the capital, the national party was haunted throughout the century by internal strife between left and right, which heated up at the start of the new millennium, this time a circumscribed closefisted family feud (cf. Högström 2011; Elmbrant 2010). Moreover, compared with participating in national decision-making in the state, party, and unions, ruling cities was always a secondary alternative for prospective candidates. The national civil service became a more rewarding career alternative than serving city hall, for both women and men. For labour movement activists, jobs in private firms have, except for trade union shop stewards, until recently been a second- or third-class alternative. Since the 1990s in Stockholm and most of its surrounding municipalities, the Social Democrats have been in constant decline; Botkyrka and Södertälje, dominated by new or non-ethnically Swedish voters, are still major exceptions to this rule.

In the 1970s, from being a class party of blue-collar men, the Social Democrats came to mobilize and promote young female political representatives, often with a background in either its national youth or student associations; later, they were also recruited directly from the growing civil service in the capital. In an insightful article from the early 1990s, two Canadian scholars concluded that, in the earthquake election of 1991, the Social Democrats had failed to mobilize the women's vote in support of the welfare state project (Jensen & Mahon 1992). In particular, the Liberal Party had a social agenda that made gender equality central. However, having to share power in a coalition that also included a new social conservative Christian Democratic Party, the socially liberal Liberals were discredited during their brief reign before the general elections of 1994. Simultaneously, the neoliberal agenda promoted by a combination of civil servants close to the Treasury and the profession of academic economists mobilized a growing segment of female pro-welfare activists. The Social Democrats were therefore backed by fairly strong and opinionated pressure groups in their attempt to return to power in the 1994 election, despite the party's open advocacy of budgetary cutbacks to bring the ever-increasing national debt payments and borrowing under control (Stark 1997). For the last time in its long rule, the party succeeded in gaining over 40 per cent of the national vote, and for a while considered a formal coalition or informal understanding with the Liberal Party. In the end, after months of uncertainty, as mentioned it was the agrarian Centre Party that again came to its rescue. This tacit coalition, institutionalized at the Ministry of Finance, did not survive the next election, even though the Social Democratic party remained at the helm.

Figure 4. National elections 1988–2010.
Election results as percentage distribution

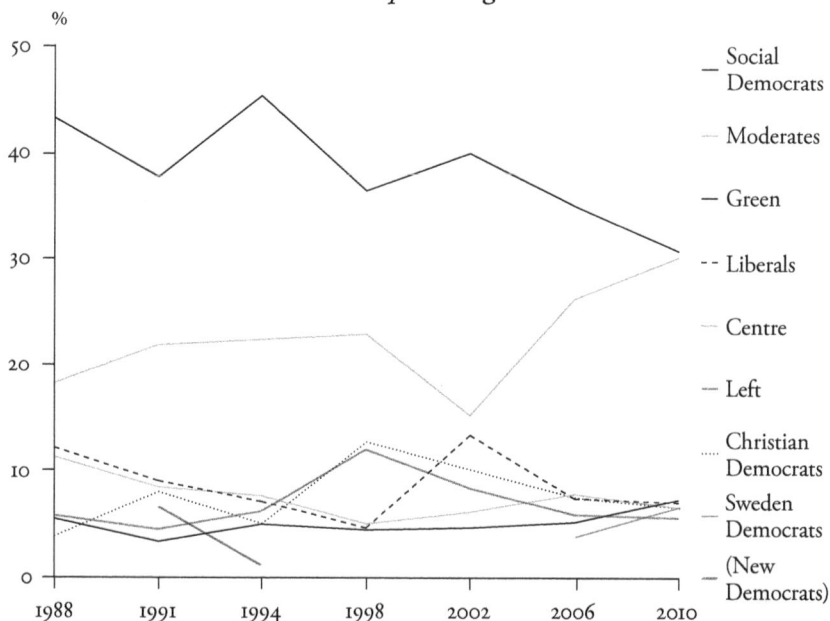

Popular culture including a rich working class literature was a characteristic of Swedish 20th century public life. The break-up of the intellectual hegemony of the movement-state, in particular the decline of the working class movement, was early on envisioned in prophetic but never fully acknowledged novels written by the best pundits in the fourth generation of Social democratic intellectuals (Strand 1982; Svenning 1979; cf. Hitchens 2011). It took a while before their worst premonitions came true. The most recent period of Social Democratic success began in 1994. Movement and party identification were still basically anchored in the social stratification of Swedish society, particularly among large segments of female white-collar employees, who supported the centre-left (although this changed in the 2010 election as a majority of the gainfully employed voted with the "Blue Labour" Alliance for Sweden). Although farmers are numerically marginal today, their role in electoral politics and associasional life remains crucial to an understanding of the development of the Swedish welfare state, especially in its formative years, but also during its most recent restructuring in the 1990s and early 2000s, when an informal coalition between the Social Democratic and Centre parties initially prevented financial collapse and blatant neoliberalism, followed by the birth of "Blue Labour" in a second round.

Table 1. Parliamentary seats 1988–2010[a]

	1988	1991	1994	1998	2002	2006	2010
Social Democrats	156	138	161	131	144	130	112
Left	21	16	22	43	30	22	19
Green	20	–	18	16	17	19	25
Centre	44	31	27	17	22	29	23
Liberals	44	33	26	17	48	28	24
Moderates	66	80	80	82	55	97	107
Christian Democrats	–	27	15	42	33	24	19
New Democrats	–	24	–	–	–	–	–
Sweden Democrats	–	–	–	–	–	–	20

a. See also distribution of parliamentary seats 1928–1948 (volume I, p. 95) and 1945–1986 (volume I, p. 207).

Apart from the New Democratic Party, two new parties appeared on the national political stage in the 1990s: the Christian Democrats on the right and the Greens on the left, at the same time as the Communists became the sole left party after a drawn-out reconfigurational process. Moreover, right-wing populist movements and the feminist movement have tried to challenge the existing political order; and the feminist movement has thoroughly penetrated the established political parties, including the newcomers. Since the 1990s, attempts have been made to establish pensioners' parties, with some success in a few municipalities, but not at the national level. However, the process of interest articulation in recent decades has gone beyond the conflictual traditional corporatist configuration of party politics, agriculture, the labour market, and the old popular social movements. Nevertheless, the logic of collective action is still applicable to most sectors of society, and voluntary national associations with regional and local branches, often with access to governmental financial sources, have mushroomed in the open spaces of the imagined welfare community of civil society.

For twelve consecutive years following the crisis of the 1990s (1994–2006), despite ups and down in national elections, the Social Democrats remained in power to clean up the mess. After Sweden was on the brink of financial collapse, the Social Democrats restored the confidence of international investors in the possibility of financing a large welfare state, not only through borrowing but also through general taxation. In 1996, two years into this process, the Centre Party lent its support and for two decisive years became a major force behind the restructuring of the welfare state. After a poor electoral showing for both parties, the leadership of the Centre Party had to go. In 1998, the Social Democrats shrewdly managed to gain the tacit support of the Green Party (also courted by the Liberals) and the Left Party, which had been extremely successful in this election under a colorful feminist leader (cf. Schyman 1998). In the 2002 election, it was the poor showing of the (old) Moderates that stood out. For twelve consecutive years, the Social Democrats continued in their earlier long-standing role as the national party dating back to the early 1930s, although it never managed hegemonically to reach out to the pivotal electorate of newly-arrived Swedes and their native-born offspring. Altogether, this was the period of global restructuring under the terms of the "Washington consensus". In contrast to the Blairite "third way" taken somewhat later in the UK, the approach taken by the Swedish Social Democrats was closer to the domestic "third way" of the early 1980s, a "formula three" adapted to the preconditions of the new international order or community in which Sweden became a leading exporter of military technology and a de facto NATO member through the Partnership for Peace. The backbone of the movement was still the unions, in alliance with the many strongholds at the local level of government, or ILWCs, and supporting common pool resource institutions.

Moreover, in the 1990s and early 2000s there was no "war of the roses" between government and unions, which reflected the gradual weakening of organized labour on the labour market. Nevertheless, the Swedish Social Democrats managed to remain in their own fortress, or institution of institutions, at both the central and local levels, with the city of Stockholm as the obvious weak link in the chain. Furthermore, the party, not to mention its youth organization, was decreasing in membership, leading to a predicted end of the membership party by 2013. The Social Democrats continued to exercise their influence, apart from via the unions on the labour market, through the central state apparatus and an impressive number of local and regional governments run by the party, either alone or in coalition with centrist parties – i.e., the Liberal, Centre, and Green parties, but excluding the Christian Democrats or Moderates (with perhaps one exception) – or the Left Party. However, it was mainly at the central level that the Social Democrats survived as a national party, although in many respects it retreated into the house of power where its various constituent institutions continued their infighting over scarce budgetary resources and career positions. Though successfully continuing a prudent economic policy and soon creating a budget surplus, the party was haunted throughout the period by its two grand promises from the 1990s. The first was its 1996 pledge to cut unemployment in half, which it achieved for only a few brief months in 2002. The second was its 1998 promise to restore employment to its pre-1990 level by 2004, which it nearly accomplished in 2005. Labour market integration policy was still carried out in an ambitious attempt to combine social and system integration, or a quality of life with a quality of government approach in which legal residency and citizenship obligations and rights were thoroughly divorced from "nativist" conceptions of ethno–national belonging. Despite some setbacks, particularly in the first half of the 1990s, when double-digit unemployment figures affected such issues as the acceptance and social integration of refugees from war-torn former Yugoslavia (particularly Bosnia and later Kosovo), the work-first principle as the normative foundation of the welfare state remained strong.

The parties to the 1996 informal coalition were losing their character as movements by the end of the century, despite the Social Democrats being a national party that remained in power until 2006. This was when, in tandem with the Moderates, the new national leadership of the Centre Party engineered an oppositional work-to-welfare "coalition of the willing" to take over the helm. Clearly within these parameters, after twelve consecutive years of Social Democratic cabinets, at the end rather tired or even decadent, a newborn four-party coalition – the Alliance for Sweden, led by the Moderates (formerly the Conservative

Party, remodelled as "New" or "Blue Labour" along Ukainian lines) – took over the helm. In 2006, for the third time during the era of established representative democracy since 1932, a right-centre coalition of four parties gained a majority in parliament. As indicated above, before the election, the Alliance for Sweden advocated an even stronger emphasis on the work-first principle or active labour market policy, even at the expense of the sound public finances achieved by the former central government during the years of recovery and reconstruction after the worst crisis since the Great Depression. In fact, the success of the new government can be largely attributed to its reiteration of the work-first principle and its adherence to the social integrationist approach. This is not to say that all is well in Sweden: Income inequality has grown since the 1980s, and more recent evidence suggests that the increase in low-wage jobs is largely a result of new labour market policies (notably labour market deregulation) and tax policy, with the creation of new types of jobs for the working poor. Moreover, as in Danish and Norwegian political experience, an undercurrent of ethnic nationalism is making itself felt, most noticeably in the southernmost part of the country. This influenced the electoral process of 2010 with the advent of another new political party, the Sweden Democrats, wielding the swing vote in parliament. Nevertheless, social cohesion, compromise, and coordination between conflicting societal actors so far remain fundamental pillars of the polity and culture of Sweden.

In 2010, the end of the Social Democracts' status as the national party was most obvious in its defeat in the general election as part of the previously mentioned hastily assembled top-down three-party opposition alternative to the incumbent cabinet. From this most recent election emerged a severely wounded Social Democratic Party, although it remained the largest party in parliament, roughly equalling the main governmental party, the Moderates. Both parties had 30 per cent of the votes, which represented the Social Democrats' worst result since 1914. In the six general elections between 1991 and 2010, Social Democratic support ranged between 30 per cent and 45 per cent, with the 1994 figure of 45 per cent coming close to the average for most of the twentieth century. The earthquake election of 1991 reduced party support by almost 10 per cent to a level not seen since 1928, and this poor showing was repeated in 2006 and 1998. Apart from its 1994 popular vote, only the 2002 figure of 38 per cent, which was still comparatively low, indicated improvement.

After the 2010 election, the hollowness of the Social Democratic parliamentary group became apparent. The female party leader from 2007, the party's first female leader who had to drop out of the 1996 leadership contest after dirty infighting, was considered finished by large segments of the movement and had to go, while the party's municipal strongholds of Göteborg and Malmö remained intact. In some municipalities, such as Kalmar, the party even gained in popular vote, and it was from the vicinity of this Copenhagen suburb that in late 2010 the Stockholm leadership was challenged and temporarily defeated. Compared with developments in neighbouring Denmark and Norway, where the Social Democrats have reappeared as national governors/inheritors, the party may eventually regain some of its former strength in Sweden, although it is unlikely to become the dominant force it was in the mid to late twentieth century. This is not least due to its failure to move from mobilizing gender to mobilizing minority ethno–nationality; as mentioned, the latter is a much more diverse group of clans and tribes that vary in time and space in terms of their relationship to the former national party (cf. Dahlström 2004; also Dahlstedt 2005).

At the turn of the century, the party attempted to court this group through the national programme mentioned in chapter 2; namely, the Metropolitan Development Initiative encompassing 24 neighbourhoods in Göteborg, Malmö, and five municipalities in metropolitan Stockholm, including five neighbourhoods in the capital itself. However, the programme was aborted and handed over to the involved municipalities in 2002, after fairly successfully mobilizing the suburban ethnic vote (Kings 2011, 2010; see also Lawson 2008). In 2002, there were also apparent failures, particularly in Landskrona in the vicinity of Copenhagen, but these were, at a distance from the capital, not among the seven municipalities included in the Metropolitan Development Initiative. After the election, the PM and the Treasury thought that enough had been invested in the poor suburbs, and the party could not muster enough leverage to combat this inner nucleus, or fortress, within the central state. The central state became the fortress of Social Democratic officialdom defending the interests of the party elite against a demobilized and demoralized party-movement in the ILWCs. In 2006, having temporarily satisfied the party elite, this reluctance to provide education and jobs to young people in the suburbs turned out to be an electoral disaster when southern Swedish urban neighbourhoods populated largely by newcomers and their neighbours abandoned the Social Democrats and turned to the Sweden Democrats, a pattern strengthened in 2010. Most importantly, never in modern Swedish politics have the traditional national rulers been out of power for such a long time – as of 2014 for eight consecutive years – and their prospects of recovery that year are still slim given the considerable financial resources the "first class", competent Minister of Finance inherited and carefully holds in trust. This is despite the fact that early 2013 opinion polls give the Social Democrats a fair chance.

Conclusions: the central state strikes back

To assemble at least the main pieces of the puzzle, most national trends indicate a flourishing, even happy or content, though environmentally worried society; demographics have, for most of the period, been a success story as fertility rates have been bolstered by family policy measures. Swedish civil society is a fairly vibrant national community of healthy inhabitants, though with considerable internal variation and differentiation. After the two decades under review, the new demographic composition has resulted in a socio-political outcome that may challenge the cohesion of Swedish society and state but has so far paid off in the form of growing prosperity among the great majority. The macroeconomic situation went from near-catastrophic to exemplary, though such trends will break down sooner rather than later The institutional recalibration of the central welfare state has not been particularly impressive to date, however. It has even been counterproductive in some ways, as agencies used each other as "human shields" in desperate attempts by the inner core to control any existing sub-centres of power. Throughout the period in question, fairly weak governments have been combined with an entrenched central bureaucracy, which has resulted in a narrowing of horizons and of conceptions of the available welfare policy alternatives. Two soft-state weaklings have given way to a harder society as power relationships have changed. At first, the central state saved the banks, which, with the market in the wings, came back with a vengeance, the four survivors being Nordea, SEB, SHB, and Swedbank. Later, the inner core of the state became increasingly preoccupied with its own public administration, particularly the autonomy of local government, resulting in a weakening of the movements behind the twentieth-century state. The new dual command of the central system likely reflects the shifting power relationships as one "iron triangle" transitions to another, rather than the efficiency and rationality of received wisdom. At present, this is the challenge that civil society and local government face.

The "stateness" of society is still comprehensive in its penetration ("the people's home" and the "Swedish model" of political compromise and peaceful labour market agreements), but so is the "societyness" of the state ("our state" or the "strong society"). Therefore, the Swedish welfare state consists of a number of specific welfare institutions and policy arenas that currently include supranationals and locals. The power structure is rooted primarily in the institutionalized class divisions, and interests generated by the advent of capitalism and popular social mobilization in the late nineteenth century, though a new iron triangle is hinted at. For many years, it was the relationship between the highly centralized corporatist labour market organizations that stood out: the Employers' Association recognized the national organization of blue-collar trade unions as their sole counterpart. The Social Democrats' long reign, either alone or in coalition with political support from both the right and the left for most of the twentieth century, has given rise to the global notion of a decommodified social democratic welfare regime and even the social-democratization of the world (cf. Judt 2009; cf. Berman 2006).

Hence, it is a "big" welfare state – in terms of spending, the numbers of union members, and the numbers it employs – with a comprehensive set of provisions conditioned primarily on age, citizenship, and residence. It is a state that embeds market dynamics and is therefore itself embedded in an imagined welfare community in which monetary relationships thoroughly imbue everyday life, a state that takes responsibility for a range of measures intended to ensure the wellbeing of its citizens. It does this, for instance, by providing publicly funded education for children and adolescents, access to health care, shelter, and housing over the lifespan, financial support for periods out of work, and personal social services in the event of disability or other personal hardship. In many respects an honorable achievement for the electorate, it is ultimately unsatisfactory, as full employment was never restored, and other welfare programmes, such as sickness insurance, face intense popular criticism. A new, in various ways "blue" Swedish labour has seen the light of day in state and society.

Long after the defection of its most flamboyant standard-bearer, "Feldt's guerrillas" proved victorious in the politics of welfare and warfare. However, it took a while to turn a public welfare administration into a tax-financed welfare market. The detour through the reign of Bildt and Westerberg (1991–1994) and furthered by Persson and Johansson (1996–1998) meant that the central state returned to the top–down Myrdal approach and abandoned the previous, more bottom–up road towards civil welfare society envisaged by Möller (Minister of Social Affairs, 1932–1951) and slightly modified and continued during the Erlander, Hedlund, Sträng, Palme, and Carlsson stewardships of the "strong society", "common sector", and even "social investment paradigm". Of course, there was also centralization, as when the municipalities decreased from over 2,000 (1952) to around 300 (1974), but this was part of the Möller programme to create viable CPR utilization under popular control. In the early 2000s, dynamic, conservative re-centralists struck back at this approach without diminishing the number of units, although they tried and partly succeeded in reducing the number of county councils (cf. Hort 2004a). So far, some municipalities have managed to remain true to the ILWC, while others have surrendered to the subaltern strategy devised by the present leadership of the National Association of County Councils and Municipalities – a merged entity that replaced the previous two, sometimes competing and almost always slightly different voices of local government. In recent years, the joint association has worked in close cooperation with the national cabinet, the association being the long arm of the Ministry of Health and Social Affairs, in sharp contrast to its previous independence, whether the government was centre-left or -right (cf. Ramel 1994). In other municipalities, the Social Democrats in particular have utterly failed to uphold their legacy of competence, Norberg and Norrtälje being cases in point.

The archaeological opening of this chapter was the macro-sociological relationships between the three fundamentals of the modern republic, i.e., territory, throne, and tribe. Researchers in neighbouring Norway, where the historical compromises that came to form the twentieth-century welfare state were not that different from the Swedish pattern, dubbed this the "iron triangle" of business, farmers-fishers, and labour. In this iron triangle, power and the state were inscribed in a way fairly similar to that of twentieth-century Denmark, where the first two were almost indistinguishable, while in Copenhagen, the modern radical cultural intelligentsia and the archaic royal household and its entourage constantly competed over the third position in this triumvirate. Initially formulated in neo-functionalist equilibrium terms, as a generalized figure of thought, the iron triangle caught the imagination of a generation of social researchers (Mjøset 1991). In Sweden, where academic researchers were more ambivalent and reluctant to speak truth to power, it is perhaps more appropriate to use the words of its early post-war longstanding premier, quoted at the start of this chapter, who said that this state was the "strong society", or the amalgamation of the imagined national and the local welfare community of movements, parties, and peoples (Olsson 1991; see also Ruin 1990).

This configuration lasted throughout the century, although the balance between the national and local levels tilted towards the latter by the end of this era, as discussed in chapter IV in the previous volume and to be continued in chapter 4 of this sequel. It was during this time that the "order of things" went from critique to practice, and the deep state establishment started to strike back at the threatened break-up of the economic and fiscal power and resources of the nation-state and some of its constituent societal parts; moving backwards when the church turned forwards, the Lutheran ethic returned in an emerging Schumpeterian or even post-Fordist workfare state (cf. Sassoon 1996; Jessop et al. 1991). At the local level, however, many, but far from all, of the previous CPRs have remained within the ILWCs.

Into the 2000s, a different, more circumscribed, Swedish iron triangle began to see the light of day at the national level. The three corners to which, in recent decades, declining social movements and political parties have had to pay respect comprise: first, the Treasury, including the Bank of Sweden; second, the private banks and the financial sector, including bank-controlled big businesses; and, third, the elite professions including academic accountants and those making big money in law and lobbying firms and think-tanks, self-employed pension investment advisers, and the upper echelons of the mass media. In contrast, a new street-level welfare administration was in place throughout the country at the end of the 1980s, when their masters, the parliamentary party structure, began to fundamentally crumble, reflecting deeper cleavages in the society–state relationship. There was also the coming of new generations with more distant experience of the hardships of the pre- and early post-war periods and of popular movement discipline, but subjectively closer to the environmental challenges of a mass consumption risk society. Over the last two decades, the most likely emergent conflicts of welfare society have been evident in a multifaceted battle over ideas and practices, which can be summarized as a new discourse of money, politics, and power. In particular, the legislative language of welfare reform and its associated public debate have changed remarkably over the last two decades compared with the previous era of social reforms in Sweden. No longer just an extension of social benefits and programmes, although various free lunches have sometimes been on offer, it is the proponents of welfare adjustments, cutbacks, downsizing, and retrenchment policies – whether centre, left, or right – who have tried to capture the meaning of responsible welfare reform or recalibration.

From the fierce battles between the advocates and critics of civil society over the 1994 public election-campaign struggle between academic economists, on the one hand, and feminist activists and pundits, on the other, to the 2006 campaign's competing formulations of the work-first principle – beneficiaries versus wage-earners, scroungers versus hard-working salaried white ethno–national Swedish (young male) employees – runs the red thread of an emerging world of supermen and women – i.e., the state leadership of not always secular Others. Demographics, economics, language, and politics went hand in hand in turning the futures of aspirations, dreams, and expectations around, if not upside down.

4. Civil Society: Challenging the Welfare State since the 1990s

The 1864 freedom of association reform spurred the growth of the "free churches", Protestant churches that had broken away from Lutheranism, including Baptists, Methodists, and other evangelical groupings. The free churches attracted members from all strata of society, especially the industrial and rural working classes. The 1864 reform also facilitated the emergence of other organized groups in civil society, such as the labour unions, the temperance movement, and consumer organizations (collectively known as the popular movements).

Anderson, K. (2009). "The Church as Nation? The Role of Religion in the Development of the Swedish Welfare State", in Van Kersbergen & Manow, p. 218.

Introduction: the invention of civil society in an imagined welfare community

The topic of this fourth chapter of the sequel is civil society. After a Gramscian springtime in the mid-1960s, this notion gained wider currency in Sweden from the early 1990s. In a genuine dialectical somersault, the czarist East was replaced by the post-Soviet Far North where "the state was everything", society by contrast a suppressed nothing ("backward", "primordial and gelatinous" in the language of *Prison Notebooks*). The Atlantic West, now in reality the Euroatlantic West-southwest, remained as it always had been: civil society balanced in a proper equilibrium with political society (or the state), the latter "only an outer ditch", the former a robust, sustainable, or "sturdy" system of "fortresses and earthworks" (Gramsci 1971:238). Gradually, the Swedish communality – the hegemonic welfare state, which was neither a "progress machine" or "prototype of modern society", in the words of David Jenkins (1968) and Richard Tomasson (1970), respectively, nor an imagined welfare community or communities of equals and unequal – became a coercive and totalitarian Leviathan where the invisible hand, the regimented Foucauldian individual, had lost its freedom of action. A critical concept had become a weapon of mass deception. The civil society challenge was born.

This chapter takes up where the first chapter in the original 1990 edition began, providing wider discussion of the birth of popular social mass movements or "free churches". This approach is familiar from the previous two chapters, as the discussion focuses on the relationship between the welfare state and civil society. It also addresses the issue of privatization, treated in chapter IV in the original book and in chapters 2 and 3 of this sequel. It discusses the relationship between modern society and the state, or welfare society and the welfare state, in particular, examining the relationship between the "etatization" of society and the "societalization" or "marketization" of the state. Simply stated, has the modern state taken charge of society, or has society conquered the state? If there is no simple answer, then how, where, and why have associations, firms, forces, and movements in civil society challenged the welfare state since the early 1990s? Moreover, if there is a trend towards a tax-financed welfare market society, how has this been mitigated during this period by the illiberal, yet mostly tolerant, community of "free churches"?

Approximately one decade after the international community proclaimed the advantages of the welfare society, in Sweden civil society challenged the national welfare state consensus. This critique of the welfare state was dual-faceted, evident in two general practices: the expansion of for-profit welfare outlets, and an emphasis on non-profit, voluntary activities in civil or welfare society. The key to understanding this dual-faceted practical critique of the welfare state is the existence of an imagined (Swedish) national welfare community comprising hundreds, if not thousands, of local welfare communities. These communities are united through national (i.e., civil society) "new corporatism", as well as through about 300 secular municipal and/or regional authorities with independent power of taxation. In addition, there are the tax-financed but reinvigorated historical institutions of the Lutheran church, in particular some 2,000 parishes of the former state church. Once a stronghold of the old regime, they are now, not without consternation, being transformed by a Northern, intersectional, primarily feminist form of liberal theology into standard-bearers of human rights and social justice (Eriksson 2012; see also Swedish Church 2009 and Jeppson Grassman 1994).

The pressure on the welfare state was localized, but the national consensus came first. Meanwhile, Möller's construction of this new state followed suit at another level of society. In the Swedish Constitution, the local and regional levels of government are of equal standing, and their roles are deemed so essential they are enshrined in fundamental law. As the first paragraph of the 1974 Instruction of Government explains: "All public power in Sweden proceeds from the people. Swedish democracy is founded on the free formation of opinion and universal and equal suffrage. It shall be realized through a representative and parliamentary polity and through local government. Public power is exercised under the law". A few years after the new constitution was launched, the OECD clergy all over the Western world sought to prevent excessive social spending, rather than having lay people claim constitutionality and take command of local or national government through collective action. Fifteen years later, the Swedish parliament, in what might be considered an act of excessive central state power, put a cap on municipal spending. The new national budget law also made the MPs of the national assembly subservient to the professional party elites, who were retained by good pay and promoted for loyalty (cf. Pålsson 2011; also Gahrton 1985). At the end of this period, after the 2008 financial meltdown, even the earlier irresponsible Left Party was forced into this conformism in exchange for a future place in the political sun.

The steps taken at the beginning of chapters 2 and 3 above permit the elaboration of a societal model that goes beyond simple accusations of being a municipal or local government "hugger". The notion of civil society as defined here is not a catch-all concept. Instead, it strictly reflects the forms such society has taken in contemporary Sweden in relation to the welfare state over the last two decades (cf. Olsson Hort 2001). The main focus of the concept is on the relationship between the local welfare state, voluntary associations, and for-profit companies providing tax-financed welfare services. However, this relationship exists at the micro-level of society, here viewed through the lenses of comparative, historical, and institutional macro-sociology. The notion embodies part of the civilizing process once envisaged by Norbert Elias (2000), recognizing that civility and civilization are not identical (cf.

Ferge 1999; also Olofsson 1999; Gough & Olofsson 1999). Hence, the individual is not an armed cowboy, as in Anglo-American ideological discourse, in which the distinction between individuals and families is blurred. In everyday civil society, men and women occupy gendered positions that bond people through various social relationships, ranging from reciprocal household obligations to collective action outside the intimate sphere. In modern capitalism, this can also be a social democratic class society. Through their biographies and habitus, human beings create and recreate their present and future, under conditions prepared by their predecessors; successors take up their roles under specific geophysical and moral-spiritual conditions and locations. There is also a spatial dimension to Scandinavian society that makes relevant the idea of civility and imagined communities.

In contrast to civil society, the concept of imagined welfare communities is a heretical reading of twentieth-century secular enlightenment thought at the local, national, or European level. In this chapter, the institutions, associations, and citizens of the kingdoms of the Far North are considered imagined national welfare communities, comprising many imagined *local* welfare communities. In Sweden, this imagined national welfare community extends from the Danish border in the south to the Norwegian border in the west – even as far as the Faroe Islands and Iceland – and the Baltic–Finnish border in the east. Demographically, it encompasses everyone from the aboriginal Samis in the North, to the recently arrived Euro Turks and other abrahamite congregations predominantly living in the big cities of the South. The concept stands in opposition to the dominant mode of thinking in the Swedish capital and its academic vicinity, where any attempt at either breaking up or enlarging the national polity (except via the EU) is considered blasphemous (for an exception, see Wetterberg 2010). Today's free churches are not the same as earlier ones, or those that may come in the future. Nevertheless, the experience of that kind of freedom, necessity, and possibility creates other possible freedoms and liberties, regardless of what present governors either tolerate or prohibit. The change in the relationship between sacred and secular local government in Scandinavia has not been previously analyzed, or has been distorted in an inward-looking disciplinary language of governance and governmentability. This ecumenical approach is the starting point for a long journey through a landscape under constant transformation (for a sober journalistic account, see Mattsson 2010; also the more electrolytic Greider 2001).

This chapter looks further into the workings of contemporary Swedish civil or welfare society and makes more predictions about the future than do the previous chapters. It starts with the privatizations of the 1990s and the first decade of the new millennium. The first section assesses the impact of private markets on the current welfare sector and the role of for-profit business organizations within it. The second section reconsiders the relationship at the local level between government and the non-profit voluntary welfare sector. Since 2000, the Church of Sweden (formerly the Lutheran state church) has been the largest voluntary membership association with more members than the three national unions taken together. The third section traces the growth of political civil society at the local level and also discusses the recent breakthrough of an ethno–nationalist political party in representative assemblies, along with tribal, ethno–national, and post-colonial welfare. Section 4 considers resistance to welfare cutbacks and anti-austerity protests emanating from civil society with the aim of defending an embedded society–state relationship within an imagined national or local welfare community. Section 5 contrasts the notion of civil society with its historic liberal–conservative counterpart, i.e., the bourgeois–Christian society, attempting to examine the republican–secular nature of contemporary challenges to imagined local and national welfare communities. Out of this comes the alternative notion of a republican–secular social formation, situated in contemporary imagined civil society or national welfare communities where recently the bellicose right has made its presence felt. A few concluding remarks on the hibernating route from the non-profit take-off to the for-profit bonanza ends this fourth chapter of volume II, or the sequel.

Civil society as a tax-financed welfare practice

Entrepreneurship was encouraged throughout the welfare sector with the advent of the 1991 non-Social Democratic regime (the first under a Moderate/Conservative PM since 1928). State monopolies in ICT were opened up to vibrant completion in the epoch of the spectacle. In particular, activities financed, organized, and produced by local government were strongly encouraged. The deregulation of strictly regulated public welfare programmes in education and in services to the disabled, elderly, families, and children changed the restrictions under which private contractors had operated in the 1980s (discussed in chapter IV, of volume I, and in the 1993 postscript). Non-profit and for-profit enterprises became contractors to the public sector. Intervention through national political decision-making was influenced by the social-liberal and centre parties (Löfgren 2013; also Gratzer forthc., Ahn & Olsson Hort 2003, Sutton 1996, Cohn 1992). At the same time, think tanks aligned with the Moderate Party, major banks, and the Employers' Association launched the Social State project. Through this project, the notion of civil society reached public discourse, explicitly challenging the briefly almost sacred concept in comparative welfare state research of decommodification, and the social democratic welfare regime type (Zetterberg 1995; see also Bambra 2006; Room 2000). A practical and theoretical public-sector reform agenda – new public management – therefore turned the Swedish public sphere upside down.

In rereading the postscript to the 1993 edition of this book, it is noteworthy that today's middle-aged rulers – Borg (Minister of Finance since 2006) and Kristersson (Minister of Social Security in 2010) in particular – had already entered centre stage on the intellectual welfare scene early on (see also Hort 2004a). Only the present Prime Minister Reinfeldt (since 2006) is not discussed in the earlier work. Notably, he wrote a booklet attacking the prevailing welfare state consensus, *The People Asleep* (*Det sovande folket*, 1993), edited by his spin doctor Per Schlingmann. This was reissued by his foes in 2008 as an internet facsimile. The first line of the first paragraph is worth quoting: "The Moderate's alternative to the strong state of the Social Democrats is confidence in civil society". He was a born-again, compassionate neo-conservative, having ousted the neo-liberal national leadership of the Moderate youth association (Kristersson, in 2010 Minister of Social Security).

Twenty years later, the result is impressive: a publicly financed, private welfare system in education, health, and personal social services, including a labour exchange. This has emerged parallel to the old public welfare system, and is financed out of it. The Heritage Foundation has recently awarded Sweden high marks for these achievements. Competition has increased between private and public providers, but so have concentration processes in the new private business sector. For-profit firms have expanded at the expense of non-profit philanthropy, and a fair share of tax money has been transformed into stock dividends. These four political parties – apart from the Moderates also the Liberal, Centre and Christian Democratic parties – were unable to remain at the helm, and saw the Social Democrats back in power in 1994. They had to wait until 2006 (three full election cycles) to return to power. However, it is the effects of their early breakthrough in the 1990s that figure most prominently in this current account and assessment, as the national decisions made in the early 1990s mostly remained in force from 1992 to the time of writing. These decisions made it possible for individual county councils and municipalities to pursue their own agendas and strategies. The making of a modern civil society in Sweden thus occurred within a generous, imagined, cross-cultural, tribal, if not ethno–national welfare community.

There was a second for-profit take-off, this time in education and health as a business, after the 2006 change of government when the rules changed in favour of private education providers (Turner 2010; see also Jarl et al. 2010 and Björklund et al. 2005). Primary and secondary education business insiders talk about "the big five", similar to the "big five" in manufacturing in the 1940s, namely, Academedia, John Bauer (JB went bankrupt in June 2013 with more than one billion SEK in debts; its CEO nevertheless immediately launched a new school company), Pysslingen, Baggium, and Kunskapsskolan, with Engelska (International English Schools) as an important sixth-place competitor. These companies almost completely conquered the publicly funded voucher market in the 2010s. After 2006, the municipalities were no longer allowed to spend more money on children in public education than in private, and some started their own "free schools" in an attempt at branding and competition. At first, private schools were a big-city phenomenon, but after 2006, there were at least one or two competing private school alternatives in every medium-sized Swedish city and town. Private non-profit schools run by mostly tribal linguistic and/or religious congregations in civil society have given voice to feelings of fear and unrest in liberal ruling circles, as well as among the ethnic national–populist forces of the imagined welfare community. The arrival of the big-five education businesses heralded the carving up of the market, thereby more or less ending competition from smaller private education providers. For instance, one of these big education companies was owned by the wife of one of the most outspoken neoliberal pundits, who was himself a board member. In the preschool sector, following the early test case of the 1980s (see Pysslingen in chapter IV in the preceeding book), there are still a number of parents' and worker-owned co-ops spread across the country. However, there is also a tendency here towards the dominance of established education firms. Taken together, private education, including the small sector of non-profits, controls about a quarter of the market (roughly 40 per cent of upper secondary schools in 2013). The rest of the schools are publicly provided, and all, including the above-mentioned private schools, are almost 100 per cent publicly funded.

The voucher system has become the dominant mode of financing, although some municipalities also contract out their schools. In a controversial case, the municipality once run by the former wife of the 2006–2013 PM sold the main upper-secondary school to its principal at below market value. A court ruling against this sell-off of public property had no effect, as municipalities are effectively above the law. The voucher system was only gradually phased into operation in the early 1990s. It then slowly increased until the aforementioned "take-off" at the end of the last decade (Allelin 2012). Most recently, in Stockholm there are signs that the popularity of private schools has reached its climax. Outside the compulsory school system, there is also a market for immigrant language education as well as some specialized schools in the cultural sector focusing on paying young adults. In tertiary academic education, incentives to encourage students to pass exams speedily were introduced in the early 1990s, and students are restricted as to the number of semesters for which they can obtain state study loans. With the exception of the Stockholm Business School and two undercapitalized non-profit universities that are endowed with previous wage-earner funds, this sector is entirely publicly funded and provided. Beyond that, there has been no move towards privatizing the university system.

In the health sector, the privatization of hospitals and clinics operated by the regional county councils has been a bone of contention between left and right, with reducing queues as the main official reason for the move. In the late 1980s, the centre-right parties proposed and later implemented guarantees regarding treatment for a limited number of surgical operations. This was done to establish maximum waiting periods. If a county makes a patient wait longer than the benchmark waiting period for treatment, the patient has the freedom to go to a private provider. Alternatively, the patient can go to another county, and send the bills to the county of residency. This guarantee created a whole new category of publicly subsidized patients for private commercial providers. Some counties began extending their existing arrangements with for-profit providers in order to deliver on their promises. Most hospitals are still run by regional governments, and thus tax financed, just as are most health services. To top up this funding, user fees have always been a minor part of the public system (see chapter 2 in this book). A small, commercial for-profit private health sector survived the tremendous increase in public health demand during the early post-war decades (see in particular chapter IV in the first book). Through the joint company Praktikertjänst, private practitioners became major sub-contractors in the provision of health services during this period (see also chapter III in that book).

In the early 1990s, the new national government allowed county councils to create a secondary role for private providers, by contracting out and increasingly hiring private companies to provide services to their residents. In the big cities, a growing share of the health sector came to be operated by private providers, although the main hospitals were still run by the county councils. The 1994–2006 Social Democratic government made some moves to prevent further privatization of public health. Nevertheless, during the non-Social Democratic county council regime of 1998–2002, an alternative Stockholm model paved the way for a confrontation between regional and national governments. Regional governments tested the limits of the commercialization of public health. They also privatized other "non-welfare" or infrastructural parts of their operations, such as public transportation. A few minor but soon profitable hospitals in Stockholm were taken over by private firms.

The 2006 national government has since allowed further privatization of the health sector, and the public sector nationwide has continued to use privately provided health services parallel to the public system. Most county councils have gradually contracted out out-patient clinics, creating more individual freedom of choice in selecting general practitioners. More recently, there has been a trend towards the concentration of private medical service provision among a smaller number of private health companies. This privatization is nearly at the same level as in the education sector, and the Wallenberg investment group has publicly declared that it intends to become a major player in the health-care market. A fairly tightly cost-controlled medical service system, though with an emphasis on generously subsidized drug prescriptions, has created demand for out-of-pocket medical services. The growth of private medical practices has generally been a large-city phenomenon, visits to private medical practitioners still being rare in smaller communities, especially in northern Sweden. The exception is dental care where commercial private practitioners organized through Praktikertjänst dominate the slightly publicly subsidized market.

Voluntary groups, non-profit organizations, and charitable agencies are virtually non-existent in the modern Swedish health-care system. The most notable exception is the Swedish Red Cross, which runs an HIV clinic and a trauma clinic in Stockholm, as well as a nursing college. Otherwise, Swedish civil society in health is commercial and organized on a profit-making basis, though largely publicly funded. In addition, there have been a small number of nationwide drug stores since 2010. Among these is one chain run by the Swedish Co-op, owned by the retail cooperative movement. This new oligopoly has broken up the monopoly of Apoteket AB, the government-owned national pharmaceutical retailing company. This was already envisaged in the 1995 accession agreement with the EU, but delayed for more than a decade. Another intervention in domestic health policy, the break-up of the government alcohol monopoly, was also long delayed. Sweden was exempted in the alcohol retail sector while production, run by Vin&Sprit and at the time extremely successful with Absolut on the global market, was up for sale. This finally occurred in 2008, with at first Pernod Ricard (which acquired Vin & Sprit, including the Absolut brand) and later Finnish Alko taking over what remained of local brand names, including the Danish ones once bought by Vin & Sprit.

Before 2011, privatizing tax-financed social services to the disabled and elderly was less controversial, although some civil society organizations of pensioners had voiced concerns early on. Non-profit, voluntary welfare organizations had been active in this area in the 1970s, and on a smaller scale even earlier (as indicated earlier in this book). The national civil-society disabled associations had grown in significance and strength, thereby challenging charity and empowering their members when publicly provided services were enlarged in the 1980s (see chapter IV in the foregoing volume). The new 1991 government joined with these groups to support a proposal to encourage small enterprises in a sector in which the public sector – through local authorities as providers – had come to dominate. The 1991 government promised more choice of providers and types of services through either a voucher system or by contracting out service delivery. These measures were almost immediately implemented in some Greater Stockholm vanguard municipalities such as Nacka and Lidingö (Sparks 1995). Other municipalities gradually followed suit. An array of privately provided, but in many cases publicly funded, services came into existence during 1980s and 1990s.

With the growth of pensioner income, a new market emerged. Already in 1992, a company named Svensk Hemservice made headlines by operating service apartment buildings for senior citizens in Stockholm, doing so on a contract basis to save public payer money. However, the company did not have a good record from another vanguard municipality. The affluent suburb of Danderyd realized that, as a result of contracting out part of their services for elderly people from 1989 to 1991, these services had become much more expensive than those provided in-house (Olsson Hort & Cohn 1995). The mix of voluntary membership associations, local government, and new private enterprises became significant ingredients in modern Swedish civil society. This was furthered by the advent of the 2006 government, its 2007 individual tax deduction (RUT), and the 2008 freedom-of-choice law (Statskontoret 2012a; Szebehely 2011). In this sector, it did not take long before welfare scandals were in full bloom. Controversial Carema Care was the first company embroiled in such a scandal in late 2011. Since then, other companies registered in tax havens from Guernsey to Luxemburg have become notorious household names in Sweden: Attendo, Frösunda, Humana, Solhaga, Team Olivia.

The privatization of manpower services also started at the beginning of the 1991 "freedom of choice revolution in welfare politics" (Blomqvist 2004). The aim was to come to terms with structural imbalances in the economy, extend the scope for individual action, and release creativity and private initiative. This was contested terrain, as it reached into the centre of modern society. In an imagined national welfare community, the most important civil-society organizations (apart from employers' organizations) are the manual blue-collar worker trade unions. With the end of the public labour exchange monopoly, new companies have stimulated the expansion of flexible labour (see chapter 3 on economic and demographic correlates above). Moreover, housing is another realm of privatization, in which flexible shelter is re-entering the scene for young adults and the homeless. Otherwise, the housing market – ownership instead of tenant-status – has gained momentum at the expense of housing policy (see chapter 2).

This overview of the development of contemporary Swedish civil society has stressed the increasingly for-profit nature of welfare practice in Sweden. In contrast, chapter 2 gave an overview of the public system, including the regulation and financing of such services (whether publicly or privately provided). Both public and private service provision are financed out of the public purse, which raises a number of questions about the relationship between the two. In an attempt to go beyond the contemporary social science discourse about the relationship between social policy and civil society, I will try to highlight the intricate build-up of an imagined national welfare community and elucidate the manifold historical relationships between society and state.

*

The Church of Rome had traditionally assumed responsibility for the care of the poor and sick and for education. With the onset of the Reformation, divergent patterns evolved across Europe. The break with the Roman Church brought about a certain fusion of secular and religious powers in the Northern states, particularly in the Lutheran monarchies. The property of the Church and the religious orders was confiscated and the clergy was incorporated into the bureaucracy of the territorial state. Thus, a concept of public welfare provisions was able to develop relatively early in the North, at least partially legitimized by the Protestant Churches. The same may be assumed for the development of a concept of corresponding citizen's obligations towards the state, probably still an important factor in mobilizing the necessary resources without excessive state pressure. (Flora 1986:XVIII)

Are the episcopate and the municipality part of Swedish civil society?

Why examine the dioceses and the municipalities in civil society? According to Flora (1986), and further emphasized by Anderson (2009) at the start of this chapter, these units are bottom–up, even lay organizational units, as compared with the hierarchical, military–industrial form of central-state ordering. This is where the inhabitants approach public authority – or "society" in the Nordic vernacular (cf. Jacobsson 2010). The secular municipality and the parishes are at one end of the scale, the county councils and former state church dioceses somewhere in the middle, and central state at the other end. In a society with no prefectures, there are no sharp boundaries. The idea that somewhere along this continuum civil society penetrates the state is anathema to discursive insiders, if not to political sociology. However, scholars of comparative politics, government, public administration, policy, and political science generally hesitate to draw such a line in societies where the distinction between private and public is so blurred that such an initiative would enrich present-day social research. In other words, this would be an inquiry into Scandinavian distinctiveness or "exceptionalism".

In the Scandinavian public sphere, the trade unions as a subject have been absent from the dominant civil society discourse. However, a combination of corporatist thinking at the macro-level, blended with individual worker rights at the micro-level, has opened up an avenue. This idea is foreign to Anglo-American, global civil-society thinking, which constantly hampers the free-spirited sociological imagination of the far north of Europe (cf. Wennerhag 2008 for a local exception). Moreover, a definite society–state cleavage resonates well with rigorously defined social scientific practice and does not challenge the supposed rationality of this academic field. Nevertheless, an analytical approach should stick to rational reasoning, emphasizing collective action in a changeable institutional setting (Rothstein & Broms forthc.; Österberg 1993). A short answer that deserves considerable elaboration is not possible here and is in any case the object of a vast social science industry focusing primarily on NGOs and the attendant international INGOs operating in global civil society and struggling with an elusive shadow: society, its configuration or structure and constituting elements "present in their absence". At an empirical level, a preliminary theoretical answer can be made through an inspection of the North European/Scandinavian welfare states with large, non-monolithic public sectors that developed over the last century. This answer particularly stresses the fairly clear distinction between central and local government in a welfare capitalist environment.

Central governments have the power to levy taxation in countries all over the world. In Sweden, local governments have independent powers to do so, too. They also have substantial leeway in using the money so raised. Nevertheless, the national parliament has sometimes intervened to turn municipalities and county councils into controllable budgetary units. This is Swedish/Nordic "devolution". Furthermore, both levels of government operate through a number of fairly independent agencies. At the local level, a plethora of public authorities provides municipal services (see chapter 2 in this book), but central government agencies also do so in specific cases. An example of this, that has already been mentioned, is the one-time jewel in the crown of the Swedish welfare state, the National Labour Market Agency, and its local Employment Service. This is perhaps the most important example, as it is directly concerned with the most pressing demographic component: the workforce. In addition to this agency, there is the central state (Social) Insurance Office. Moreover, both local government agencies and central government agencies at the local level can form partnerships with one another, and with private agencies. These partnerships may be either non-profit or for-profit (public–private–public partnerships). These are to be distinguished from traditional Anglo-American two-dimensional private–public partnerships sponsored by, for example, the IMF and the World Bank.

In Scandinavia, an important avenue of partnership involves more than just single public and single private agencies. Usually, at least two public agencies responsible to two different principals (i.e., central and local government), and at least one private partner, form a joint venture. Even three public partners can be involved. The regional level is on par with the local level, so perhaps another one or two layers should be added. The complexity of government is most obvious in the independent role of the Swedish (state) church (although its limited power to levy taxes caps its material resources), as well as the possibility of forming private associations consisting of local and/or regional public bodies. On the private side, there are numerous non-profit and for-profit alternatives. As already explained in connection with the discussion of policies and programmes (chapter 2), the social welfare–industrial complex became responsible for a number of tasks quite apart from poor relief and other basics. This was restated in the discussion of the institution of the welfare state. The public sector grew and came to dominate education, health, and social services, along with other social policy needs such as housing (eg. Gustafsson 1988).

Apart from the 1971 merger of the Stockholm county councils, few changes occurred in the health and regional planning sector of local government before the crisis of the 1990s, when the regional issue again became a hot topic. This issue was resolved by the State Responsibility Commission in the early 2000s, but in most cases has yet to be implemented (Svegfors 2013). With the second round of local authority mergers in the early 1970s, roughly 300 municipalities emerged, though as many as 200 are today in great danger of demographic and financial collapse and have so far been rescued by the inter-municipal transfer system. With few exceptions, they continued as the main public local financiers and providers of welfare services throughout the 1980s and 1990s – the in-kind services previously described and in most cases prescribed by national legislation. In most cases, either the county council or the municipality became the largest employer. Nevertheless, over a 25-year period, the organization of welfare delivery changed, compared with the situation described in chapter IV in the previous, original volume. Public decentralization was most obvious in the 1990 decision to make both primary and secondary education a purely municipal task in terms of financing and provision. Other decisions also reinforced this trend towards increased municipal responsibility and employment.

However, public recalibration reached a limit. As outlined in the "New Course for Sweden", the election manifesto of the Moderate-Liberal parties of the 1991–1994 government, later adopted by the Centre and Christian Democratic parties, active measures were taken to encourage (women's) entrepreneurship in this predominantly non-profit-sector. First were preschools, later followed by compulsory education itself, particularly secondary education. Privatization also became a prospect in the health sector, including personal social services to the elderly. In the early part of this decade, municipalities either took the lead or refrained from this option, depending on their political stance. Nevertheless, the trend was set, and private initiatives have gradually increased. Since the change of government in 2006, welfare delivery has moved considerably in the direction of privately provided welfare or market development. This makes municipalities – on their way towards being CPR institutions – financially governed through national regulations.

The municipality as the fundamental territorial unit for ensuring people's welfare, support, and survival continues within the ambience of a semi-Christian monopoly. No individual in Sweden can live off the municipality alone, but every resident lives in some secular municipality. The thing itself may be almost dead: although some 80 per cent of the electorate participated in the latest general local election, only 15 per cent voted in the ecclesiastical election. In the latter case, this was despite mobilization against the threat of a breakthrough of the Sweden Democrats. Nevertheless, the municipal sector is flourishing without really being noticed by social research. However, with the recent upsurge in tax-financed, private welfare delivery and the influence of new public management concepts on local government, the media, police investigators, prosecutors, and courts have become interested in bribery and closed-door agreements between private entrepreneurs and public officials. Corrupt practices have come to the fore more frequently than in the early post-war decades. At that time, such murky dealings predominantly took place in the housing sector.

The municipal sector could also give rise to a financial crisis, but that is not very likely if Moody's or S & P's long-standing triple-A ratings can be relied upon. In the Scandinavian context, the municipality is an all-in-one solution. In the bigger cities, municipalities may also take the form of territorial subdivisions. Immigrants to North America left when these units were called parishes (*socknar*), but new immigrants are now arriving, and on and off being restricted to in terms of residency to one municipality, add all those with a good memory. Today, municipalities are where people shape their existence. Many are on their way elsewhere, but even more stay or return after, for instance, a university stint. This is where the children who will support future welfare, or be marked by misfortune if things turn out badly, are born. This is where football, floor- and ice-hockey teams exist, as well as pensioners' associations, Rotary clubs, and sewing circles (cf. Agevall 2010). This is also where the environmental battles and strives are most overt and vociferous.

The semi-rural countryside has industrial trade unions and the local branches of the Federation of Swedish Farmers. There are new and growing associations of Euro-Muslims in the suburbs, as well as racial purists. People without passports usually hide here. This is also where health clinics are operated by, for instance, Doctors Without Borders. Those who once represented the mainline political parties in parliament are still found in the municipal parliamentary chambers, though not always in step with the changing times. Norberg, Fagersta, and Kalix, for instance, are cases of recent local Social Democratic collapse. More importantly, it is often in the individual town halls that the strength of new forms of civil political association is tested, such as the Green and Christian Democratic parties, and more recently, the Sweden Democrats. When the central state has not privatized its activities or converted them into independent subsidiaries, as in the case of pension savings, it has sometimes handed implementation over to the municipalities. Exceptions include the Employment Service, the judicial system, parts of the transport services, higher education, and the (Social) Insurance Office.

However, the mandate of providing schooling and health care has been transformed and the welfare state turned into the welfare municipality at a time when the established state church became the largest voluntary association. The welfare entrepreneurs will continue to flock to the county council and municipal government, mostly to gain access to the considerable resources they control. Welfare entrepreneurs and local authorities may also band together to acquire the occasional EU subsidy, since some of the social and structural funds are custom-made for them and the partnerships they have entered into. Likewise, the associations staffed mostly by unpaid volunteer or partially paid workers (e.g., the City Mission and other Swedish church and traditional free church outlets, Catholic Caritas, mosques, the Red Cross, the Salvation Army, Doctors Without Borders, and Save the Children) will also focus their attention on municipal governments and their treasure chests (cf. Ekström 2006). Welfare is a matter of material and human resources, and of appropriating those scarce resources.

The municipal mandate is regulated, but is all-embracing in practice. Silo-style managed central state supervision of municipal activities became superficially stronger when municipal politicians complained that they had to do what was decided "in Stockholm" first and then do what their voters want. Despite this control from above, including that exerted by supervisory bodies and courts lacking the power to enforce their decisions, there is still great variation in outcome and output between municipal governments, including between their constituent local communities. This variation of practice will probably persist, and it allows the creation of distinctive local successes that can be identified as "best practices". At the same time, the exchange of ideas between municipalities will flourish via think tanks, courses, and conferences, the week-long summer political forum at Almedalen on the island of Gotland being a prime example. Local communities will shift in relative performance, some ending up in financial crisis, others remaining solvent. This has also been the case for the national church with its local congregations and affiliated organizations. However, the church is less focused on exerting central control and has greater independence in utilizing its resources. From a sociological perspective, such tendencies have obvious impacts on social relationships, for example, between taxpayers/voters and politicians, or service users and providers. In the church, the analogous relationships would be between the eligible voters and their elected laymen or between the clergy and ordinary churchgoers, while in the private, commercial sphere they would be between customers and salespeople.

These changes in welfare practice did not occur overnight. Instead, they were part of a larger international shift concerning regulation of the everyday life sphere, and public intervention in the overarching private–public relationship. In the late 1980s, Sweden was still lagging in these respects, but two decades later, the situation is different. It is worth emphasizing that the 1982 decentralization/privatization strategy (discussed in chapters III and IV in the companion volume) fell out of favour in the early 1990s. There is as yet no comprehensive overview of the variety of municipal and county council experience in these areas, but decentralization/privatization is big business in both schooling and social services, as indicated in chapter 2 of these afterthoughts. Neither voluntary associations in local communities, nor small-scale employee and customer co-ops in civil society, have gained ground with the advent of decentralized privatization. The main exceptions lie partly outside the parameters of traditional welfare-state and civil-society research, perhaps not in the non-welfare sports movement but in non-profit associations in the religious sphere, though the latter are in no sense uninfluenced by mass consumption culture.

Mapping the new "free churches" and non-profits in contemporary civil society

Since 2010, the imagined national welfare community of Sweden has belonged to European normality, with the advent of a far-right popu-list political party with anti-immigration policies as its selling point. This party had already existed at the time of the 1991 election, when it obtained fewer than 5,000 votes nation-wide (0.09 per cent or less than one per mille of the popular vote), but managed for the first time to be elected in two municipalities (one representative in each). This per-formance should be compared with its 1,119 votes (0.02 per cent) and no representatives in its first electoral participation in 1988, when the Green Party took a big step from the municipalities to parliament. Fur-thermore, the 1991 election saw the worst results for the Social Demo-crats since 1928 and until the 2010 election.

In 1991, the Sweden Democratic Party was only one of several ethno–nationalist parties. The Scania Party (Skånepartiet) took the lead in Malmö. This successful challenger of local Social Democrats became the model for national efforts to create a party able to break up the long-standing dominance of the mass movements underlying the popular state consciously pursued by big business through the Employers' Association. In Malmö, Göran Herslow was presented by the Scania Party as the black sheep of an old-money family. The same was said of the New Democratic Party's Ian Wachtmeister, from an even older noble family that had married into the financial aristocracy of Sweden. His brother was the King's chief of staff and previously a CEO of one of the Wallenberg flagships. Both he and Herslow were educated at Sigtuna, the Swedish equivalent of Harrow.

In the 1991 election, Wachtmeister's anti-tax, anti-bureaucratic, and slightly anti-immigrant New Democratic Party entered parliament with almost 6 per cent of the national vote. Wachtmeister's co-leader was Bert Karlsson (a show business figure, once the man behind Euro-vision-winner Carola), who pursued his own agenda at the expense of the common good of the party. The New Democrats became a popu-list pro-welfare party, which almost completely ruined itself through factional infighting between its two leading figures, but also among a hastily assembled group of MPs from most corners of society. It partly disintegrated at the end of the electoral period. By 1993, the possibil-ity of "the emergence of a more openly racist, anti-immigration party than New Democrats" was proposed as "racist candidates have already done quite well in some local elections" (Olsson 1993, not included in the third, 2013 imprint):

> Traditionally, social policy and immigration policy have been closely con-nected in Sweden, and immigrants have quickly been included in the fairly generous welfare system. In the early 1990s, this contributes to the inherently explosive potential of the issue from a welfare state perspective. Since the late 1980s, both central and local authorities have tended to be more restrictive and exclusive as regards social benefits in-kind and cash. (p. 367)

However, it took 16 years for the parliamentary breakthrough of an ethno–nationalist populist party to become a reality. Even at a time of deep economic recession, the Sweden Democrats gained little with the demise of the New Democratic Party, which was still by far the largest of the right-wing populist parties in 1994. In the 1994 election, the Sweden Democrats won some 14,000 votes and elected only one more municipal council representative. Their increase was smaller in the 1998 election, when they won almost 20,000 votes (0.37 per cent of the popular vote) in the national election and elected eight rep-resentatives in five municipalities. Their participation in the first EU election in 1999 was a disaster, when they won fewer than 9,000 votes (0.3 per cent), compared with 28,000 (1.13 per cent) in the following EU parliamentary election in 2004. The Sweden Democrats' take-off at the local level occurred in the 2002 election when 49 representatives were elected to the boards of 29 municipalities, leaving behind other far-right aspirants such as the "browner" National Democrats (cf. Rydgren 2002). Still, the party only gained a stronghold in southern Sweden, and only after it under a new national leadership (alumni of Lund University History Department) started to collaborate with the extremely successful Danish People's Party. In the 2006 election, it became a real alternative, but its national campaign was overshadowed by the right–left divide, which brought the four-party "Blue Labour" Alliance to national power. In the southern municipalities, the Sweden Democrats were elected to all but one municipality (i.e., the Moderate Party stronghold of well-to-do Vellinge in metropolitan Malmö). The Sweden Democrats had gained seats in 144 municipalities nationally, although their 281 representatives were not always there in person. Well over 162,000 people (2.93 per cent of the electorate) voted for the party in the national election, compared with almost 150,000 (2.77 per cent) in the county council elections. The Sweden Democrats were elected to 16 seats in three councils for the first time.

These figures should be compared with the most recent election results: In 2010, the Sweden Democrats won parliamentary representation for the first time, winning 5.7 per cent of the national vote and electing 20 MPs. The party is now represented in most municipalities and county councils, the one exception at the county level being northern Västerbotten (Umeå). The party has seats in 27 municipalities but no human representatives. Borgholm is one of these municipalities, where an expelled Moderate Party farmer re-entered the municipal council after being written in by an anonymous Sweden Democratic voter following the rules of the election law book .

The long road to national recognition of the new parties – the Christian Democratic, Green, and Sweden Democratic parties – started at the local level. The Sweden Democrats are on their way to becoming the Swedish equivalent of the Danish People's Party, although it remains to be seen whether they will end up closer to a Norwegian-style Progress Party. The Danish People's Party was severely wounded in the 2011 general election, which may make it a less attractive model for a Swedish counterpart. Although it is an extremely centralist party, local forces always surprise even the most astute commentators on Swedish society and politics. However, it is too early to detect signs of such a current. Its next-of-kin, the National Democrats, are represented in only two municipalities, Södertälje being among them, but remains a constant thorn in the side of Sweden Democrats .

Another significant turning-point in civil society relationships was the new institutional state–church relationship. Since 2000, a decisive and drastic institutional transformation has occurred in Sweden: The Lutheran Swedish Church has formally separated from the state, resulting in the largest civil-society organization in Sweden, with roughly six million initial members. This made it much larger than LO (the Swedish Trade Union Confederation, for manual trades) or the Swedish Cooperative movement, each with roughly two million members (Friberg 2005). Even the combined membership of the three major national trade union congresses – LO, TCO, and SACO – does not match this figure. The welfare work of the church and its role in educating professional social workers dates back to the first half of the twentieth century, as previously noted. Surveys by civil-society researchers also indicate that Church of Sweden activities attracted many more volunteers at the end of the 1990s than at the beginning of the decade (Jeppsson Grassman & Svedberg 2007:149; see also Yeung 2006). The picture of elderly church-goers may still be true for Sunday mass, but otherwise does not capture the reality of church involvement. Christian activists now come from a new, predominantly youth movement The partition of the church from the state reinvigorated this to such an extent that it caused some alarm both within and outside the church. This concern has particularly been voiced by critics noting the absence of canonical orthodoxy, regarding women clergy in particular. Gay marriage was also a bone of contention before finally being approved in 2009. In 2013, 64 per cent of the Swedish population are members of the former "state church" – belongers rather than believers – and an even larger percentage pay regular fees to this organization. Actually, almost all taxpayers must pay a certain amount of money to this association, as part of a welfare package including a burial plot in a church graveyard. Moreover, regular elections to the governing bodies of the Swedish church take place every fourth year, and all traditional political parties are involved in the church via lay activists. In the 2009 elections, they even joined forces to stop the racist Sweden Democrats from gaining a foothold in the church.

Researchers have concluded that a vibrant civil society can exist side by side with the welfare state; this stands in contrast to social state critics who claim that citizen passivity is the main feature of Swedish society. In the 1990s, the social movement networks got a new public image, as numerous activities and associations were recognized as important players in civil society. Except by voluntary, informal "helping thy neighbour" surveys conducted by royal commissions and well-endowed research projects, most research found that unpaid volunteer activities were more prevalent in the cultural than the welfare sectors. In that sense, professional welfare provision was a salient aspect of Swedish civil society. Voluntary welfare work also increased in the 1990s, which was interpreted in light of a slimmed-down welfare state. For instance, a growing number of active pensioners and young people took part in voluntary welfare work through the churches. In the big cities, homelessness became an interest of the non-profit welfare sector, where shelters were provided mainly by the City Mission and the Salvation Army. These shelters were partly financed by local government, but also by voluntary financial contributions. Even soup kitchens became a regular feature of everyday life in some Swedish cities, organized by young Red Cross volunteers and the religious associations.

It is noteworthy that much of this civil society research was carried out at the private Stockholm Business School (Wijkström & Lundström 1997) and at public and private institutions of higher learning geared to educating professional social workers, in particular the one supported by the Swedish Church (Ersta Sköndal 2011: see also Svedberg et al. 2010). At the turn of the millennium, a state commission under the direction of a former Social Democratic minister and popular movement figure increased our knowledge of civil society in Sweden, and this line of inquiry has been followed up by research councils and funds. The place of virtual activities, social media in particular, in civil society later came to the fore after the success of the Pirate Party in the 2009 European election. As late as 2010, the Minister for Integration and Gender Equality set aside money for social research into civil society; the task of distributing these resources was assigned to a committee chaired by Bo Rothstein.

Welfare protests in civil society
during and after the *decennium horribile*

May 1 – International Workers' Day, or May Day – is a national holiday in Sweden. Since the early 1900s, it has been a celebration and manifestation of working-class solidarity and unity. Since the early 1940s, the Swedish flag has flown alongside red banners to commemorate wartime unity and the day that parliament circumscribed wage slavery or the right to laziness and leisure. Labour laws, welfare issues, and work regulation as well as pay rates usually come to the fore on this day. All across the country, the Social Democrats and affiliated organizations – particularly trade unions and women's, pensioners', and youth organizations – mobilize their members and core supporters despite being the traditional political rulers of the country, and defenders of national labour accords. Demands, slogans, and speeches carry a special meaning on this day – the managers of politics and union affairs have to look into the eyes of the thousands of people who have elevated them to public leadership positions. For decades, the Social Democrats have socialized and gathered in the park behind the Royal Library in Stockholm to chant slogans while marching up King's Street, to the Swedish Trade Union Confederation's headquarters on the "red" Norra Bantorget ("northern railroad square"). There they listen to the party chair or the LO (TUC) chair, sometimes also the party secretary. In Göteborg, a similar ritual takes place, with the march extending from Heden – a former military training ground – along the Avenue to Götaplatsen, where the masses gather between the main philanthropic cultural institutions, the city theatre, art museum, and concert hall to listen to one of the top three leaders of the labour movement; otherwise, the local boss will take the opportunity to address his home audience. It is not that different in Malmö and other cities around the country, although fewer usually participate and the speakers are often of a different calibre. Having said that, the chairpersons of the women's and youth organizations always make an appearance somewhere in the country. During the long Social Democratic rule, activists and an increasing number of paid professional officials managed to inject energy into a movement at the King's table (Billing et al. 1991; Engman 1999). In particular, 1 May has served as a test of the prospects and strength of the labour movement in election years.

Since the late 1960s, a new – street-fighting – generation of leftists challenged the traditional International Workers' Day activities and started to organize their own rallies. These marches were similar to the earlier anti-Vietnam war demonstrations, which were accepted early on by the political establishment, despite some initial skirmishes with police and the larger social order. For example, future Nobel Peace Prize Laureate Le Duc Tho marched side by side with Olof Palme on 1 May 1973 in the Stockholm Social Democratic rally. In addition, the Left Party communists started to organize separate May Day demonstrations, and during the 1970s the bigger cities often had at least three, sometimes four or five, different 1 May rallies – anarchists, Maoists, Trotskyists, and other groupuscule "ists" each had their own outdoor activities. Since the 1980s, however, the far left has diminished in importance, and only in Göteborg has it maintained visible 1 May activity. The Left Party with its orchestras has continued to demonstrate on its own in several municipalities throughout the country, despite decreasing interest in this event as the party has increasingly become an open supporter and a possible coalition partner of the Social Democrats. Notably, in recent decades, the religious right has tried to organize pro-life marches on 1 May. On this side of the political spectrum, the right also took to the streets to protest various wage-earner fund proposals, and 4 October has become its day of demonstrations. In 1983, almost one hundred thousand businessmen and women marched from Stureplan – the financial district of Stockholm – to the government quarters at the Royal Castle. A decade later, when wage-earner funds began to be used to fund academic research and training, this movement withered away.

Over the last two decades, other types of demonstrations and actions have arisen in the form of welfare or anti-austerity protests, either on the streets or in public places (Schierup et al. forthc.). Earlier still, the early 1970s saw some minor upheavals; for example, the housewives in the working-class suburb of Skärholmen, Stockholm, protested against raising food prices. The Social Democratic government had earlier managed to dismiss such events as communist provocations, but with the advent of centre–right governments in the late 1970s, the Social Democrats started to address the same audiences. In particular, the child day-care movement uniting young parents and Left Party activists protested the long queues for day-care in most municipalities, spurring a substantial increase in new day-care centres, although the system was still characterized by shortage until the early 1990s (Sundbom & Sidebäck 1984; see also chapter III in the previous volume). The struggle to increase investments in child day-care by building new facilities was typical of the imagined local welfare communities in Sweden. Moreover, demonstrations against nuclear power became a common green civil society activity in Sweden starting in the late 1970s. People in Sweden were also prepared to take to the streets, sign petitions, and express their concerns and opinions at times other than election day or in letters to the editor, particularly in the 1990s, when the nation was hit by the worst recession since the Great Depression (cf. Alapuro 1999). In particular, networks of protesters increasingly started to organize single-issue campaigns even before the Internet emerged. Many former ultra-left activists turned their skills towards protesting austerity in innovative ways at the national level, as was most evident in the case of feminists fighting the welfare cutbacks supported by professional academics, bankers, and economists. The feminists were backed by musicians and other cultural figures, making the struggle against austerity especially colourful and vibrant (Holmberg 2012; cf. Debord 1970). The *decennium horribile* also gave rise to cultural–political events, spurred by activist networks and usually supported by local union and civil society activists, including young social Christians and Muslim proponents of sobriety. The fine arts have also been affected. In 2007, for instance, the Stockholm Museum of Contemporary Arts featured the participation of Olle Baertling – the Swedish futurist and constructivist artist and contemporary equivalent of El Lissitzky or Malevitch – in the 1961 May Day Parade (cf. Brunius 1990). In 2011, the same museum featured the contribution of peace activist and artist Siri Derkert to Sweden's society and environment, not least her work for the Metro stations in downtown Stockholm.

With the return to power of the Social Democrats in the mid-1990s, this wave of protest temporarily came to a halt, or was limited to May Day orderliness. Local struggles did not stop completely, as the urban sprawl intermittently prompted youth rebellion, although not comparable in scale to that occurring in the big cities of Europe: Reclaim the City, ATTAC, and, later, Occupy Wall Street all gave rise to fairly small public gatherings in Sweden (cf. Sörbom & Wennerhag 2012; also Boreus et al. 2012). Feminist actions such as burning bank notes to symbolically represent the gender gap in earnings have had greater impact, attracting supporters such as ABBA's Benny Andersson and a PR mogul. In particular, growing dissatisfaction with the workings of the sickness and unemployment benefit systems has made these systems national bones of contention. Welfare protests have not yet turned into street riots, or led to general strikes. However, after the advent of the "Blue Labour" Alliance in 2006, uninsured former beneficiaries of the national insurance system have frequently gone public to voice their concerns and misgivings. With stricter rules governing the welfare system, even terminal patients have suffered from bureaucratic ruthlessness. Such cases have made public scapegoats of both the Minister of Health and Social Affairs and the Director-General of the Insurance Office, who were ridiculed in the media by comedians and columnists. As mentioned, the latter agency is no longer a credible part of the INWC (see chapter 3). The deficiencies of the social insurance system made the government severely vulnerable leading up to the 2010 election, although it was not only the respectable opposition but also the populist challengers that captured voter attention. After the election, the Minister of Health and Social Affairs had to step down, but the new one – Kristersson – has had a difficult time countering a united opposition with a majority in parliament (see also chapter 3). Moreover, although the Pirate Party has not yet addressed welfare issues, social media in general have helped form numerous networks advocating against austerity measures in this branch of social insurance, reproduced also in commercial mainstream and right-wing media.

Adieu to civil society: enter bourgeois–Christian society?

Is it time to say farewell to the idea of civil society as an independent branch of research? In a fascinating reconsideration of the rationale of civil society, Apostolis Papakostas (2011 and 2012) proposed that members of voluntary associations (including political parties) have become expendable. In contemporary post-political mass culture, professional organizational elites can simply replace one group of followers with another; Greenpeace is the ultimate innovator in this. Involving the dioceses and municipalities in civil society does not transcend this rationale, which gives strategists' spontaneity an institutional framework that limits available opportunities and options. Perhaps there is still hope for investigations of the relationship between new corporatism, voluntary associations, non-profits, for-profits, and government;

if not, it is time to leave this endeavour behind. Given that the social sciences are heavily influenced by a parochial Anglophone culture, what kind of practical society–state relationship is there to offer social research at the dawn of the new millennium?

The examination of the welfare state presented here was expressly long-term in outlook; perhaps a medium-term examination would have been a more modest, and manageable, analytical choice. Today's social welfare state exists between the experiences of yesterday and the expectations of tomorrow. As a model, it began to crack in the 1980s, and in Sweden was almost on the brink of financial collapse in the 1990s. The idea of the social welfare state as a possible union between the home, a strong society, and a shared public sector was doubted by many. It was explicitly rejected by vocal and articulate forces both within Sweden's borders and abroad: Its time was past, it was claimed, and the space it occupied was either too large (i.e., "the strong state") or too small (i.e., due to globalization). A new and harsher order emerged, emphasizing the difference between private and public, and erasing the line demarcating commerce from cooperation. Instead of members of collective households, each person became an island, a number on the civil registration list, and an impersonal "Hello" from the Social Insurance Agency (according to a 1990s ad from this agency, nowadays the Insurance Office).

Nevertheless, the welfare state has displayed a remarkable resilience, and ability to frustrate its enemies. The systemic shift towards a welfare market society is perhaps almost fully implemented, and both welfare entrepreneurs and non-profit civil-society activists are flocking to local governments. The fairly uniform insurance "company" that farmers, employers, and employees created at least fifty years ago has tortuously been adapted to changing circumstances. Swedish agricultural subsidies became part of the CAP of the European Union (EU), and the supplementary pension became the "freedom of choice" premium scheme of financial big business. At the same time, local government and civil society denied the roots of this model in the Nordic topsoil, and instead of challenging the welfare state, partnership became the watchword. One unwanted and unforeseen bastard child was born of this, namely, the ethno–nationalist current in political civil society. This current is stronger in Denmark and Norway than in Finland and Sweden, but not by much (cf. Andersen & Björklund 2008). Other unforeseen civic currents may be waiting in the wings.

In the current situation, another discursive turnaround may be in sight: the reappearance of the bourgeois–Christian society. This concept is contemporary with Adam Ferguson and the Enlightenment tradition. It was later transformed by Max Weber and others into an analytical tool with which to treat the relationship between the economy and religion as the foundations of modern Western society (cf. Colletti 1973). This notion has been interchangeable with bourgeois–liberal–conservative configurations of community and society from Hegel onward (Žižek 2012; see also Jameson 1981), and continues to be treated as such in contemporary First-World social research. The ascendancy of civil society in Swedish public discourse occurred at the time of the great crisis of the 1990s. The dominant mode of thinking has been intellectual jihadism or cultural struggle against an oppositional "Other" in a clash of civility and civilizations. In Sweden, and perhaps all over Scandinavia, such a conservative reaction within the former state church is one possibility, but it is less likely after sixty years of feminization of its workforce and lay followers. An alternative Nordic republican–secular approach belongs to a stream of thought followed by a minority of radical Spinozans, but has yet to have a broader impact. While the former points to an era of ethnic nationalism, the latter seems closer to any civic form conceivably available for the future, whatever the present rulers of China, Colombia, Egypt, Iran or Saudi Arabia – or any contemporary warlord – might say, or whatever the hopes of export-driven Northern salesmen and women. In any case, this is the civil society where the old movements lost energy and became part of a fragmented world of successors – the lost world of social democracy.

After yet another end of history – i.e., 9.15 – is it time to say farewell to civil society in favour of bourgeois–Christian society? From a sociological perspective, the idea of bourgeois–Christian society is a foreign and long-forgotten concept that is preferably avoided in any analytical dissection of the Swedish welfare state. Even movements within the largest civil or welfare society associations seem to take such a stance. However, regressive insular forces may make it necessary to take up this thread in the future. Nevertheless, most recent developments in Sweden point in a direction that shifts the society–state relationship in the direction of republican–secular affairs. Demographic, economic, and political factors are all embedded in a civic national culture that must compete and struggle with an ethnic nationality. This makes Rousseau, as a critic of civil society, still relevant to any examination of the universality of the welfare society notion, whatever particulars are trying to influence its impact on the future of humankind (cf. Rahe 2009). This is the optimistic, yet preliminary, end note on for- and non-profits, and on the various historical "free church" layers of Sweden's imagined communities, before considering the global spread of the Nordic model. Paradoxically, however, the first element of this pair – bourgeois – points backwards, while the second – Christian – points forwards.

The sell-out of Sweden Incorporated: from take-off to bonanza – a summary

Something is rotten in the state of Sweden. Welfare has survived, but in its vicinity is a stinking carcass. Tax-money is disappearing to tax havens, until recently with the approval of the Privy Council, chaplains to the King, and court jesters. In September 2011, the symbolic corpus of Trofim Lysenko finally arrived in Stockholm. For more than sixty years, the Centre for Business and Policy Studies (SNS in Swedish) has been an established and mildly provocative middle-of-the-road think tank supported by centrists in big business. Earlier that month, the SNS published a research report including contributions from several distinguished experts and social researchers in the field of welfare. The report, published in-house as a book, stressed the lack of any empirical evidence supporting the hypothesis that exposing previously public welfare services to deregulation, privatization, and market competition had led to increased effectiveness. Cautiously, the research director – a female economist of some standing and an editor of the report – concluded that the results were inconclusive and that there was a dire need for more research (Hartman 2011a).

On 7 September 2011, the report was publicized in an op-ed article in the leading Stockholm newspaper *Dagens Nyheter*, authored by the editor of the report and emphasizing the "absence of evidence" (Hartman 2011b). The same day, at an open seminar organized by the SNS and moderated by a Swedish media intellectual leading proponents of the welfare deregulation and privatization establishment were invited as discussants. However, the seminar got somewhat out of hand, as the defendants of the new order accused the report's authors of "bad research". Among the most aggressive critics was the respected CEO of Svenskt Näringsliv (formerly the Employers' Association) and former Bank of Sweden governor. At the end of the seminar, the CEO of the think tank stepped in with the intention of calming the waters and to prevent further conflict. Before the audience, the economic research director and editor of the report was explicitly silenced by her boss. A few days later, the research director left "at her own request" for a research position at Uppsala University, the oldest and in many respects most prestigious Swedish centre of higher learning. The SNS's most senior political scientist, another research director, followed suit, and with him the contract for the following year's Democracy Report (since the early 1990s, an annual publication of this think tank, which also publishes an annual Welfare Report, whose reputation was now threatened). In the interim, these wheelings and dealings had become a "Lysenko affair" in the blogosphere, with the business community effectively alleging forged research results. On Friday, 23 September, the SNS's CEO posted an apology to the two outgoing research directors on the centre's official website. On Saturday, seven members of the consultative standing forum of this think tank, six of whom were academic economists, published another op-ed article in *Dagens Nyheter* openly defending the freedom of social research. Two days after the apology, the SNS board met, chaired by the CEO of the Söderberg investment group, one of the most important historical investment firms in Sweden (one of the "fifteen families"). The board decided that the CEO had to leave. SNS had to save its own damaged reputation, but there were other factors. Since the early 1990s, SNS had been where most of Sweden's new constitutional direction had been thought through, and the legitimacy of that project was suddenly on trial.

Welfare capitalism is nothing new in the far north of Europe – after all, for more than 150 years, Sweden has been "Wallenberg land" – but its present form and battles have been both astonishing and thought-provoking. Its modern iteration arose in the mid-1980s, when big business intervened and established private child day-care centres, and Pysslingen (the name taken from Astrid Lindgren's literary universe) became the first welfare company, operating under the auspices of Electrolux, the multinational Wallenberg-owned home appliance manufacturer. At that time, however, the reply from the national party and government was resolute, even abrupt: No public money from the municipalities should be paid to such for-profit companies. Young children were sacrosanct human beings, who were to be protected from the predations of profiteering. This was akin to a somewhat later legislative initiative to protect women from prospective (criminalized) buyers on the sex market (see also chapter IV in the original volume). Since the early 1990s, however, various national governments have, in different forms and modes, adjusted to the demands of several emerging markets, if not the last mentioned type of market place. Therefore, as of 2013, it is common to find publicly funded for-profit welfare enterprises in child care, education, health, and other personal social services. It was the economic effectiveness of this experiment that the big business think-tank researchers mildly called in question, causing a rift in the public mind when the for-profit welfare entrepreneurs on the respectable right made Stalinist research demands. Nowadays, such evaluations of tax-money are the task of honest and scrupulous state inspectorates.

From the foregoing chapters – 2 and 3 – it follows that the Swedish welfare model is sustainable and the Swedish welfare state has survived during a period of hibernation. What about the civil society challenge? The demographic section of chapter 3 of this sequel presented a fairly happy and healthy class society. Swedes, like all Scandinavians, live longer and give birth to more children than do most other people on this earth. This is substantiated by several investigations into happiness and subjective wellbeing. The Swedish population is also fairly critical of its welfare administration and markets, and is not afraid of pointing out that the stresses of modern adult life do not easily go hand in hand with contemporary institutions and policies. Nevertheless, most people make significant contributions to the public sphere. Civil society in Sweden has often been considered a structured national totality on which numerous voluntary associations have put their stamp. Today, apart from a rejuvenated former state church, sports and other leisure associations stand out in contrast to earlier popular social movements such as the political movements of revivalists, teetotallers, farmers, and workers. In terms of members, the trade unions are still very important and a major base for the political wing of the working class. This is seen in the selection of the latest Social Democratic Party chair and prospective PM. Nevertheless, the unions operate predominantly inside the workplaces, and in general do not reach out to the wider public sphere, except during elections and on May Day; they are closed except to labour market insiders. Although only about 20 per cent of union members are particularly active in union affairs, the unions collectively act as an insurance company serving their wider community of members. The associations for farmers and entrepreneurs perform a similar function.

The key roles of local authorities and of Lutheran church parishes, in their regional and national configurations, have also been emphasized in these pages. In many respects, the latter two form the backbone of civil society evident all over the country, perhaps more so in the less sparsely populated areas. There may well be two civil societies, one urban and another semi-urban/rural, though the importance of this dichotomy should not be overestimated. The municipalities finance various voluntary associations ranging from Alcoholics Anonymous to shelters for battered women (e.g., Helmersson Bergmark 1995). Meanwhile, the former state church, organized into some 2,500 parishes in 13 dioceses, and the "people's palaces" provide shelter and serve as meeting halls, as do the municipal libraries. The Lutheran church also undertakes a great deal of community and social work, serving an increasing number of disabled, elderly, and poor people. Its youth association is probably closer to the everyday lives of young people than are the similar, well-funded organizations close to the established political parties. Needless to say, such a topic is a matter for future research; for instance, to what extent do the new pentecostal churches in Sweden compete with the old ones and between each other (cf. Bäckström 2011)? However, the traditional revivalist free churches have declined in recent decades while other abrahamite congregations have prospered. Moreover, the tax-financed, voluntary, historical educational associations are still around and finance activities ranging from armchair travelling to zoo-keeping. Over the last two decades, the EU has become a co-sponsor of such activities and contributed to the viability of civil society in Sweden (cf. Hansen 2011). The variation of the imagined local welfare communities has probably increased due to the emerging cultural Europeanization, increasing globalization, and heterogenization of Swedish demographics and society.

This chapter has discussed the transformation of the Swedish imagined national welfare community in the face of the challenges posed by the appearance of civil society over the last two decades. In another genuine reversal, under the umbrella of the Nordic model and with a strong emphasis on economic prudence, the welfare state has managed to shake off its Eastern baggage while retaining its proper "Western" equilibrium between civil and political society. So far, the price the Swedish Social Democrats have had to pay is that of loosening their ties with the associated movements and becoming a centralized welfare administrative party at a growing distance from a recomposed taxpaying and working electorate – plebeian as well as middle class. Red politicians have turned into blue plutocrats. The central state bureaucracy, once in a state of confusion, has gathered strength, though this may not be the case forever. After a half-century long pause, the traditional party of the right, the Moderate Party, has re-emerged as an alternative national party. For how long is another question.

Figure 5. Social welfare industrial complex:
IN/LWCs meet the CPRs in 2013

SCALES OF GOVERNANCE AND GOVERNMENT		Social welfare–industrial complex (common pool resources)	
		Top-down	Bottom-up
Imagined welfare communities	Supra-national	European law and directives Re-judicialization	Subsidiarity Redistribution
	National	Macroeconomic steering/deregulation/ Retrenchment	Re-regulation "Reforming"
	Local	Privatization/ Recalibration	Decentralization/ Retrenchment

Moreover, civil or welfare society have been analysed in light of the appearance of both for-profit welfare enterprises encouraged by political power at the national level, and non-profit voluntary associations involved in delivering culture and welfare at the local level. The argument made here is that these two tendencies are knit together by local and regional government and by the parishes and dioceses of the former state church. In this chapter, for-profits were first discussed, followed by an investigation into the historical build-up of an imagined local welfare community. This paved the way for a view of the municipalities and renewed free churches as the crucial links between for-profits and non-profits, as the joint challenge to an imagined national welfare community organized through "new corporatism". This was followed by a scrutiny of the current role of voluntary associations, particularly the role of the non-profit welfare agencies, and of the ensuing transformation of civil society in the wake of a changing pattern of migration and ongoing cultural–republican secularization, including welfare protests against permanent austerity and volatile sustainability.

Is there a configuration of forces outside and within the boundaries of the (central) state and market, in which local welfare agencies act interdependently with civil society or the local (imagined) communities? Local government is the key to understanding this configuration, a key that transcends class and ethno–national ghettos in Sweden. This was also where civil and political society challenged and reinvigorated the institutions of the welfare state, including the long-standing rule of the national party. The new political parties of the late 1980s and early 1990s – the Green and Christian Democratic parties – grew and prospered at the local level of society and politics before taking the crucial step and establishing themselves as parties on the national level. The Greens did so in the university towns and cities, and the Christian Democrats did so in certain semi-urban religious strongholds. The exception was the rapid rise and fall of the New Democrats. However, in their shadow, the Sweden Democrats first emerged at the local level in southern Sweden, before finally entering parliament in 2010. Whether or not this will reinforce the imagined national welfare community – perhaps as a bourgeois–Christian society – at the expense of the republican–secular imagined local welfare communities is a question for the future and for future research. When the notion of a bourgeois–Christian society again surfaces, will the forces of modernity come forward with an alternative concept nearer the republican–secular topography? Is there a local correspondence between the everyday life sphere of human existence and the social order specific to the model social welfare state, as hinted at in the opening quotation of this chapter?

5. A Republican–Secular Society under the Umbrella of the Nordic Model? Notes for a Comparative Survey

> It is widely thought that the Nordic countries have found some magic way of combining high taxes and lavish welfare systems with fast growth and low unemployment … Yet, the belief in a special Nordic model, or "third way", will crumble further in 2007.
>
> *The Economist* (2006), "The World in 2007", Annual edition, p. 44.

Introduction: a contested model in the epoch of the post-colonial spectacle

Economics, geography, and politics all matter, as do time, language, and perceptions of contemporaneity. Human institutional and social relationships are formed in the intersection between material/physical space and chronological/real time. Both are reciprocally influenced by moral/spiritual topography in which welfare models may figure or not. In February 2013, as these pages were on their way to the publisher, *The Economist* claimed to have found the magic way or the next supermodel – in the Far North. Nevertheless, it is necessary to move behind and beyond the mediations of the era of the spectacle when all that is solid is instantly consumed, digested and thrown up whether academic or vulgar.

With the fall of the Berlin wall, one Baltic nation-state went into the abyss (DDR) while three or four others appeared on the stage (i.e., Estonia, Latvia, and Lithuania, and perhaps also Russia). All states, including welfare states, are thus also survival units, which as institutions and nations may opt for dissolution or unification depending on the workings of a broader state system (cf. Kaspersen 2008). It is in the context of such an international organizational system that the previously crippled Nordic imagination has prospered in recent decades in sharp contrast to the time when, for instance, Nordek was conceived. Nordek, the proposed 1971 economic union between the five Nordic nation-states, was finally turned down by Finland after a supposed "*njet*" from its superpower neighbour to the east. The notes to come hint at some issues that are in dire need of further comparative investigation, as was done in the thoughtful works of, for instance, Meagher & Szebehely (2013), Salminen (1993) and, before him, Heckscher (1984).

More than 20 years have passed since the collapse of the communist regimes in Central and Eastern Europe – the "totalitarian welfare state" or the "structural model of welfare" in the words of Harold Wilensky (1975) and Ramesh Mishra (1976), respectively. This heralded the neo-liberal transition from Soviet-style socialism to late modern or post-modern contemporary global communist capitalism, with China at the forefront after the break-up of the Sino–Soviet world in the late 1950s. The European social model briefly had its day in the sun following Jacques Delors' grandiose plans, before ending in September 2008. In contrast, after a purgatorial decade for the Finnish and Swedish welfare states, the Nordic model throve in the first decade of the new millennium and continues to do so in the second (cf. Hilson 2008) – particularly in the aftermath of the global/American financial meltdown. Not only have the words of the Dane Gösta Esping-Andersen travelled the world, so have the feminist ideas of a generation of Scandinavian social researchers. From Buenos Aires to Havana, and from Hanoi to Seoul, not to mention in Beijing and Shanghai, the Nordic model has been held up for scrutiny by Anneli Anttonen, Drude Dahlerup, Barbara Hobson, Birte Siim, Martha Szebehely, and Kari Waernes as well as Jörgen Goal Andersen, Olli Kangas, Stein Kuhnle, Joakim Palme, Stein Ringen and Göran Therborn. They have all followed in the steps of an earlier generation led by Alva and Gunnar Myrdal but perhaps most prominently by the golden generation of Norwegian social researchers (Mjøset 1991).

The common resources possessed and utilized by imagined welfare communities consist of a set of rights, both to claim and act, and a set of obligations or duties to contribute and pay taxes. These obligations concern not just money, i.e., taxes, but the common good or human dignity. The right to claim comprises legitimate appropriations from the community and its polity for services and support. The right to act concerns not just the political right to vote on election day; it also includes labour legislation as well as family and gender law, extending the right to act of children, employees, and the self-employed, including farmers and sometimes also people leaving the countryside, usually for the insecurity and poverty of the urban informal sector, and perhaps women in particular. The right to claim reduces the patronage discretion retained by administrators, bosses, businessmen, middlemen, and politicians. The right to act on the part of social subordinates is intended to restrict the powers of employers, fathers, husbands, and parents. The relationship between these two sets of rights differs between the four Nordic countries, but this is not the place to unnecessarily stress these differences.

The Nordic welfare model can be briefly summarized by listing its common characteristics:

– Broad-based preventive measures directed towards the poor and destitute.
– Comprehensive child allowances for all families with children.
– Free or inexpensive education in publicly owned educational institutions.
– Free or inexpensive health, old age, and disability care.
– Universal old-age pensions.
– Income programmes, including benefits for the disabled, housewives, the ill, orphans, and the unemployed.
– Human shelter through general housing policies.

It is a well-developed model in which not only social but also fiscal welfare figures preeminently.

Before and after World War II, historical compromises were achieved all over far-northern Europe. These were facilitated by the historical freedom of small landowners and fishermen, and the absence of excessive state powers due to the special relationship between tribal congregations, the Protestant churches, and the absolutist monarchies (cf. Yeung 2006; also Stenius 1997). Throughout Scandinavia, a movement developed that combined growth and welfare for the good of the great majority.

This model and its constituent common pool resources (CPRs), located in imagined-cum-factual communities, will again be the main focus of this brief overview of the most recent decades. However,

Table 2. A macro typology of welfare models and the social division of public social and fiscal welfare

	RESIDUAL MODEL		STATUS MODEL		INSTITUTIONAL MODEL	
	Social division of welfare		Social division of welfare		Social division of welfare	
DIMENSIONS	Public social welfare	Fiscal welfare	Public social welfare	Fiscal welfare	Public social welfare	Fiscal welfare
1. Target group	Poor	Taxpayers (groups of taxpayers)	Economically active	Taxpayers (groups of taxpayers)	All citizens	Taxpayers (groups of taxpayers)
2. Most important system of rules	Selective (discretion)	Selective (taxpayers)	Selective (work)	Selective (taxpayers)	Universal	Selective (taxpayers)
3. Criteria for assignment of benefits	Discretionary needs assessment	Rights (tax law)	Rights	Rights (tax law)	Rights	Rights (tax law)
4. Level of benefits	Minimum standard	Normal standard (generous)	Normal standard	Normal standard (generous)	Normal standard	Normal standard (generous)
5. Most important source of financing	Taxes	Tax expenditures	Insurance premiums	Tax expenditures	Taxes (and premiums)	Tax expenditures
6. Degree of redistribution	Probably modest	Small (regressive)	Moderate	Small (regressive)	Probably relatively large	Small (regressive)
7. Degree of social control	Strong	Small	Moderate	Small	Small	Small
8. Status of receivers	Low	Normal (high)	Normal	Normal (high)	Normal	Normal (high)
9. Social expenditures as percentage of GNPa	Low (less than 10 %)	High/medium	Medium (10–20 %)	High/medium	High (more than 20 %)	Low
10. Status of social policy in relation to the economy	Marginal	Strengthening the marginalization of social policy	Inferior	Enforcing inferiority	Relatively equal status	Strengthening the economy in relation to social policy

Source: Ervik (2000)

* Social expenditures are here defined as including both direct public expenditures and fiscal welfare spending in the form of "tax expenditures".

written in the spirit of the 600-year-old Union of Kalmar, celebrated as late as 1997, and of the region's labour market, fairly open since 1954, the region's human tribal components and their intermittent relationships to territory and throne will be highlighted throughout these pages. Without excessive state pressure in imagined communities at different levels of civil society in the tributary states, CPRs have been assembled throughout Scandinavia (see also Knudsen 2000; Knudsen and Rothstein 1994; Grell 1992). Although variation within these imagined welfare communities is subsumed under the nation state heading, local cooperation and government are not entirely absent. More than one thousand municipalities are involved; there is a similar number of dioceses, with several thousand geophysical parishes within these four Augsburg confessional kingdoms. This reaches back to the archaic order and the early formation of Christendom in far-northern Europe. In addition, there were the nineteenth-century "free churches" of farmers, labourers, revivalists, teetotallers, and suffragettes, although the teetotallers have always been of minor importance in Denmark (cf. Sulkunen et al. 2000). In Finland, the pietists remained within the established church. During the Tsarist era, an Orthodox church saw the light of day in Helsinki and the Eastern border regions, areas that had to wake up to post-Soviet immigration. A third layer of new, urban and rural systemic social movements is also perceptible: ethno–national abrahamite migrants, eugenicists, evangelicals, feminists, Greens, New Age adherents, and sports fans. Finally, there may be a fourth twenty-first-century layer of virtual movements as part of the imagined communities of the Far North – i.e., pirates of various kinds.

This chapter starts with the imagined community of Denmark and ends with Swedish civil society, before a few concluding remarks on the universality of the Nordic model in the context of comparative research. The constituent parts of this model and the larger European social model have conquered the global imagination. What comes out of the ensuing picture is only a brief look at its variety.

The flexicurity of the Danish model

Policy diffusion in the Far North has a long history, predating the advent of best practices and learning by global examples. After the Great Depression, the Nordic countries made their marks on the international scene and continued to do so for a long time. Denmark did so first. It was the leading light of Scandinavian welfare reform, with agricultural protection, labour market measures, and increased social spending as part of the deal between the collective interests of farmers and labourers. Agribusiness throve in a Grundtvigian setting (Christiansen et al. 2006). Nazi occupation changed the intra-Nordic order. Gustav Möller, like his internationally more well-known contemporaries Per Albin Hansson and Ernst Wigforss of East Danish (Scania) origin, imported into Sweden the ideas and visionary plans of the Danish social engineers Bramsnaes and Steincke. This laid the foundation for another welfare system very similar to the Danish one. Only a decade after the end of the Second World War, Sweden came to symbolize the Nordic welfare model in the works of UK Labour politician Anthony Crosland (Anderson 1961). Full employment and high-quality public health and social services became a hallmark of this model, as well as high taxes and generous insurance benefits. This was much better than what Harold MacMillan and Sir Alec Douglas-Home could offer the British electorate.

However, the Danish model also had an urban radical profile including enlightened civil servants and urban intellectuals with a background in the resistance movement. This conjured up images of early day-care for children, cigar-smoking Copenhagen feminists leaving the kids for the job, and libertarian old-age care that made the more respectable Swedish social institutions look lacklustre. Throughout the 1950s and 1960s, Denmark remained in second place, with a welfare system fairly similar to the Swedish one. However, at the end of the 1970s, an anti-tax uprising was led by the solicitor Mogens Glistrup and his populist political party. In the 1980s, Denmark saw the reappearance of high unemployment, but no further extension of active labour market measures (Nørby Johansen 1986; see also Miller 1991 and Mortensen 1995). The social insurance system had to take responsibility for all the unemployed without the necessary means to bring them back into the labour market. It was therefore possible for university students to continue their studies while receiving grant-level unemployment benefits. However, the mainstream political parties – the Social Democratic, Social Conservative, Venstre, Radical Left, and Socialist Left parties – took the heat and defended the system, with the exception of study allowances. Meanwhile, the labour market organizations renegotiated to the benefit of the employers, who now had more flexibility to lay off employees at times of low demand. Denmark was the first Nordic country to embrace neoliberal social policies, making it the pioneer of Nordic new public management (cf. Regeringen 1997; for the broader picture, see also Mathieu 1999).

Flexicurity became the new Danish watchword, Lego and Maersk, the brand-names of its accumulation regime. Denmark's was a flexible labour market, backed up by a traditional Nordic social security safety net and the cradle-to-deathbed local social services. Together with strenuous efforts to balance the budget and control an escalating public debt, the imagined welfare communities (at the level of local, regional, and national governments, as well as the labour market organizations) succeeded in bringing Denmark back into the Nordic family of nations (Kaspersen 2008; see also Kvist et al. 2011, Abrahamson 2010, Andersen 2007, and Jensen 2005). When the state tried to reorganize its internal institutions – the welfare municipalities – its success was limited to the peninsula of Jutland. The prosperous ILWCs around Copenhagen remained indifferent and rejected central state management of civil society. In their contribution to *The Handbook of European Welfare Systems*, Christoffer Green-Pedersen and Michael Baggesen Klitgaard (2009) summarize the development of the Danish system under the heading "Between economic constraints and popular entrenchment: the development of the Danish welfare state 1982–2005":

> Twenty-five years of reform developments have in some ways adapted the Danish welfare state further to the universal ideal of the Scandinavian type of welfare state ... It may be seen as a paradox that this accommodation implied significant retrenchments in unemployment benefits, early retirement, social assistance and disability pensions ... Prior to the reforms, Danish unemployment benefits were extremely generous and probably as close to a genuine "citizen-wage" as any Western democracy has ever been, which was recognized as a fundamental threat to the strategic solidarity and thus political legitimacy of the universal welfare state. (p. 148)

Moreover, throughout this transformation, Denmark was always at the top of Richard Estes' happiness index, long before this had become a lucrative social science business. At the end of this period, in the 1990s, growth returned, high taxes persisted, and unemployment decreased considerably, and maybe the happy Danes would argue that their welfare benefits and services were "lavish". The Danish miracle – also beneficial to young Swedish jobseekers in the south, and to the southern Swedish housing market – survived almost until 9.15. The contradictions of the Danish welfare paradox are still around in neoliberal globalism, sustained by a territorially imagined welfare community of cultural radicals, devoted royalists, and quarrelling tribalists who are defending a national currency, though tied to the Euro. Many of these also have a second home in rural southern Sweden. The exception is the foreign-born, who suffered from another turn to the political right in the late 1990s when welfare benefits were no longer universal but ethnified, with higher reimbursement rates for native Danes. After a general election in 2011, this apparent injustice was removed by a new left-leaning government. A year later, after an election in Egypt, Denmark again became an exporter of its welfare model (Hajighasemi 2012).

Finland: a model that cracked but was temporarily sustained by the Nokia cell phone

Twentieth-century Finnish history is exceptional, marked by civil war, war with the Soviet Union and alliance with Hitler's Germany (Alestalo et al. forthc.). In the late 1980s, Finland was the latecomer that looked to the West and became a close Nordic family member. As of 1991, it was free and independent, soon an EU and Eurozone member state, though not fully integrated into the Atlantic community via NATO. Nor is the Swedish speaking community of Åland fully integrated with the republic of Finland, its current suzerain. There is clearly more to add on the history of what once was the eastern half of the Kingdom of Sweden.

In the first half of the nineteenth century after conquering it, Czarist Russia embarked on massive fortifications in an archipelago in the south-western part of present Finnish territory. During the Crimean War, these fortifications were destroyed and seized by the British and French navies ruling the Baltic waves. After the October Revolution, in 1917 the Ålanders wanted to join Sweden and accordingly petitioned its king. However, the newly independent Republic of Finland rejected this proposal and instead offered home rule under Finnish sovereignty. The issue was resolved by the newly founded League of Nations, which in 1921 drew up an international convention, signed by ten states, that confirmed and guaranteed the status of the independent region, the demilitarization of 1856, and also neutralized Åland. The compromise was supplemented by an agreement between Finland and Sweden on how these guarantees were to be realized; the Norwegian Nobel Peace Prize committee awarded the Swede Hjalmar Branting the medal for his efforts in brokering this agreement. This convention has since become an admired global example of a peaceful and successful solution to a minority conflict that also involved several nation-states. Furthermore, similar to the Faroe Islands and Greenland – under Danish jurisdiction – the Åland Islands have since 1970 had their own representation in the Nordic Council. In advance of the Finnish EU entrance, the Autonomy Act was revised and agreed upon by both parties, and Åland has since continued to conduct its own domestic affairs, including education, health, the promotion of industry and welfare, and policing, though its courts are part of the national system. Moreover, when Finland joined the EU in 1995, the Ålanders had the opportunity to stay outside but gave their consent. A special protocol to the Treaty of Accession between the EU and Finland states that Åland shall be regarded as a third territory with respect to the purchase of land, doing business, and indirect taxation. Today, Åland is an example of an advanced imagined welfare community with a vibrant civil society.

The achievements of the Finnish welfare state were a success story of the ruling Agrarians and their many political partners: the conservative Unity Party, the Swedish People's Party, the Social Democrats, and even what remained of the former Communist Party (for a while led by a Swedish-language poet). The political landscape of Finland was one of consensus-seeking large majorities. For decades, the Agrarian Party had been the constant broker between the various interests within this coalition, mindful of a Swedocentric big business in lumber and timber waiting in the wings.

Finland built a welfare system similar to the Swedish and Danish ones, with specific characteristics reflecting historical choices (cf. Hiilamo & Kangas 2009; also Tripp 2000). On the one hand, there was a local community welfare system, including general social services, special services for certain populations, and income security for those in need; on the other hand, there was a rights-based income security system at the level of the imagined national welfare community. Both education – publicly funded and provided from primary to tertiary – and universal public health care were outside the social protection system. Housing and agricultural policies were similar to the Swedish ones. Both deserve to be mentioned in this context as, after 1945, the Finnish state and municipalities had to provide land to Karelians fleeing Soviet-conquered land in the East. Although it is more centralized in some respects, in others the Finnish welfare system is more decentralized than its Swedish counterpart. This is exemplified by the affluent Swedish-speaking community on the island of Åland, which since 1995 has also been something of an EU tax haven and has a high degree of self-determination over social welfare affairs.

Moreover, Nokia started to conquer the virtual world in the 1990s. This began after the collapse of the Finnish economy in the wake of the break-up of its superpower neighbour, the Soviet Union. Forestry survived while the dockyards and similar heavy-industry Soviet exporters went bankrupt (cf. Kosonen 1993). Despite a turbulent crisis, with municipal or voluntary soup kitchens popping up all over the country, the national and local institutions of the welfare state survived, testifying to the sustainability of the welfare state in the worst years of an employment and fiscal crisis. Millenarianism aside, the secular apocalypse had to wait for another time; there was life after Soviet death. Nokia caught the imagination of post-modern aesthetics and economics, proving that Finland had found a way to combine high taxes and a not-so-lavish welfare system with fast growth, if not low unemployment. Matti Kautto and Matti Heikkilä concluded that the Nordic model stood on "stable but on shaky grounds" (1999). Six years later, Olli Kangas was much more optimistic when he and Joakim Palme dared to ask whether the most brilliant future of the Nordic model had passed (2005). At that time, Nokia cell phones were outcompeting Ericsson on the consumer electronics market, and most Finns felt relieved after having being severely wounded a decade earlier. Kangas and Palme even included a chapter on the relationship between the Nordic model and the information society in their UN-sponsored message to the world (Himanen 2005; also the co-author of a book in 2002 with Manuel Castells). Otherwise, it was the usual suspects who argued the case for the future of the welfare state. This is also true with the latest output from the community of Nordic comparative welfare state researchers, where Finland remains at the forefront (Kvist et al. 2011).

Finland's success stands tall, but is still marred by historical ethno–national tribal impediments. Even the Swedish-language minority, although fully eligible for all social benefits and services, has difficulties protecting its social rights. In recent decades, local struggles over scarce resources have been bitter and hard-fought between the two recognized ethno–national communities. Nevertheless, the majorities of both groups belong to the same religious congregation and speak the same language of atonement, although in two different tongues. A new populist anti-Nordic party saw the light of day in 2011: the (True) Finns attacked the followers of the Swedish People's Party and the EU consensus (Jungner 2011). Furthermore, Finland has remained a fortress regarding modern global migration, despite sharing an American immigration history with its neighbours. It is also part of the 1954 passport-free internal Nordic labour market, whereby half a million Finns left for Sweden, although many have since returned and resettled in Finland. Though the country has not managed to avoid global migration, the number of immigrants and their children differ considerably from that of Norway, and even more so from that of Denmark or Sweden. Comparative research indicates that its educational system is first class.

The Finnish welfare state and its local extensions made a full-scale comeback after an economic backlash against them in the early 1990s (cf. Kangas & Saari 2009; Saari 2001). However, despite recurring populist movements and parties, there was never a full-scale *political* backlash against welfare in Finland, and support for the welfare state has consistently been strong there (Kroll 2005; Kroll et al. 2000). Finland had difficulty making ends meet after 9.15. In the aftermath of the American financial meltdown, the national debt reached alarming levels, although far from PIIGS levels. In defending its national interests, Finland's national government has been regarded by the dominant EU players as a naysayer. By 2012, however, Nokia had sunk to penny-stock status, outcompeted by Apple, Samsung, and other Asian companies. All that is solid melts into air.

Norway: saviour of the Nordic model during the *decennium horribile*?

In 1990, however, it was not an individual business company – Statoil or Hydro – but the entire nation-state and its shared North Sea oilfields that had made its way to the top of the welfare rankings. The Norwegian CPR was already an imagined national welfare community and had gradually been building a joint framework since the break-up of the dynastical union with Sweden in 1905, particularly after 1945 (Sejersted 2005; Åmark 2005). The early post-war emphasis on economic reconstruction was obvious in the OEEC-sponsored medium-term plans (Kuhnle & Hort forthc.). There was also the continued unification of a large number of imagined local welfare communities. Along the west coast of Norway, a welfare state emerged that, in axiological terms and cosmopolitan outlook, differed from its neighbours. The social engineers in Oslo envied the Swedish welfare system, but also looked at the Danish model and beyond. Norway was a laggard, if not comparable to Finland, and it was a while before its poor-law system was replaced by a universal social-security model (Lödemel 1997). Even the Norwegian supplementary pension system, which was so controversial in Sweden, was passed by parliament with general approval (Hatland et al. 2011, Ervik 2000). Moreover, the social housing policy through the State Housing Bank made home ownership possible for a great majority of Norwegians (Esping-Andersen 1985).

The Norwegian welfare state has enlarged its activities over the last two decades, particularly in the domain of family policy, where it has served as an example for Germany (Lappegård 2011; Skovedal Lindén 2009). The welfare municipality acquired a status comparable to its Danish prototype, although possessing more resources. As with the other Nordic countries, a national association of local governments is an important lobby for a regional policy that is independent of European directives (Nagel 1991). In other areas such as work activation, and income maintenance, there have been incremental changes with a mostly egalitarian redistributional profile (Helgesen 1997).

This system has incrementally adapted to the winds of transformation, but it would be a tremendous exaggeration to speak of the "fall of the welfare state" in Norway (Wahl 2011; see also Mjøset et al. 1994). No Nordic welfare state has fared better than Norway over the last two decades, whether governed by the centre-right without the support of the populists, or the centre-left coalition of labour, farmers, and left Greens. Norway is the richest country of the four family members, and it is still an egalitarian society where the gospel of neoliberalism has been kept in check through decades of welfare-state recalibration and restructuring. That does not preclude the existence of a pro-welfare but tribal neo-nationalist populism that took its toll on 22 July 2011 in the darkest moment in Norwegian labour movement history.

In twentieth century Norway, there was always more to the welfare state than social democracy. Moreover, the Norwegian pattern of society–state relationships in its imagined welfare community is similar to those of the other Nordic countries. There was also the old state structure of the church, which was divided early and remained more conservative for a longer time than in the other Nordic countries. There were also the nineteenth-century free churches of atheists, farmers, fishermen, labour, revivalists, teetotallers, and suffragettes. In recent decades, this has been enlarged by a wide-ranging network of new social movements in civil society, centred in the imagined local welfare communities. The Lutheran work ethic has remained strong and oil wealth has been saved to a degree that puts any consideration of public debt outside the orbit of hegemonic imagination, whatever the current populist party said or did, the Petroleum Fund being firmly in the hands of the respectable centre whether left- or right- leaning. Voluntary welfare has been part of this moral platform as a complement to tax-financed or organized social-welfare institutions, and this residual system has prevailed longer in Norway than in Denmark or Sweden (cf. Kuhnle & Selle 1992). Moreover, occupational welfare, in cooperation with employers and trade unions, replaced earlier paternalistic welfare regimes in the factories. With the advent of an extremely affluent society, social movements and ecclesiastical institutions returned to the scene, as providers of welfare to special populations and as significant defenders of CPRs in areas that had earlier been organized through outside reciprocal arrangements. In other words, Norway became the last Soviet state – in the words of a male Swedish Social Democratic Minister of Industry. It is a matter of dispute whether this "kibbutz Sovietness" also includes the state feminism that has permeated Norwegian – and Nordic – welfare society-state developments in recent decades.

Sweden: from Mr. Crosland's to David Cameron's dreamland?

In the previous three chapters, Sweden already occupied centre stage, and in a brief overview such as the present one, its relationship to its "umbrella" will only be touched on. After the *decennium horribile*, Sweden returned to the scene with a new economy in ICT revolution. It was not yet big business in Sweden, but its young entrepreneurs caught the imagination of the world at large – at odds with the emerging tax-financed welfare business actors. The anti-authoritarian and free-spirited Swedish school system was suddenly open to scrutiny and given a fair share of the credit for the success of Swedish innovators in the third industrial revolution of information and communication technology. Sweden has risen to the top, not only in human welfare indices, but also in economically oriented global competitive rankings. This is the country the present leader of the former Empire is fondly looking into pleasing his hosts. British Prime Minister David Cameron was probably not given a copy of international best-seller *Bitterbitch* (Sveland 2011), an account and assessment of gender equality by a member of a younger cohort of feminists who recently conquered the emancipated world, when he briefly visited Stockholm in 2012.

Sweden and its welfare state have not fully recovered from the awkward decade of the 1990s and the Norwegian race to the top. It is still difficult to accept the more than century-long surrender of its westernmost Atlantic province, although the "tribe" has a reasonable attitude towards its benign neighbours. Job opportunities on the free Nordic labour market and westward labour mobility have became so common that they are taken for granted and easily forgotten as a cause for the diminished social spending.

In the late 1980s, the Swedish model was considered world-class. Two decades later, it was a slimmed-down version of the original model the Social Democrats handed over to their welfarist successors. Several sets of institutional change in particular became international export goods. On the one hand, the 1990 tax reform should serve as a model for others to follow, according to international organizations. The same is true of the pension reform a decade later. The new urban policy measures of the early 2000s have also been highlighted, at least in the European Union (EU). After the financial meltdown of 2008, Sweden's bailouts of private banks in the early 1990s were back on the international agenda. The worst deficiencies of the system were already evident in the early 1990s, in the absence of a return to high-quality active labour market measures and a less-than-universal sickness cash benefit insurance system.

More than half a decade after the transition to a new political order, it is a second- or third-class version of the original regime that is up for scrutiny. This is clearest in the collapse of the coverage rate in unemployment insurance. Looking at the Swedish welfare system from the perspective of education, the Social Democratic decentralization of the early 1990s, paired with the more recent neoliberal privatization, have combined the worst of two worlds of welfare capitalism. Instead, the Finnish school system became a best practice in the far north of Europe (Allendinger et al. 2010). In Swedish elderly care, one scandal after another has contributed to further distrust in the welfare system.

Thus, the apparent trend towards a tax-financed private welfare-market society has put the imagined welfare community on trial, in a letter to the editors of *Economist* after the Supermodel appeared juicily, reiterated by a professor in urban planning at the Stockholm Royal Institute of Technology:

> According to Bagehot British politicians look longingly at Sweden's approach to the public-private provision of welfare services (March 16th). One factor he did not mention, however, is that Swedish schools, hospitals, clinics and so on, have been sold for paltry sums, well under their real market value. The new private owners have made profits that are far above the returns found in other parts of the economy. In Sweden privatized schools can close when there is a drop in the number of students attending and the owners can merely declare insolvency and start a new school under a new name. Patients are often forced to move from one hospital to another or sent home prematurely. Elderly people in care centres who are incontinent forgo having their pads changed because the owners say it costs too much. Another big shortcoming of privatized services has been the lack of adequate monitoring by the public authorities. British politicians should properly monitor the impact of the Swedish model first before falling in love. (Abdul Khakee 2013)

The national welfare community in particular is under scrutiny, although corrupt practices have been evident on local markets. Compared with the other Nordic countries, the Swedish welfare system no longer stands out, except possibly for parental insurance and similar gender-equality programmes. Denmark is close behind in terms of gender-neutral child- and family-friendly policies. Norway has been catching up, and Finland has made a remarkable return to the top end of welfare capitalism. Comparing the Nordic countries, the paradox is that the more Swedish politicians and top civil servants invoke "world class", the less evidence there is of such an edge. From a wider comparative perspective, however, the Nordic countries stand out, whatever index is scrutinized. This says more about the state of welfare in the rest of the world than about Scandinavia.

Conclusion: the resurgence of the Nordic model

In the first and start of the second decade of the new century, the Nordic model surged. It is a distinct, unified model of the Far North, beyond a preoccupation with minor differences. Norway led the way, overshadowing Denmark; Finland and Sweden soon followed suit and were able to participate in friendly family-of-nations competition and coordination. As the European model dwindled, the Nordic welfare model regained momentum. It is no coincidence that there is a Nordic, blurred Beveridgean–Bismarckian road from the vacillating post-colonial Labour of Mr. Crosland to the resolute neo-imperial "Blue Labour" of Mr. Cameron. Thus, there is no interruption in the Etonian surveillance of the Far North. Simultaneously with a brief visit to Stockholm in 2012 by the British PM for a Baltic–Nordic meeting of North European PMs, the Joint Committee of the Nordic Social Democratic Labour Movement (SAMAK) succeeded in persuading the Swedish Patent Agency to authorize "The Nordic Welfare Model" as its brand name as part of launching a long-term research project sponsored by this association and led by the Norwegian research institute Fafo. The business-sponsored Norwegian think-tank Civita protested immediately and an intense social media conversation began about the wisdom of the action taken by SAMAK and the Swedish Patent Agency. To many, this was a suspect sign of sectarian thinking within the respectable left, or a show of its entrepreneurial spirit.

Several Scandinavian researchers, quite apart from lobbyists and pundits, were actively involved in this public debate. The stakes were high, as the model was a crown jewel for all involved, having made considerable inroads on the international stage (cf. Svensson 2013; Hort 2007). Even the World Bank had espoused the experience of the social and political system of these countries (e.g., Marshall & Butzbach 2003). After the 2007 credit crunch and the near collapse of the Western banking system, the bailout of banks in Sweden in the early 1990s was upheld as a prototype for others to follow. Instead of crumbling further, the Nordic model reached a new zenith and continued to ascend during the subsequent Eurozone crisis (cf. Bildt & Borg 2011). Thus, there is currently added value in securing a copyright for this model. SAMAK's infringement on freedom of thought poses hard questions to the Nordic political and research communities, including Fafo, the research wing of the Norwegian Labour movement. However, this affair also indicates that Nordic social democracy is not acting short-sightedly: The new research project is to last until 2030 and is to consider the types of movements that will exist in the meantime throughout the Far North, but also in the larger Eurasian and global context. The research findings will perhaps be of considerable interest to a suspicious global polity in an international research area that still attracts considerable attention.

The geography of comparative welfare state research and its temporality give a hint as to the global ups and downs of its research object.

In this sequel, the focus has been on the third generation of this kind of social research, pointing also towards an incoming fourth. This chapter places special emphasis on Sweden in the larger family of nations. Is Sweden just one of many European welfare states, or part of a separate, if related, Nordic model? Amidst the hypocrisy generated by the launching of the Euro and the enlargement of the EU, there was also talk of a European social model, in contrast to the American example. Between the drafting of the Maastricht Social Protocol and the UK's signing of this document in 1997, a European social policy discourse emerged. Still, the Protocol's measures were confined to intra-Union migration, while welfare policy remained a national task with agriculture as the obvious exception. Despite this, various soft-coordination initiatives were promulgated by the former Swedish Director-General of the EU Employment Directorate, a former NLRB/AMS chieftain. With the escalation of the Eurozone crisis, it was no understatement to conclude that the social solidarity between the member states of the monetary union was weak, and talk of a European social model soon came to an end. Instead, it is the welfare model of the Far North that has travelled around the globe. While the PIIGS, maybe even France after the presidential and parliamentary elections of 2012, belong to the bad guys – in gendered language – the Nordic countries are the good girls. It is under the umbrella of the Nordic model that Sweden with its Janus-faceted social welfare state has continued to attract worldwide attention.

In the midst of the first decade of the 2000s, the four Nordic countries made their mark on a range of best practices indices, from gender equality to wellbeing. It was widely thought that the Nordic countries had found some magic way of combining high taxes and lavish welfare systems with fast growth and low unemployment, as *The Economist* complained in 2006. However, the neoliberals have not come away empty-handed, as tax-financed for-profit welfare has flourished in Sweden. Moreover, underemployment, unemployment, and deindustrialization are still social problems in the politics of the third industrial revolution that created space for non-profit or voluntary welfare delivery relating to the special Nordic church–state relationship. The sustainability of the dual-faceted Nordic model has been demographically, culturally, and politically prospering on the outskirts of Eurasia. Growth is fragile or volatile, but continues to mobilize resources, monetary as well as human. Taxes are still high, and welfare benefits and services are not always that lavish or generous. Nevertheless, the model comprises a transnational imagined community of four ethno–national "tribes" (five, if the Swedes in Finland are counted separately) and two main languages (Finnish and the Scandinavian dialects, or languages). It subsumes thousands of imagined local welfare communities, sustained by old and free churches. There are also the virtual communities of the lay social movements and networks in civil society, as well as the exposure of "welfare scandals" and other public discontent by critical social media and even the European Parliament. Moreover, it is no longer only the in the "people's places" and the municipal town halls, but also in the old parish halls and houses that one hears lamentation over the ways of the world. For an emigrated member of this nation, the grim conclusion from the 2010 Swedish election is that the celebrated welfare model produced two cabinet alternatives – one "new" and the other red-green – and one (inward-looking but welfarist) opposition, recalling the pathways of late twentieth-century Denmark and Norway (cf. Andersen & Björklund 2008; also *Arkiv* 2013). Most likely an innovative blend of obligations and rights embedded and constructed out of welfare legislation in Denmark, Finland and Norway would be far superior to the present Swedish system, and invigorate the imagined local welfare communities of the Far North of Europe. Its central state is obsolete, its Stockholm centered intellectual welfare universe a province of the past, national patriotism at present an impediment to civility and civilising social action and change. Whether a modern Northern republican–secular society is in the making is a different issue.

2015 and Beyond: The Global Advance of the Eurasian Social Welfare State?

> The experimental reforms linked to identity adaptation and more pervasive democracy will surely be more practical within sovereignties less constrained by expansion and belligerence. Part of that route has already been tried out in northern Europe, among populations less afflicted by warfare, status and the need for self-sufficiency. Small Brazils, as it were, which have taken the giant wave of globalisation with decisive success, losing little of their identity but gaining in many other ways.
>
> Nairn, T. (2007). "The Enabling Boundary", *London Review of Books*, 18 October.

Modernity and enlightenment thought are forward-looking artefacts actively encouraging human beings to seek and make a future. In contrast, archaic and religious perceptions are either backward-looking or status quo oriented, a golden age or heavenly kingdom being a typical representation in which the present is a casual and immaterial abode (cf. Herrin 1987). Modernity accentuated the idea of worldly progress spurred by anticlerical and peasant uprisings. The Revolt in the Netherlands set in motion a number of upheavals that in the end became the bourgeois revolution, the era of republican–secular enlightenment and nationhood in the midst of imperial ambitions, colonialism, and human slavery. Bismarck built a Reich, Beveridge built and rebuilt an empire, and FDR shaped a New Deal out of a victorious revolution and a coercive but unifying civil war. The "ten days that shook the world" underscored the idea of worldwide earthly emancipation, an idea, however, that met forceful and violent resistance. Utopian dreams and the communist scenario haunted the well to do and the rulers of the day. During the twentieth century, working-class politics proliferated, making previously solid social relationships less sustainable, necessitating and provoking creativity and social innovations. In between empire, revolution, counter-revolution, and world and civil wars, in the far north of Europe, movements and social reformers set out on a road that intermittently met with curious engagement. The historical compromise between civil society, capitalism, and the welfare state came to symbolize these ambitions.

A quarter of a century ago the Swedish welfare model peaked. The first edition of *Social Policy and Welfare State in Sweden* covered a century of welfare state construction. Creative welfare intellectuals in civil society were profiled in the first chapter, while the second elaborated in detail on the social forces underlying the political alternatives. While these analyses treated the early formation of the Swedish welfare model, the third and fourth chapters highlighted the postwar enlargement of social policies and related public institutions, tracing their phases, sequences, and parallel trajectories. The perspective was long term, yet short-sighted. During *der Augenblick* of writing in the late 1980s, the neoliberal wind had not yet reached hurricane force; only a few years later, the postscript to the second edition of the first book had to take issue with the near-collapse of state finances and the withering away of a nearby empire. In a penetrating assessment and lucid account of Swedish "thin rationality", Agneta Hugemark (1994) pointed out the inherent ambiguity in the analysis of the last "period of adjustments" in chapter three of the original edition of *Social Policy and Welfare State in Sweden*. Thus, the reverential tone in the original analysis of the postwar epoch is a suspect sign of difficulties evaded, and might even be interpreted as intending to down play pressing concerns and burning controversies. The recent triumphalism of the obscurantist–rational critics of the normative foundation of the welfare state bears witness to the symbolic cultural–economic and political power of the global think tanks and their attendant environments (Freeland 2012). This paradigm differs greatly from the social investment, common pool resource (CPR) approaches with their common origin in "Polanyian embeddedness".

The 1990 book's initial approach contrasted with the doomsday perspective of the 1980s – the dismantling of the welfare state. Its "Introduction" presented the comparative welfare-state literature available in the late 1980s. Chapter 1 of this book outlined and discussed the shift from second- to third-generation research under the influence of gendering and racialization processes (Zakharov 2013). The conclusion was that this research has geoculturally expanded to an extent not foreseen by an inward-looking discipline. In a decade or so, it transcended the first generation's initial 64 surveyed welfare states around the globe. Instead, the North Atlantic/Pacific worlds of welfare capitalism became parts of the global range of capitalisms. This research branch reached out to most parts of the globe as the sustainability of the welfare state was thoroughly demonstrated during the turbulent 1990s. Globalization brought to the fore first the European social model, and later the more peripheral, seemingly robust and sustainable Nordic welfare model.

The survival of the social welfare–industrial complex in Sweden is analyzed in chapter 2 of this sequel. This is done in relation to the previous post-war welfare-state growth that was elaborated upon in chapters II and III in the original book. With the exception of housing policy, the current tax-financed public welfare system does not superficially look that different from the earlier one, despite cutbacks and retrenchment. Most similar is perhaps agricultural policy, where the welfare of farmers is no longer safeguarded at the national level, and the CAP umbrella of the European (Social) Union has been put up in an attempt to shelter an imagined supranational welfare community. Nevertheless, almost every other policy area in Sweden has undergone major deregulation and/or recalibration, due to more publicly financed, private delivery of welfare benefits and services. These include education, pensions, health care, and old age and disability care, where a market has boomed in recent years. Old age and disability care were previously under the auspices of the county councils and municipalities. Now the latter have become financiers, and just one of a multitude of providers. Universality has prevailed but selectivity has become more pronounced. High taxes are still characteristic of the system, but CPR institutional redistribution has become tilted towards the well-to-do and the insiders on the labour market. Re-regulation is still a possibility, hinted at through the discussion of both policy evaluation and welfare scandals. But much more than that is probably needed to turn this Titanic in other directions.

The temporality of the third chapter of this sequel differs only marginally from that of the second. It examines the relationship between state, economy, and society over the last two and a half decades compared with similar interdependencies during the early post-war period.

Favourable recent demographic developments are examined in light of the historical child-, family-, and work-friendly policies in Sweden. A sequential analysis of the sustainability of the welfare state, its deconstruction and reconstruction, survival and hibernation are highlighted through examining the impact of the initially less favourable economic conjuncture and its aftermath on the previous welfare regime and its larger imaginary settings. The transformation of the popular state into a gradually more centralized elite apparatus is exposed through the changes in the institutional set-up of the central welfare state agencies, the decline of the social movements and political parties, and the construction of an "inspectorate state" delivered under the auspices of fiscal prudence and new public management reaching beyond the previous limits on the freedoms of local government. However, the crucial mid-1990s roles of the feminist movement and the former agrarian Centre Party (later replaced by the Green and the Left parties) are pinpointed in an attempt to identify creative conservatism and the transformation of the minor parties of the centre into neo- and military–liberal strongholds. An "iron triangle" of the Treasury/Central Bank, merchant banks, and the political–entertainment industry emerges from social democracy, reaching far into academic research and teaching. This is the new power discourse as well as the new world of labour and welfare: a world of low pay and increasing gaps between the new rich and less rich, a new world of Swedish red plutocrats and perhaps an escapist middle class – rebellious plebeians struggling against an on and off nearly silent majority.

Chapter 4 examines civil society, and continues where both the introduction began and the fourth chapter of the preceeding volume ended. It focuses on the concurrent impact of the movements, or free churches, underlying the social welfare–industrial complex, as well as the impact on the social programmes and policies of its predecessors. In particular, the rejuvenated old tribal–national church, and more recent free church successors in this realm of practices and thought, such as the feminist, Green, and various other new movements and congregations of gendered and intersectional, even ethno–national, peoples are highlighened. For-profits, non-profits, and voluntary welfare organizations in civil society are under surveillance here. Some of this includes trends leading to the emergence of a tax-financed welfare-market society with the attendant problems of corporate concentration – oligopoly – and corrupt practices situated between the public and the private – i.e., the collusion of economics and politics (ESO 2012). This chapter also returns to a pair of concepts introduced in the second chapter of this sequel: CPRs and imagined welfare communities (whether local, national, or supranational). It discusses the blurred private–public relationship in Scandinavia from the perspective of a larger, nonlinear civilizing process in which the monarchical bourgeois–Christian society presumably gives way to a modern republican–secular order of equals and unequals within the confines of organized imagined communities.

It is time to reintroduce the Nordic welfare model under which the Swedish welfare society and state have transformed themselves over the last two decades. In chapter 5, the main characteristics of the Nordic model are reiterated and recent developments in the four Nordic countries are briefly compared: Norway stands out as the leading light of imagined welfare community control over CPRs and social investments. The differing comebacks of Denmark and Finland are noted. The dual-faceted nature of the Swedish welfare state is not that different from the other Nordic welfare systems. However, the most recent triumphalism of the global libertarians is a silent reminder of the fragile nature of CPR sustainability in imagined welfare communities. In hindsight, the operation may have been successful, but did the patient die? It is too early to write off the entire Nordic welfare model, but the decline – or hollowing out – of the Swedish welfare state is a matter of fact.

Whatever the gravediggers might say, the welfare state is still alive in Scandinavia and in many other parts of the world. There have, however, been setbacks. Life and humanity, under late modernity, are in transformation or at the start of a new era (cf. Therborn 2012). Almost twenty-five years have passed since the first article in this book was published. At that time, Ronald Reagan and Margaret Thatcher were leading two of the most vociferous anti-welfare-state governments on the globe, and Friedrich von Hayek and Milton Friedmann were their presiding over lights. Both argued for a small state, less social spending, limited politics, and market solutions as the replacements for welfare institutions. Only the market solutions have been implemented to some extent, though not if the small state of the EU is taken into account. For many people on the margins or outside the "Washington consensus", the limits of political and social thinking have been on the agenda. In contrast, the global neoliberal crisis is recent, akin to the financial meltdown of late 2008. The crisis of the welfare state dates back to the first comparative study in this field of social research, *The Welfare State and Equality*. It was soon codified by the OECD (1981), embracing the Japanese "welfare society". The welfare state became a bone of contention in politics, as well as in the social sciences, with the advent of the new global order.

Figure 6. Conceptual map: Imagined welfare communities and CPR institutions between civil society and the social welfare state

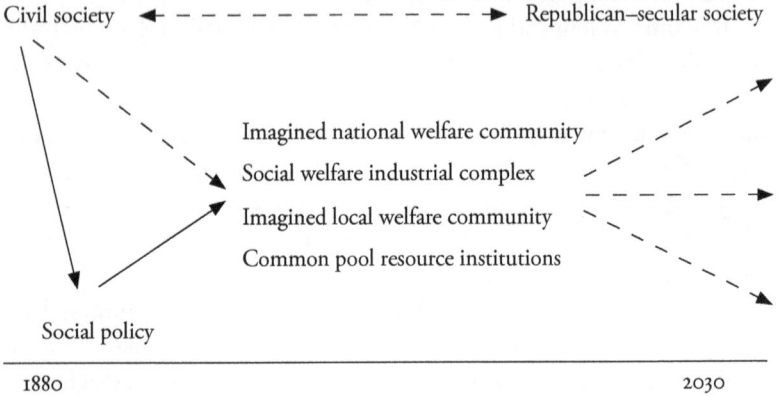

Civil society ◄ – – – – – – – – – – – – ► Republican–secular society

Imagined national welfare community
Social welfare industrial complex
Imagined local welfare community
Common pool resource institutions

Social policy

1880   2030

Ideas and practices that opposed state interference in the economy and society gained momentum worldwide, at the expense of the early post-war paradigm. Outside the heartland of the welfare states, social planning became obsolete; inside the heartland, social engineering became circumscribed past recognition. Structural adjustment programmes came into being whenever international organizations, such as the IMF and the World Bank, got the upper hand. The ILO, ISSA, UNDP, and UNESCO were relegated to junior partners on a "global Wall Street". Welfare was regarded as created by the regimented singular individual operating on the free market, not by mobilized and organized citizens and denizens participating in fair and free elections outside the control of corrupt oligarchs, plutocrats, and other robber barons. There was no such thing as society or aspiring social popular mass movements. Apart from social services in a broad sense (such as education in Sweden), well-funded pension programmes became the most obvious targets for ravenous global adventurists and speculators who demanded immediate, positive research results and no dissident or contrarian thinking – not to speak of their appetite for money, profits and recognition. Moreover, with the end of the Soviet empire, the "structural welfare state model" disappeared. This made other models less communal and more totalitarian. Instead of being the last Soviet state or "iceberg society", Norway is perhaps the most prosperous kibbutz, or the twentyfirst-century New Lanark, a new semi-republican Jerusalem while the historical antecedent is worse off than since the age when the Crusaders went to Palestine. The common horizon is still alive far from its original adobe.

Exploring the future implies being prepared for the unforeseen, including interdependences and transgressions between examined models. The social risk protection that Bismarck instituted at the dawn of the labour movement and that spread through Europe more than a century ago has proven robust, despite constant warnings of over-insurance, lack of efficiency, and unsustainability. The appearance of a new global labour reserve, and the withering away of full employment at the centre of working-class politics, paved the way for another world. Capitalism might be an abstract system of social relationships, but its equilibria have always rested on human social forces. That the present constellation of global political manifestations will remain in the future is predictable, but its horizons are uncertain. Nevertheless, with many people transformed from industrial wage-earners into urban investors or borrowers directly exposed to the highly volatile stock- and bondmarket/interest rate fluctuations, the need for adequate social protection and services has become greater than ever. Popular support for CPRs, including financing through fairly heavy taxation, has remained strong throughout the neoliberal era (Svallfors 2007 and 2011; cf. also Nilsson 2013). Thus, the welfare state "survived" in north-western Europe, but changed during its hibernation. A blend of left- and right-wing retrenchment has taken its toll throughout Europe. This is less so in Scandinavia and at the centre of continental Europe, where popular resistance has been antagonistic to any insecurity/poverty regime. Social Europe and the Nordic model re-entered the global arena as new, more modest, welfare states arose in other parts of the world. The Nordic model regained positive attention during the first decade of the new millennium, when new social movements such as the Greens supported an extension of a generous welfare state. This was a civilized version of workfare with basic income security and work- and family-friendly policies. For a time, the great majority of the feminist movement was the welfare state's most vocal defender, followed by the gay movement's defence of human dignity. In contrast, representative associations of numerous ethno–national communities immigrating to the Far North took varying positions on the matter.

The Epoch of the Spectacle is rapidly moving ahead, and so is the welfare regime type. As late as December 2006, this welfare model was declared "dead" by an up-beat *Economist*. Seven years later, however, its corpse is still breathing, even ballooning, although sometimes proving an embarrassment to government officials and corporate and financial headquarters. With global turmoil so close behind, is it perhaps too soon to proclaim the end of an era? The welfare state as a state form, imagined community, and research topic has definitely moved beyond its original borders into Africa, Asia, and Latin America. Moreover, it has recently made minor inroads in the form of health insurance reform under the American Obama administration. Nevertheless, it is pertinent to remember that such advances have not always been the case. The Nordic welfare-state laboratory re-entered the global arena parallel to the emergence of new, modest, "productivist" welfare states that came to fruition where the developmental state first appeared. In the years to come, the amalgamation of these developmental and welfare states will likely deserve a separate, transnational study. The incomplete welfare state revolution is likely not the end of the story, but perhaps a continuation of a nonlinear and in no sense evolutionary civilizing process. The future of social policy is uncertain, although more likely in other parts of Eurasia than in Scandinavia. As dusk falls over the imagined welfare communities and their CPRs, the owl of Minerva is spreading its wings. Far away, on the other end of the continent, birds sing, it's dawn, the sun is rising over nascent social welfare states yet sorely grim human societies plagued by graft and insecurity.

Figure 7. The interdependency of CPR-institutions and tax-financed welfare after Poor Relief in Imagined Welfare Communities. The case of Sweden Incorporated plus EU/CAP

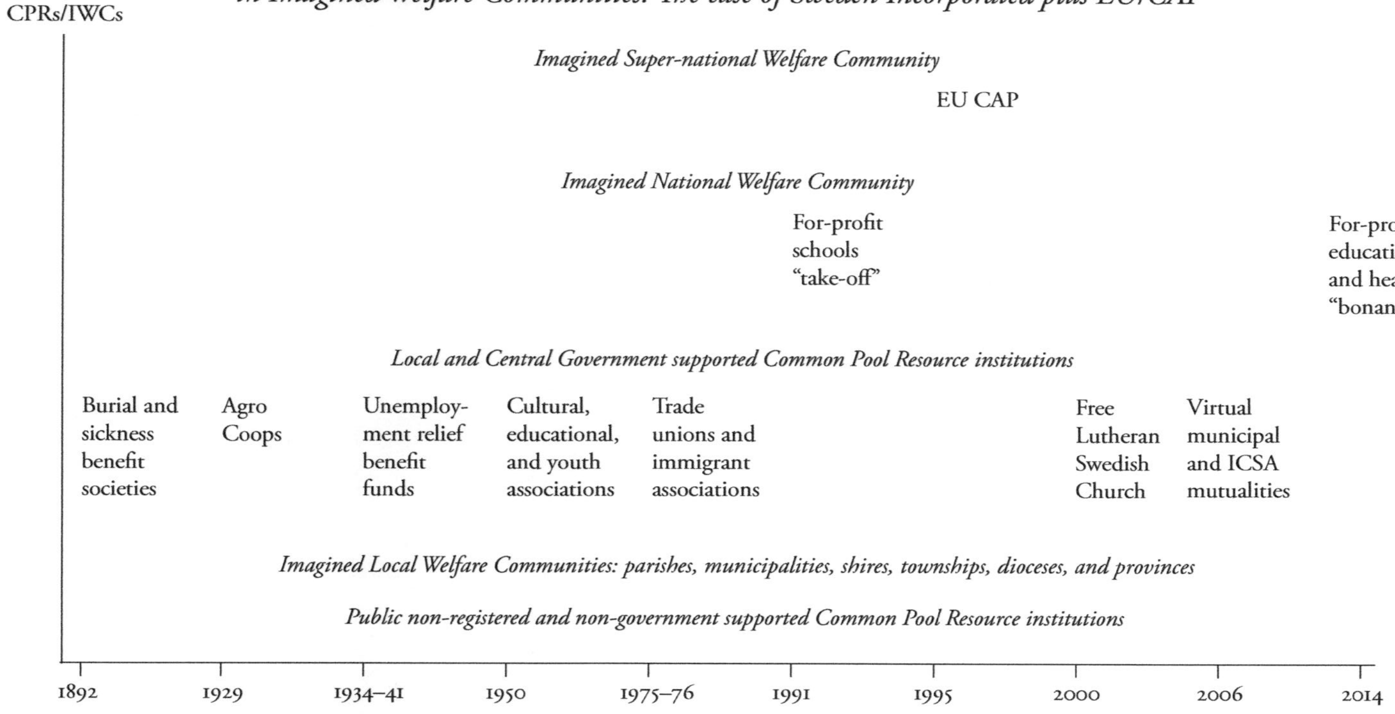

Appendix. In the Tracks of the Welfare State: Research by Walking Around

> It's hard to fathom the 12-inch minds of people even though one can see through 12-foot waters.
> Korean proverb

Methodologically, this sequel largely follows the guidelines for chapter III in the original book, which were based on a set of indicators documented in my contribution to *Growth to Limits: The West European Welfare State since World War II* (Flora 1986–7), in particular its institutional synopsis in volume IV – formally also an appendix to the dissertation's chapter III (Olsson 1990) – "The Development of the Postwar Welfare State" or "Sweden" in volume I in the Flora series – the focus of which was on changes in policy and programmes, or "resources and clienteles" through inspecting subsequent documents of the type of material present in the appendix volume (institutional documents, laws, evaluation and research reports, statistics, etc.). However, as stated in chapter 3 of this sequel, the aim here has been, analytically, to go beyond "Rokkan schema" and explore the archaeology of common pool resource institutions in civilizing and embedding processes in imagined welfare communities. In a survey that claims to be both rational and realistic, this necessitates an approach that is flexible and allows even for intuition, which was facilitated by participation in other types of research collaboration.

Moreover, in the mid-1980s, I was a member of a research team led by Walter Korpi, collecting data on social rights and the rules of social insurance institutions in 18 advanced countries, Belgium and Sweden being my special responsibilities. For two decades, these two countries have by now been captured in numerous equations in social scientific articles published in peer-reviewed journals by members of a growing stock of researchers (cf. Korpi & Palme 2007; also Ferrarini et al. 2012).

While a detailed but half-baked manuscript on the Belgian road from nation-state to welfare state half the size of this sequel stayed in the drawer (this was before the global escalation of the perish-or-publish rush), chapter II in the foregoing volume to some extent reflects my own contribution to the early stage of the controversial Stockholm Social Policy in an International Perspective project. Chapter II represented part of an exchange with historian Peter Baldwin, whose erudition and writings I still admire, and from which I hope I have learnt. Well into the 1990s part-time, I continued to contribute to the data-collecting of the Stockholm Social Policy projects, and the two major projects, Flora's and Korpi's, strengthened my awareness of the fallacies and potentials of social research.

Until very recently this type of project has not been a fulltime pre-occupation of mine. Since the early 1990s, in addition to other and often more pressing academic and professional duties, I have still tried to follow social policy-making in Sweden – somewhat later also elsewhere, particularly in East and South-East Asia, the Baltics, and Eastern and Central Europe – through following official documents and public debates and through working with devoted doctoral and masters students. I kept an archive that has grown over the years. Away from Sweden for a year in the mid-1990s, my time at UC Berkeley broadened my perspectives on social welfare practices, theories, and methodologies. Not being in Sweden rendered inquiry into domestic issues more difficult, but the appendix to C. W. Mills' *The Sociological Imagination* (1959) early inspired me to keep an ongoing diary, or research log. In the late 1990s, several years' work at the University of Bergen also facilitated comparative, cross-cultural and national research. Some of these jottings found their way into articles written along the way, while others remained in reserve in the archive.

Some of the ideas and statements presented in this volume were originally but often prematurely outlined in lectures, seminars and other oral communications, and articles published after the previous postscript went to press in early 1993. Sometimes sources not cited in detail in this sequel are made explicit in some of these earlier publications in which the material underlying the conclusions is hopefully scrutinized to an extent not always possible in the present manuscript. Almost all of the written interventions are available in English, exception for those dealing with the "new" Swedish urban policies focusing on ethnicity, (social) exclusion, growth, inclusion (or assimilation), migration and urbanity which were intended mainly for a domestic audience. Another, minor, exception is a review of the large output of the Swedish Welfare Commission published in a Norwegian journal (Hort 2002). Otherwise, reports from that and similar state commissions have been meticulously followed and digested over the years, as have other relevant documents from parliament (and, since 2003, from its independent National Audit Office – "3R"), the government and the government's central welfare state agencies and bureaucracies (including its former audit agency RRV) though no other reviews like the one just mentioned have been produced.

This is also the case for the scrutiny of a select number of local authorities, either in the metropolitan areas or among the median types of the Ostrom kind, and more recently one or two in the interim (Kalmar and Växjö). Likewise, output from the major civil society associations, including the national assemblies of local and regional government – for some years merged into one lobby group (SKL) – have been examined, often with the generous help of doctoral students, research assistants and student aids (e.g., Kings 2010; Ramel 1994). The six-year evaluation of the Metropolitan Development Initiative offered an excellent opportunity to delve into the daily working of community organizers, local officials and politicians (Hajighasemi et al. 2006; Urban 2005). With the tacit approval of local contractors the wheeling and dealings of the MDI-secretariat and its political commissariat, or metropolitan delegation, the under-secretaries of state from five ministries, were closely monitored by the supposedly local evaluators. Taken together, the background to much of what was discussed in chapters 2–4 above is based on the inspection of over two decades of relevant official documents: for instance, each year some forty or fifty State Commission papers are produced by several ministries connected with welfare provision, and Statistics Sweden (SCB) annually produces and publishes information on almost every aspect of society, though following-up earlier time-series is often expensive and sly for those without free access.

Moreover, two decades of conversations with over one thousand civil society activists, local decision-makers and employees in various responsible positions in local authorities (particularly in the "segregated" communities of metropolitan Stockholm, the municipalities of Eskilstuna and Västerås, and local government in the counties of Kalmar and Kronoberg – as well as slightly fewer civil servants and national politicians (particularly at the National Audit Office, more recently also the National Agency of Public Management, and the ministries of Education, Finance, Health and Social Affairs, Integration, Justice, Labour, and Migration – have contributed to this inspection of welfare state developments in Sweden. Walking through the corridors, and negotiating the landscapes of welfare, was often an eye-opener also for its seemingly well-prepared office worker, making ethnographic field trips a necessary complement to any legal exposition or statistical computation. As well as studying documents and figures provided by officials or protagonists, we formally and informally interviewed decision- and policy-makers – politicians and civil servants – as well as civil society activists and employees of business and voluntary (welfare) associations including the Swedish Church and its clergy (especially the diocese of Växjö), which are duly acknowledged in what has been presented above. Confidential exchanges have been secured in the archive (for an insightful sociological analysis – in Swedish – of the arduous task of deciphering interviews, see Bergman 2009). Over these decades I have visited a number of parishes and almost every second municipality in Sweden, and usually gained access to those helping make welfare work, civil society activists, welfare entrepreneurs, local politicians as well as local government and church employees. Nine years of membership in the research and development committee of the National Association of Local Authorities facilitated this interlocution.

Apart from an introductory presentation and the summary remarks at the end, this sequel is divided into five chapters. An outline of chapter 1, first drafted for a global overview of welfare and politics, reviews the global comparative welfare state research literature (cf. Hort och Therborn 2012). The second chapter investigates the social policies and programmes of the Swedish welfare state, and is an updated, more comprehensive, but briefer summary of three articles written in the first years of the new millennium for a series of books edited by Neil Gilbert (2000) and Niel Gilbert and Rebecca van Vorheis (2001 and 2003) (see also Olsson Hort in Riegler & Schneider 1999). This summary is enriched by material from contributions to *The European Handbook on welfare systems*, a cross-national volume on old age policy and a companion volume on the comparative study of child welfare written at the end of the 1990s and 'oos respectively (Schubert et al. 2009, Aspalter & Walker 2008, Gilbert 1997 and Gilbert, Parton & Skivenes 2010). Chapter two addresses issues first touched on in two of the original articles in the first volume – chapters III and IV – but adapted to the new world of welfare in the years succeeding both the "Short" and the "Long Twentieth Century".

This scrutiny of the Swedish welfare state is a fairly sketchy patchwork of policies and programmes, offering more of an outline to direct further research than a conclusive account and assessment by a single author. At the end of chapter 2, the key role of the financing of welfare state programmes and policies came to the fore to an extent not foreseen in the first volume. Hence, I think it is pertinent to underline the still provisional and incomplete character of these pages and the following chapter in particular in relation to some of the hypothesis advanced (e.g., the implications of the shift "from a welfare state to a tax state", and finally "to a market administration"). The imagination and power of "creative destruction" should not be underestimated. The third chapter approaches the institution of the welfare state from the perspective of broader demographic, institutional, political and socio-economic processes as were done in chapter III in the first book. Again, this chapter is also based on conversations with involved participants, and to some extent also on sociological "participant observation". When the stakes are high, it should be no surprise that battling academic ideologues, economic and institutional power-players, and political opponents use whatever support they can garner from social scientists – some more willing than others to support one side or the other. In writing up this chapter, I also benefitted from sojourns in the late 1970s and 1980s at both *Aftonbladet* and *Dagens Nyheter* and, from 1983, being the editor of *Arkiv för studier i arbetarrörelsens historia*. More recently, colleagues at the Institute of Contemporary History at Södertörn, Håkan Blomqvist in particular, have often shared their thoughts on current Swedish affairs with me.

The fourth chapter explores the micro-level of modern society focusing on the topic of civil society. Though the concept is a guiding principle in chapter I – as made explicit by for instance Margaret Weir in her generous review of the book in *American Journal of Sociology* (1991) – after the publication of the second edition, several attempts were made to develop a formal model that overcame the shortcomings of the figure presented in chapter IV of the original volume (p. 253) (e.g. in Berghman & Cantillon 1993). In particular a piece written for a book on the normative foundation of the Nordic welfare state edited by Nanna Kildal and Stein Kuhnle (2004) serves as a forerunner, though it has been almost completely reworked to fit into the present mould, further articulating the idea of imagined welfare communities (ILWCs and INWCs) and common pool resource (CPR) institutions, even "dynamic conservatism".

The material and sources are similar to those used in the original book and are analysed accordingly in chapters 2–4. Over twenty Swedish government budgets have been tabled for parliamentary approval, as have a similar number of supplementary (spring) economic–political propositions. The ministries of education, health, labour, and social affairs – over the years organized and re-organized in various combinations and enlarged by the creation of new central welfare ministries such as gender equality, integration and migration (with housing back in late 2010 after almost twenty years in the cold) and under their auspices new, old, renamed and scrapped central state agencies and boards – have presented major as well as minor proposals and propositions pertaining to the areas under review here. Under their respective jurisdictions, apart from propositions to parliament, each year state commissions presented a handful of reports for public discussion and for responses from selected institutions and organizations. Other relevant documents, such as parliamentary debates and committee reports as well as documents from the central agencies and other important players have also been consulted. The archives of the world of business, however, are still closed. Moreover, the increasing output of the social research industry – often financed by the Social Science Research Council and its predecessors – has, given the limitations of a humble worker in the garden of social inquiry, been taken into account. Of course, more than one report may have slipped past my eyes, or simply put aside after a brief glance, but both the more controversial and substantial ones have usually been hinted at by more than one advisor, for which I tender thanks here. Summarizing the three closely related chapters, chapter 2 is an overview, based on previously employed classifications, neither a final judgment nor a reconstructed taxonomical system, leaving the order of things almost as it was: observing or "seeing a few things systematically". In that sense, this chapter is not the archaeology of existing social programs nevertheless written in an effort to explore their futures (cf. Hort 2013; see also Edenheim 2010). Chapter 3 attempts to go beyond the social democratic regime type, and chapter 4 takes up the threads from chapters I and IV in the original volume. Chapters 3 and 4 were particularly enriched by conversations, interviews and research participation – "ethnographic oral histories" – which provided additional information beyond that conveyed in official documents, public debates and statistics.

CPR-institutions and imagined welfare communities are not restricted to the Far North of Europe, and hopes for an alternative and better future for many on earth are expressed throughout the globe. The fifth chapter steps out of the local Northern context and focuses on the remarkable global spread of the "Nordic model" – not only from Sweden but from Denmark, Finland and Norway as well – over the last decade, as discussed in some earlier works co-authored with Scandinavian colleagues, or alone (e.g., Alestalo, Hort & Kuhnle forthc.; Hatland et al. 2003; Kuhnle & Hort 2005; Hort 2005). The foundations of this chapter, growing output from Nordic research in this field, also include domestic and transnational media coverage both of the miraculous rebirth of the Nordic model and its actors, as well as conversations with INGO and NGO activists and academic celebrities involved in the dissemination of research results, ideas and visions in this field of social action and inquiry.

References

Abrahamson, P. (2010). "Continuity and consensus: Governing families in Danmark". *Journal of European Social Policy*, vol. 20, no. 5, pp. 399–409.

Abrahamson, P. (2011). "The welfare modeling business revisited: The case of East Asian welfare regimes". In: Hwang, G.-J. (ed.) (2011). *New Welfare States in East Asia*. Cheltenham: Edward Elgar.

Agevall, O. (2010) "Dragspelskampen: Statsbidragen, bildningsförbunden och det folkliga musicerandet 1947-1960". Paper presented at the Annual meeting of the Swedish Sociological Associasion, March 10–11. Halmstad.

Ahmad, E.; Drèze, J.; Hills, J. & Sen, A. (eds.) (1991). *Social Security in Developing Countries*. Oxford: Oxford University Press.

Ahn, S.-H. & Olsson Hort, S. E. (2003). "The Welfare State in Sweden". In: Aspalter, C. (ed.) (2003). *Welfare Capitalism around the world*. Hong Kong: Casa Verde.

Ahrne, G. (2006). "Stater och andra organisationer". In: Ahrne, G. (ed.) (2006). *Stater som organisationer*. Stockholm: Nerenius & Santérus.

Aidukaite, J. (2004). *The Emergence of the Post-Socialist Welfare State – the case of the Baltic States: Estonia, Lativa and Lithuania*. Dissertation series, no. 1. Huddinge: Södertörn University College.

Aidukaite, J. (2009a). "Transformation of welfare systems in the Baltic States: Estonia, Latvia, Lithuania". In: Cerami, A. & Vanhuysse, P. (eds.) (2009). *Post-Communist Welfare Pathways: Theorizing Social Policy Transformations in Central and Eastern Europe*. Basingstoke: Palgrave MacMillan.

Aidukaite, J. (ed.) (2009b). *Poverty, Urbanity and Social Policy: Central and Eastern Europe Compared*. New York: Nova Science.

Alapuro, R. (1999). "On the repertoire of collective action in France and the Nordic countries: A perspective". In: Bouget, D. & Palier, B. (eds.) (1999). *Comparing social welfare systems in Nordic Europe and France*. Paris: MIRE ("Copenhagen Conference", vol. 4).

Alber, J. (1982). *Vom Armenhaus zum Wohlfahrtsstaat: Analysen zur Entwicklung der Sozialversicherung in Westeuropa*. Frankfurt: Campus.

Alber, J. & Standing, G. (2000). "Social dumping, catch-up or convergence? Europe in a comparative global context". *Journal of European Social Policy*, vol. 10, no. 2, pp. 99–119.

Alestalo, M. & Flora, P. (1994). "Welfare States in the Periphery – Peripheral Welfare States?". In: Alestalo, M.; Allardt, E.; Rychard, A. & Wesolowski, W. (eds.) (1994). *The Transformation of Europe: Social Conditions and Consequences*. Warsaw: IFiS Publishers.

Alestalo, M.; Hort, S. E. O. & Kuhnle, S. (forthc.). "The Nordic Model: Conditions, Origins, Outcomes, Lessons". In: Kuhnle, S.; Yinzhang, C.; Kettunen, P. & Pedersen, K. (eds.) (forthc.) *The Nordic Welfare State – A Basic Reader*. (in Japanese; 2010 Chinese edition Shanghai: Fudan University Press).

Allelin, M. (2012). *Eleven som konsument, skolan som företag och utbildning som vara - det fria skolvalet utifrån elever boende i förorten*. Bachelor thesis. Gothenburg: Department of Sociology and Work Science.

Allendinger, J.; Ebner, C. & Nikolai, R. (2010). "Education in Europe and the Lisbon Benchmarks". In: Alber, J. & Gilbert N. (eds.) (2010). *United in Diversity*. Oxford: Oxford University Press.

Andersen, J. G. (2007). "Conceptualizing Welfare State Change". CCWS working paper. Aalborg: CCWS. (Mimeo.)

Andersen, J. G. & Bjorklund, T. (2008). "Scandinavia and the far right". In: Davies, P. & Jackson, P. (eds.) (2008). *The Far Right in Europe: An Encyclopedia*. Oxford: Greenwood.

Anderson, B. (1998). *The Spectre of Comparisons: Nationalism, Southeast Asia and the World*. London: Verso.

Anderson, B. (2006). *Imagined Communities*. 3rd edition. London: Verso.

Anderson, K. (2009). "The Church as Nation? The Role of Religion in the Development of the Swedish Welfare State". In: van Kersbergen, K. & Manow, P. (eds.) (2009). *Religion, Class Coalitions, and Welfare States*. Cambridge: Cambridge University Press.

Anderson, P. (1961). "Sweden: Mr Crosland's Dreamland" (pt. 1) & "Sweden: Study in Social Democracy" (pt. 2). *New Left Review*, First Series, Nos. 7 and 9.

Anderson, P. (2001). "US Elections: Testing Formula Two." *New Left Review*, second series, no. 8, pp. 5–22.

Anderson, P. (2006). "Persian Letters". In: Moretti, F. (ed.) (2006). *The Novel, Volume 1*. Princeton: Princeton University Press.

Anderson, P. (2009). *The New Old World*. London: Verso.

Andersson, D. (2013). "Den offentliga tjänstens etos". In: Hort, S. E. O. (ed.) (2013). *På cykeltur genom livet*. Stockholm: Atlantis.

Andersson, J. (2003). *Mellan tillväxt och trygghet: Idéer om produktiv socialpolitik i socialdemokratisk socialpolitisk ideologi under efterkrigstiden*. Uppsala Studies in Economic History, no. 67. Uppsala: Acta Universitatis Upsaliensis.

Andersson, R. (2006). "'Breaking segregation' – Rhetorical Construct or Effective Policy? The Case of the Metropolitan Development Initiative in Sweden". *Urban Studies*, vol. 43, no 4, pp. 787–799.

Anttonen, A. & Sipilä, J. (1996). "European Social Care Services: Is It Possible to Identify Models?". *Journal of European Social Policy*, vol. 6, no. 2.

Arkiv. Tidskrift för samhällsanalys (2013), no. 2, special edition, *Det vita fältet II*.

Ascherson, N. (2000). "On with the pooling and merging". *London Review of Books*, vol. 22, no. 4, pp. 8–9.

Aspalter, C. & Walker, A. (eds.) (2008). *The Elderly in Welfare Capitalism*. Hong Kong: Casa Verde.

Bahle, T., Pfeifer, M. & Wendt, C. (2010). "Social Assistance". In: Castles, F. et al. (eds.) (2010). *The Oxford Handbook of the Welfare State*. Oxford: Oxford University Press.

Baldwin, P. (1990). *The Politics of Social Solidarity: The Class Basis of the European Welfare State 1875–1975*. Cambridge: Cambridge University Press.

Baldwin, P. (2009). *The Narcissism of Minor Differences: How America and Europe are Alike*. Oxford: Oxford University Press.

Bambra, C. (2006). "Research Note: Decommodification and the worlds of welfare revisited". *Journal of European Social Policy*, vol. 1, no. 16, pp. 73–80.

Barrientos, A. & Santibanez, C. (2009). "New Forms of Social Assistance and the Evolution of Social Protection in Latin America". *Journal of Latin American Studies*, vol. 41, no. 1, pp. 1–26.

Bendz, A. (2004). *I välfärdsstatens hägn: Autonomi inom arbetslöshetsförsäkringen*. Göteborg studies in politics, no. 88. Gothenburg: Statsvetenskapliga institutionen.

Bengtsson, B. (2009). "Housing Politics and Political Science" in: Clapham, D. F.; Clark, W. & Gibb, K. (eds.) (2009). *The SAGE Handbook of Housing Studies*. London: Sage.

Benner, M. (1997). *The Politics of Growth: Economic Regulation in Sweden 1930–1994*. Lund: Arkiv.

Berghman, J. & Cantillon, B. (eds) (1993). *The European Face of Social Security: Essays in Honour of Herman Deleeck*. Aldershot: Avebury.

Bergman, P. (2009). *Kvinna bland stålmän*. Lund: Arkiv.

Bergman, P. & Wigblad, R. (1999). "Worker's Last Performance: Why Some Factories Show their Best Results during Countdown". *Economic and Industrial Democracy*, vol. 20, no. 3, pp. 343–368.

Bergmark, Å. & Bäckman, O. (2004). "Stuck with Welfare? Long-term Social Assistance Recipiency in Sweden". *European Sociological Review*, vol. 20, no. 5, pp. 425–443.

Bergström, J. & Rothstein B. (1999). *Korporatismens fall och den svenska modellens kris*. Stockholm: SNS.

Berman, S. (2006). *The Primacy of Politics: Social Democracy and the Making of Europe's Twentieth Century*. Cambridge: Cambridge University Press.

Berner, B. (1996). "Professional or Wage Worker? Engineers and Economic Transformation in Sweden". In: Meiksins, P. & Smith, C. (eds.) (1996). *Engineering Labour: Technical Workers in Comparative Perspective*. London: Verso.

Berven, N. (2003). *National Politics and Cross-National Ideas: Welfare, work and legitimacy in the United States and Norway*. Bergen: Institute for Comparative Politics.

Bildt, C. & Borg A. (2011). "The Swedish model should guide Europe's bail-out". *Financial Times*, 12 October, p. 11.

Billing, M.; Olsson, L. & Stigendal, M. (1991). "Malmö – Our Town: Local Politics in Social Democracy". In: Misgeld, K. & Åmark, K. (eds.) (1991). *Creating Social Democracy: A Century of the Social Democratic Labor Party in Sweden*. College Park: The Pennsylvania State University Press.

Björk, L. (2004). *Vårdnadsbidraget som aldrig blev av – om välfärdsstatens förmåga till återställning*. Bachelor thesis. Huddinge: Södertörn University, School of Social Sciences.

Björklund, A. et al. (2005). *The Market Comes to Education in Sweden: An Evaluation of Sweden's Surprising School Reforms*. New York: Russell Sage.

Björnsson, A. (2012). *Arbetsterapeuterna*. Stockholm: Förbundet Svenska Arbetsterepeuter.

Blackburn, R. (2006). *Age shock: How Finance is Failing Us*. London: Verso.

Blomqvist, P. (2004). "The choice revolution in Sweden: Privatization of Swedish Welfare Services in the 1990s". *Social Policy and Administration*, vol. 38, no. 2, pp. 139–155.

Boreus, K.; Ighe, A.; Karlsson, M. & Warlenius, R. (eds.) (2012). *Ett sekel av syndikalism – Sveriges Arbetares Centralorganisation 1910–2010*. Stockholm: Federativ.

Bradshaw, J. & Finch, N. (2010). "Family Benefits and Services". In: Castles, F. et al. (eds.) (2010). *The Oxford Handbook of the Welfare State*. Oxford: Oxford University Press.

Brante, T. (2005). "Staten och professionerna". In: Jørgensen, M. A. & Rask Eriksen, T. (reds.) (2005). *Professionsidentitet i forandring*. Copenhagen: Akademisk forlag.

Breman, J. (2007). *Insecurity Regime in Village India*. Oxford: Oxford University Press.

Brenner, R. (1998). *The Economics of Global Turbulence: A special report on the World Economy, 1950–1998*. Seoul: no publisher (pirated photocopy with laminated cover).

Brunius, T. (1990). *Olle Baertling*. Stockholm: Konstfrämjandet.

Brännström, L. (2005). "The Corrosion of Trust: The Impacts of Disadvantaged Neighbourhood Conditions, Fear of Victimisation, Powerlessness, and Precarious Labour Market Positions". In: Carroll, E. & Eriksson, L. (eds.) (2005). *Welfare Politics Cross-examined – Eclecticist Analytical Perspectives on Sweden and the Developed World from the 1880s to the 2000s*. Amsterdam: Aksant.

Bull, M. (ed.) (1995). *Apocalypse Theory and the Ends of the World*. Oxford: Blackwell.

Busemeyer, M. R. & Nikolai, R. (2010). "Education". In: Castles, F. et al. (eds.) (2010). *The Oxford Handbook of the Welfare State*. Oxford: Oxford University Press.

Bäckström, A. (2011). *Welfare and religion in 21st Century Europe, Volume 1*. Farnham: Ashgate.

Bötker, P. (2007). *Leviathan i arkipelagen: Staten, förvaltningen och samhället. Fallet Estland*. Södertörn doctoral dissertations, vol. 13. Huddinge: Södertörn University.

Carlsson Wetterberg, C. (2011). *– bara ett öfverskott af lif-: En biografi om Frida Stéenhoff*. Stockholm: Atlantis.

Carrillo Garcia, B. (2012). *China and Mexico's welfare policy in comparative perspective: Rationale and forces behind the move towards universal social assistance and health insurance*. Paper presented at the Seventeenth International Seminar on Issues in Social Security, 18–20 June. Sigtuna.

Carson, M. (2005). "Paradigm drift in the Swedish Welfare State". In: Kildal, N. & Kuhnle, S. (eds) (2005). *The Normative Foundations of the Nordic Welfare State*. London: Routledge.

Carsten, J. (2004). *After kinship*. Cambridge: Cambridge University Press.

Castells, M. & Himanen, P. (2002). *The Information Society and the Welfare State: The Finnish Model*. Oxford: Oxford University Press.

Castles, F. G. (2010). "Comparative Analyses of Stateness and State Action: What can we learn from patterns of expenditure?". In: Alber, J. & Gilbert N. (eds.) (2010). *United in Diversity?* Oxford: Oxford University Press.

Castles, F. G. et al. (2010). *The Oxford Handbook of the Welfare State*. Oxford: Oxford University Press.

Castles, S. & Schierup, C.-U. (2010). "Migration and Ethnic Minorities". In: Castles, F. G. et al. (eds.) (2010). *The Oxford Handbook of the Welfare State*. Oxford: Oxford University Press.

Chang, K.-S.; Fine, B. & Weiss, L. (eds.) (2012). *Developmental Policy in Transition: the neoliberal Era and Beyond*. London: Palgrave.

Charron, N.; Lapuente, V. & Rothstein, B. (2013). *Quality of Government and Corruption from a European Perspective: A Comparative Study of Good Government in EU Regions*. Cheltenham: Edward Elgar.

Christiansen, N. F.; Pedersen, K.; Edling, N. & Haave, P. (eds.) (2006). *The Nordic Model of Welfare: Historical Reappraisal*. Copenhagen: Museum Tusculanum Press.

Chung, H. & Muntaner, C. (2007). "Welfare state matters: A typological multilevel analysis of wealthy countries". *Health Policy*, vol. 80, no. 3, pp. 328–39.

Clark, C. (2007). *Iron Kingdom: The Rise and Downfall of Prussia*. Boston: Belknap Press.

Clawson, D. et al. (eds.) (2007). *Public Sociology*. Berkeley: University of California Press.

Cockburn, A. (1995). *The Golden Age Is in Us: Journeys and Encounters*. London: Verso.

Cocozza, M. & Hort, S. E. O. (2011). "The Dark Side of the Universal Welfare State". In: Gilbert, N.; Patton, N. & Skivenes, M. (eds.) (2011). *Child Protection Systems: International Trends and Orientations*. Oxford: Oxford University Press.

Cohen, J. L. & Arato, A. (1992). *Civil society and political theory*. Cambridge, Mass.: MIT Press.

Cohn, D. (1992). *Reforming Health Care in Canada and Sweden 1975–1990*. Stockholm International Studies 92:2. Stockholm: Stockholm University International Graduate School.

Dahlstedt, M. (2005). *Reserverad demokrati*. Umeå: Borea.

Dahlström, C. (2004). *Nästan välkomna: Invandrarpolitikens retorik och praktik*. Göteborg: Statsvetenskapliga institutionen.

Dalström, K. (1987). *Brev till Hjalmar Branting och Fredrik Ström*. Introduction and commentary by Rut Berggren. Lund: Arkiv.

Dannefjord, P. (2009). *Organisationspraktiker och målförändringar: Exemplet svensk socialdemokrati*. Lund: Arkiv.

Davidson, A. (1994): *Two Models of Welfare: The Origins and Development of the Welfare State in Sweden and New Zealand, 1888-1988*. Uppsala: Acta Universitatis Upsaliensis.

Davis, M. (1986). *Prisoners of the American Dream*. London: Verso.

Deacon, B.; Hulse, M. & Stubbs, P. (eds.) (1997). *Global Social Policy: International Organizations and the Future of Welfare*. London: Sage.

Debord, G. (1970). *The Society of the Spectacle*. London: Zone

Delcroix, C. (2000). "The Transmission of life stories from ethnic minority fathers to their children: A personal resource to promote social integration". In: Arbet, S. & Attias-Donfut, C. (eds.) (2000). *The Myth of Generational Conflict: The family and state in ageing societies*. London: Routledge.

Derluguian, G. (2005). *Bourdieu's Secret Admirer in the Caucasus*. Chicago: The University of Chicago Press.

Dienst, R. (2011). *The Bonds of Debt: Borrowing against the Common Good*. London: Verso.

Dore, R. (2000). *Stock-market capitalism, welfare capitalism: Japan and Germany versus the Anglo-Saxons*. Oxford: Oxford University Press.

Douglas, M. (1986). *How Institutions Think*. Syracuse: Syracuse University Press.

Draibe, S. & Riesco, M. (2007). "Latin America: A New Developmental Welfare State in the Making ". In: Riesco, M. (ed.) (2007). *Latin America: A new developmental welfare state in the making*. London: Palgrave.

The Economist (2013). "The Next Supermodel". Leader. 2 February.

The Economist (2010). "Moderate and Happy". 18 September.

The Economist (2006). "The End of the Nordic Model". Annual edition. December.

The Economist (1991). Post election commentary. September.

Edebalk, P. G. (2011). *Gustav Möller och åldringarma*. Lund: Socialhögskolan.

Edenheim, S. (2010). "Governmental Reports and the Genealogy of Heteronormativity". In: Lundqvist, Å. & Pedersen, K. (eds.) (2010). *In Experts we trust: Knowledge, Politics and Bureaucracy in Nordic Welfare State*. Odense: University Press of Southern Denmark.

Eglinski, M. (1992). *Evaluation Research: The Swedish National Audit Bureau's Evaluation of the Labour Inspectorate*. Stockholm International Studies 92:1. Stockholm: Stockholm University International Graduate School.

Eklund, K. & Sjödin, K. G. (1990). *Läckan*. Stockholm: Tiden.

Ekström, A. (ed.) (2006). *Digital welfare*. Stockholm: Global utmaning.

Elgenius, G. (2011). *Symbols of Nation and Nationalism: Celebrating Nationhood*. London: Palgrave.

Elias, N. (2000). *The civilizing process: sociogenetic and psychogenetic investigations*. Oxford: Blackwell.

Eliasson-Lappalainen, R.-M. (2011). "En personlig betraktelse om vård och omsorg". *Socialvetenskaplig tidskrift*, vol. 18, no. 3, pp. 206–221.

Elmbrandt, B. (2010). *Stockholmskärlek: En bok om Hjalmar Mehr*. Stockholm: Atlas.

Engelstad, F. & Kalleberg, R. (eds.) (1999). *Social Time and Social Change: Perspectives on Sociology and History*. Oslo: Scandinavian University Press.

Englund, P. (2007). *En välfärdsstats uppgång och fall*. Stockholm: Atlantis.

Engman, J. (1999). *Rituell process, tradition och media: Socialdemokratisk första maj i Stockholm*. Dissertation. Stockholm: Stockholm University.

Eriksson, L.; Stenberg, S.-Å.; Flyghed, J. & Nilsson, A. (2010). *Vräkt: Utkastad från hus och hem i Stockholm 1879–2009*. Stockholm: Premiss.

Eriksson, M.-L. (2012). *Att predika en tradition: Om tro och teologisk literacy*. Lund: Arcus.

Erixon, L. (2011). "Under the impact of traumatic events, new ideas, economic experts and the ICT Revolution: The Economic Policy and Macroeconomic Performance of Sweden in the 1990s and 2000s". *Comparative Social Research*, vol. 28, pp. 265–330.

Ersta Sköndal (2011). *Current Studies at the Civil Society Institute: An Overview*. Stockholm: Ersta Sköndal University College.

Ervik, R. (2000). *The Hidden Welfare State in Comparative Perspective: Tax Expenditures and Social Policy in Various Welfare Models*. Bergen: Institute of Comparative Politics.

ESO (2012). *Svängdörrar i staten: En ESO-rapport om när politiker och tjänstemän byter sida*. Rapport till Expertgruppen för studier i offentlig ekonomi 2012:1. Stockholm: Finansdepartementet.

Esping-Andersen, G. (1985). *Politics Against Markets*. Princeton: Princeton University Press.

Esping-Andersen, G. (1990). *The Three Worlds of Welfare Capitalism*. Cambridge: Polity.

Esping-Andersen, G. (ed.) (1996). *Welfare States in Transition: National Adaptations in Global Economies*. London: Sage.

Esping-Andersen, G. (1997). "Hybrid or Unique: The Japanese Welfare State between Europe and America". *Journal of European Social Policy*, vol. 7, no. 3, pp. 179–189.

Esping-Andersen, G. (2009). *The Incomplete Revolution*. London: Pluto.

Esping-Andersen, G; Gallie, D.; Hemerijcks, A. & Myles, J. (2002). *Why we need a new welfare state*. Oxford: Oxford University Press.

Fahey, T. & Norris, M. (2010). "Housing". In: Castles, F. G. et al. (eds.) (2010). T*he Oxford Handbook of the Welfare State*. Oxford: Oxford University Press.

Falkner, G. (2010). "European Union". In: Castles, F. G. et al. (eds.) (2010). *The Oxford Handbook of the Welfare State*. Oxford: Oxford University Press.

Favell, A. & Guiraudon, V. (eds.) (2011). *Sociology of the European Union*. London: Palgrave Macmillan.

Feldt, K.-O. (1992). *Alla dessa dagar*. Stockholm: Bonniers.

Ferge, S. (1999). "And what if the state fades away? The civilizing process and the state". In: Svallfors, S. & Taylor-Gooby, P. (eds.) (1999). *The End of the Welfare State*. London: Routledge.

Ferrarini, T.; Nelson, K.; Palme, J. & Sjöberg, O. (2012). *Sveriges socialförsäkringar i ett jämförande perspektiv*. Stockholm: Socialdepartementet.

Ferrera, M. (2009). *National Welfare States and European Integration: Dilemmas and Perspectives*. Paper presented at the Symposium in honour of Peter Flora on the occasion of his 65th birthday. WZB, 6–7 March. Berlin.

Financial Times (2011). "Top Finance Minister of Europe". Leader. 8 December.

Flora, P. (ed.) (1986). *Growth to Limits: The Western European Welfare States Since World War II: Volume 1, Sweden, Norway, Finland, Denmark*. Berlin: de Gruyter.

Flora, P. (ed.) (1987). *Growth to Limits: The West European Welfare State Since World War II, Volume IV, Appendix (Synopses, Bibliographies, Tables)*. Berlin & New York: Walther de Gruyter.

Flora, P. & Alber, J. (1981). "Modernization, Democratization, and the Development of the Welfare States in Western Europe". In: Flora, P. & Heidenheimer, A. J. (eds.) (1981). *The Development of the Welfare States in Europe and America*. New Brunswick & London: Transaction Books.

Flora, P. & Heidenheimer, A. J. (eds.) (1981). *The Development of Welfare States in Europe and America*. New Brunswick: Transaction.

Franzén, M. (2009). "Between pleasure and virtue: ambivalences of public space today". *Yhdyskuntasuunnittelu*, vol. 47, no. 3, pp. 6–23.

Freeland, C. (2012). *Plutocrats: The rise of the new global super rich*. London: Allen Lane.

Freeman, R. & Rothgang, H. (2010). "Health". In: Castles, F. G. et al. (eds.) (2010). *The Oxford Handbook of the Welfare State*. Oxford: Oxford University Press.

Friberg, K. (2005). *The Workings of Cooperation: a comparative study of consumer co-operative organisation in Britain and Sweden 1860–1970*. Växjö: Acta Vexiosiana.

Frykman, J. et al. (2009). "Sense of Community: Trust, Hope and Worries in the Welfare State". *Ethnologia Europaea*, vol. 39, no. 1.

Gahrton, P. (1984). *Riksdagen inifrån*. Lund: Publica/Liber.

Garsten, C.; Rothstein, B. & Svallfors, S. (2011). Grant application to The Swedish Research Council for the research project "De policyintellektuella i välfärdsstaten". Stockholm: Institutet för Framtidsstudier.

Gilbert, N. (ed.) (1997). *Combatting child abuse: International perspectives and trends*. New York: Oxford University Press.

Gilbert, N. (ed.) (2000). *Targeting social benefits*. New Brunswick: Transaction.

Gilbert, N. (2002). *The Transformation of the Welfare State: The Silent Surrender of Public Responsibility*. New York: Oxford University Press.

Gilbert, N. & Van Voorhis (ed.) (2001). *Activating the Unemployed: A Comparative Appraisal of Work-oriented Policies*. New Brunswick: Transaction.

Gilbert, N. & Van Voorhis, R. (eds.) (2003). *Changing Patterns of Social Protection*. New Brunswick: Transaction.

Glans, K. (1986). *Från den norra provinsen*. Stockholm: Bonniers.

Goody, J. (1998). *Food and Love*. London: Verso.

Goody, J. (2004). *Islam in Europe*. Cambridge: Polity Press.

Gough, I. & Olofsson, G. (eds.) (1999). *Capitalism and Social Cohesion: Essays on Exclusion and Inclusion*. London: MacMillan.

Gough, I. et al. (eds.) (2004). *Insecurity and Welfare Regimes in Asia, Africa and Latin America: Social Policy in Developmental Contexts*. Cambridge: Cambridge University Press.

Gouldner, A. W. (1973). "Personal reality, social theory and the tragic dimension in science". In Gouldner, A. W. (1973). *For sociology: Renewal and critique in sociology today*. London: Allen Lane. First published in: Boalt, G. (1969). *The sociology of research*. Carbondale: Southern Illinois University Press.

Gramsci, A. (1971). *Selections from the Prison Notebooks*. London: Lawrence & Wishardt.

Gratzer, K. (forthc.). "Privatiseringsmanuskript". Work in progress, presented at a seminar 22 January 2013, Stockholm School of Economics. (Mimeo.)

Green-Pedersen, G. & Baggesen Klitgaard, M. (2009). "Between economic constrains and popular entrenchment: The development of the Danish welfare state 1982–2005". In: Schubert, K.; Bazant, U. & Heberle, S. (eds.) (2009). *The Handbook of European Welfare Systems*. London: Routledge.

Green, U. (2009). *Managing Laponia*. Uppsala: Department of Cultural Anthropology.

Greider, G. (2001). *Fucking Sverige*. Stockholm: Ordfront [in Swedish].

Grell, O. P. (1992). "Scandinavia". In: Pettegree, A. (ed.) (1992). *The Early Reformation in Europe*. Cambridge: Cambridge University Press.

Grönlund, A. (2004). *Flexibilitetens gränser: Förändring och friktion i arbetsliv och familj*. Umeå: Borea.

Guillou, J. (2004). *Tjuvarnas marknad*. Stockholm: Piratförlaget.

Gustafsson, B. (1988). *Den tysta revolutionen: Det lokala välfärdssamhällets framväxt i Örebro 1945-1982*. Stockholm: Gidlunds.

Gustafsson, B.-Å. (2010). "Branding public schools". In: Hort, S. E. O. (ed.) (2010). *From Linnaeus to the future(s)*. Kalmar & Växjö: Linnaeus University Press.

Hajighasemi, A. (2012). Email. 30 June.

Hajighasemi, A. et al. (2006). *Experiment, motstånd, makt: Det kommunala integrationsarbetet och storstadssatsningen i Södertälje*. Huddinge: Södertörn university.

Haggard, S. & Kaufmann, R. R. (2008). *Development, Democracy and Welfare States: Latin America, East Asia and Eastern Europe*. Princeton: Princeton University Press.

Hall, P. & Soskice, D. (eds.) (2001). *Varieties of Capitalism*. Oxford: Oxford University Press.

Halleröd, B., Rothstein, B., Daoud, A. & Nandy, S. (2013). "Good Governance and Poor Children: A Comparative Analysis of Government Efficiency and Severe Child Deprivation in 68 Low- and Middle-income Countires". *World Development*, vol. 48, pp. 19–31.

Hansen, J. (2011). *"Så fixade vi allhallen": Resursmobilisering och organisationsförtätning i ett lokalsamhälle*. Lund: Arkiv.

Hartman, L. (ed.) (2011a). *Konkurrensens konsekvenser: Vad händer med svensk välfärd?* Stockholm: SNS.

Hartman, L. (2011b). "Hur får vi konkurrensutsatt välfärd att fungera optimalt?" *Dagens Nyheter, Debatt.* 16 oktober.

Hasselbladh, H.; Bejerot, E. & Gustavsson, R. Å. (2008). *Bortom New Public management*. Lund: Academia Adacta.

Hatland, A.; Kuhnle, S. & Romoren, T. I. (eds.) (2011). *Den norske velferdstaten*. Oslo: Gyldeldal Akademisk.

Hatland, A.; Hort, S. & Kuhnle, S. (2003). "A Work-, Child- and Family-Friendly Social Policy". In: Marshall, K. & Butzbach, O. (eds.) (2003). *New Social Policy Agendas for Europe and Asia*. Washington D C: The World Bank.

Heckscher, E. (1932). "Un Grand Chapitre de l'Historie du Fer: Le Monopole Suédois". *Annales d'histoire économique et sociale*, vol. 4, no. 14, pp. 127–139.

Heckscher, G. (1984). *The Welfare State and Beyond*. Minneapolis: University of Minnesota Press.

Hedin, K.; Clark, E.; Lundholm, E. & Malmborg, G. (2012). "Neoliberalization of Housing in Sweden: Gentrification, Filtering and Social Polarization". *Annals of the Association of American Geographers*, vol. 102, no. 2, pp. 443–463.

Helgesen, M. (1997). *Attföring – en tjeneste i velferdsstaten*. Rapport no. 56. Bergen: Institutt for Administration og organisajonsvitenskap.

Heller, P. (1997). "Social Capital as a Product of Class Mobilization and State Intervention: Industrial Workers in Kerala, India". *World Development*, vol. 24, no. 6, pp. 1055–1071.

Helmersson Bergmark, K. (1995). *Anonyma alkoholister i Sverige*. Stockholm: Sociologiska institutionen (diss.)

Herrin, J. (1987). *The formation of Christendom*. Princeton: Princeton University Press.

Hertting, N. & Wedung, E. (2009). *Den utvärderingstäta politiken: Styrning och utvärdering i svensk storstadspolitik*. Lund: Studentlitteratur.

Hiilamo, H. & Kangas, O. (2009). "Trap for Women or Freedom of Choice? The Struggle over Child Care Schemes in Finland and Sweden". *Journal of Social Policy*, vol. 38, no. 3, pp. 457–475.

Hilson, M. (2008). *The Nordic Model: Scandinavia since 1945*. London: Reaktion.

Himanen, P. (2005). "The Nordic Model and the Information Society: The Finnish Case". In: Kangas, O. & Palme, J. (eds.) (2005). *Social Policy and Economic Development in the Nordic countries*. London: Palgrave.

Hinrichs, K. & Lynch, J. (2010). "Old Age Pensions". In: Castles, F. G. et al. (2010). *The Oxford Handbook of the Welfare State*. Oxford: Oxford University Press.

Hitchens, C. (2011). "Stieg Larsson: The Author who played with fire", In: Hitchens, C. (2011). *Arguably: Essays*. New York: Twelve.

Hobsbawn, E. (1994). *The Age of Extremes: A History of the World 1914–1991*. New York: Pantheon.

Hobson, B. (ed) (2002). *Making men into Fathers: Men, Masculinities and the Social Politics of Fatherhood*. Cambridge: Cambridge UP.

Hollander, A. (1995). "Social Policy: Aspects of the Relationship between General Welfare and Welfare for People with Special Needs". In: Åkerman, S. & Granatstein, J. (eds.) (1995). *Welfare States in Trouble*. Umeå: Swedish Science Press.

Holmberg, J. (2005). "Kan vi bry oss om varandra? Can we bother about each other?" In: Soila, T. (ed.) (2005). *The Cinema of Scandinavia*. London: Wallflower.

Holmberg, L. (2012). "Papperslösa i SAC: Organisering och kamp på 2000-talet". In: Boreus, K. et al. (eds.) (2012). *Ett sekel av syndikalism: Sveriges arbetares centralorganisation 1910–2010*. Stockholm: Federativ.

Holmqvist, M. (2010). "The 'Active Welfare State' and its consequences". *European Societies*, vol. 12, no. 2, pp. 209–230.

Hort, S. E. O. (2002). "Ett bokslut over Välfärdsbokslut". *Tidskrift for Velferdsforskning*, vol. 5, no. 3, pp. 168–174.

Hort, S. E. O. (2004a) "Normative Innovations from Lindbeck to Svegfors – towards a Dynamic Conservatism?". In: Kildal, N. & Kuhnle, S. (eds.) (2004). *The Normative Foundations of the Nordic Welfare Model*. London: Routledge.

Hort, S. E. O. (2004b). "Renten in Schweden – Auf dem weg zurück zur Grundrente?". In: Opielka, M. (ed.) (2004). *Grundrente in Deutschland: Sozialpolitische Analysen*. Wiesbaden: Verlag für Sozialwissenschaften.

Hort, S. E. O. (2005). "The Geography of Comparative welfare state research: A comment". *Global Social Policy*, vol. 5, no. 1, pp. 14–17.

Hort, S. E. O. (2007). "Mr Welfare State, I presume". *Bergens Tidene*. 7 December.

Hort, S. E. O. (2009a). "The growing circulation of Euroturk in pro-Turkish and eurosceptical Sweden". In: Höjelid, S. (ed.) (2009). *Turkey: From tutelary to liberal democracy?* Lund: Sekel.

Hort, S. E. O. (2009b). "Tom Nairn: Mellan nation och klass". *Arkiv för studier i arbetarrörelsens historia*, no. 98–99, pp. 217–234.

Hort, S. E. O. (2010). "Introduction". In: S. E. O. Hort (eds.) (2010). *From Linnaeus to the Future(s) – Letters from afar*. Kalmar and Växjö: Linnaeus University Press.

Hort, S. E. O. (2013). "Familje- och jämställdhetspolitiken". In: Tarschys, D. & Lemne, M. (eds.) (2013). *Vad staten vill: Mål och ambitioner i svensk politik*. Hedemora: Gidlunds.

Hort, S. E. O. & Kuhnle, S. (2000). "Growth and Welfare? A First Look at the Recent East and Southeast Asian Experience". PROSEA Occasional Paper, no. 28. Taipei: Academia Sinica.

Hort, S. E. O. & Therborn, G. (2012). "Politics and Welfare". In: Amenta, E.; Nash, K. & Scott, J. (eds.) (2012). *The Wiley-Blackwell Companion to Political Sociology*. London: Blackwell.

Hosseini-Kaladjahi, H. (2002). *Stora fiskar äter fortfarande små fiskar: Helhetsutvärdering av storstadssatsningen i Botkyrka kommún*. Fittja: Mångkulturellt centrum.

Hosseini-Kaladjahi, H. (2003). *Satsning ger resultat: Utvecklingen i Fittja 1999–2003 enligt en enkät bland de boende*. Tumba: Mångkulturellt centrum.

Huber, E. & Stephens, J. (2005). "Welfare states and the economy". In: Smelser, N. & Swedberg, R. (eds.) (2005). *Handbook of Economic Sociology*. Second edition. New York: Russell Sage.

Huber, E.; Mustillo, T. & Stephens J. (2008). "Politics and Social Spending in Latin America". *Journal of Politics*, vol. 70, no. 2, pp. 420–436.

Hugemark, A. (1994). *Den fängslande marknaden: Ekonomiska experter om välfärdsstaten*. Lund: Arkiv.

Hultgren, P. (2011). *Det dubbla statushandikappet och sjukförsäkringens moraliska praktiker*. Linnaeus University dissertations, no. 39. Växjö: Linnéuniversitetet.

Hultgren, P. (2007). *Sjukskrivningspraxis på vårdcentralen*. Växjö: Sociologiska institutionen (lic).

Högskoleverket (2006). *Invandrarakademi och aspirantutbildning – erfarenheter av kompletterande utbildning för invandrade akademiker*. Report 2006:35 R. Stockholm: Swedish National Board of Higher Education.

Högström, A. (2011). "Ett rike av denna världen: Zeth Höglund som pacifistisk journalist, visionär poet, revolutionär agitator och socialdemokratiskt borgarråd". *Arbetarhistoria*, vol. 35. no. 4, pp. 10–27.

Immergut, E.; Anderson, K. & Schultze, I. (eds.) (2005). *The Handbook of West European Pension Politics*. Oxford: Oxford University Press.

International Herald Tribune (2006). "Elections in Sweden". 12 September.

Isaksson, A. (2006). *Den politiska adeln*. Stockholm: Bonniers.

Jacobsson, K. (ed.) (2010). *Känslan för det allmänna*. Umeå: Borea.

Jameson, F. (1981). *The Political Unconscious*. Ithaka: Cornell University Press.

Jansson, P. (2003). *Den huvudlösa idén: Medborgarlön, välfärdspolitik och en blockerad debatt*. Lund: Arkiv.

Jarl, M.; Persson, S. & Fredriksson, A. (2010). *New public Management in public education: a catalyst for the professionalisation of Swedish school principals*. Paper presented at the Sociology Seminar, 26 April. Linnaeus University.

Jenkins, D. (1968). *Sweden – the Progress Machine*. London: Robert Hale.

Jensen, J. & Mahon, R. (1992). "Representing Solidarity: Class, Gender and the Crisis in Social Democratic Sweden". *New Left Review*, First Series, no. 201, pp. 76–100.

Jensen, P. H. (ed.) (2005). *Velfaerd – dimensioner og betydninger*. Copenhagen: Frydenlund.

Jeppsson Grassman, E. (1994). *Third Age Volunteering in Sweden*. Stockholm: Sköndalsinstitutet,

Jeppsson Grassman, E. & Svedberg, L. (2007). "Civic Participation in a Scandinavian Welfare State: Patterns in Contemporary Sweden". In: Trägårdh, L. (ed.) (2007). *Civil Society in Northern Europe: The Swedish Model Reconsidered*. New York: Berghans Books.

Jessop, B.; Kastendiek, H.; Nielsen, K. & Pedersen, O. K. (eds.) (1991). *The Politics of Flexibility: Restructuring State and Industry in Britain, Germany and Scandinavia*. Aldershot: Edward Elgar.

Johansson, H. (2001). *I det sociala medborgarskapets skugga*. Lund: Arkiv.

Johnson, B. (2010). *Kampen om sjukfrånvaron*. Lund: Arkiv.

Judt, T. (2009). *Ill fares the land*. New York: Heinemann.

Jungner, A.-C. (2011). *Baltic Worlds*, blog.

Kangas, O. (2010). "Work Accidents and Sickness Benefits" In: Castles, F. G. et al. (eds.) (2010). *The Oxford Handbook of the Welfare State*. Oxford: Oxford University Press.

Kangas, O. & Palme, J. (eds.) (2005). *Social Policy and Economic Development in the Nordic Countries*. London: Palgrave.

Kangas, O. & Saari, J. (2009). "The Welfare System of Finland". In: Schubert, K.; Bazant, U. & Heberle, S. (eds.) (2009). *The Handbook of European Welfare Systems*. London: Routledge.

Karvonen, L. & Kuhnle, S. (eds.) (2001). *Party Systems and Voter Alignments Revisted*. London: Routledge.

Kaspersen, L. B. (2008). *Danmark i verden*. Copenhagen: Hans Reitzels forlag.

Kautto, M. et al. (eds.) (1999). *Nordic Social Policy: Changing Welfare States*. London: Routledge.

Kenworthy, L. (2010). "Labour Market Activation". In: Castles, F. G. et al. (eds.) (2010). *The Oxford Handbook of the Welfare State*. Oxford: Oxford University Press.

Khakee, A. (2013). "Letter to the editor". *The Economist*. 30 March.

Kildal, N. (ed.) (2000). *Den nya sociala frågan*. Gothenburg: Daidalos.

Kildal, N. & Kuhnle, S. (eds.) (2004). *The Normative Foundations of the Nordic Welfare States*. London: Routledge.

Kings, L. (2010). "In Defence of the Local". In: S. E. O. Hort (eds.) (2010). *From Linnaeus to the Future(s) – Letters from afar*. Kalmar and Växjö: Linnaeus University Press.

Kings, L. (2011). *Till det lokalas försvar: Civilsamhället i den urbana periferin*. Lund: Arkiv.

Kings, L. (2012). "Förorten och föreningen". In: Wijkström, F. (ed.) (2012). *Civilsamhället i samhällskontraktet*. Stockholm: European Civil Society Press.

Kings, L. & Kravchenko, Z. (2012.). *Carrots and Sticks: Housing Policies for Youth in Russia and Sweden*. Paper presented at the Sociology Seminar, February 20th. Huddinge: Södertörn University College. (Mimeo.)

Kjellberg, A. (2011). "Trade Unions and Collective Agreements in a Changing World". In: Thörnqvist, A. & Engstrand, Å.-K. (eds.) (2011). *Precarious Employment in Perspective: Old and New Challenges to Working Conditions in Sweden*. Bruxelles: P.I.E. Peter Lang.

Klitgaard, R. (2012). "The Quality of Government". *Perspective on Politics*, vol. 10. no. 3, pp. 855–857.

Knudsen, T. (2000). "Tilblivelsen af den universalistiske velfaerdsstat". In: Knudsen, T. (ed.) (2000). *Den nordiske protestantisme og velfaerdsstaten*. Aarhus: Aarhus universitetsforlag.

Knudsen, T. & Rothstein, B. (1994). "State Building in Scandinavia". *Comparative Politics*, vol. 26, no. 2, pp. 203–220.

Korpi, W. & Palme, J. (2003). "New Politics and Class Politics in the Context of Austerity and Globalization". *American Political Science Review*, vol. 97 no 3, pp. 425–446.

Korpi, W. & Palme, J. (2007). *The Social Citizenship Indicators Program (SCIP)*. Stockholm: Swedish Institute for Social Research, Stockholm University.

Kosonen, P. (1993). "The Scandinavian Welfare Model in a New Europe". In: Boje, T. P. & Olsson, S. E. (eds.) (1993). *Scandinavia in a New Europe*. Oslo: Scandinavian University Press.

Kravchenko, Z. (2008). *Family (versus) Policy: Combining work and care in Russia and Sweden*. Dissertation series, no. 27. Huddinge: Södertörn University.

Kroll, C. (2005). *Välfärdspolitikens offentliga ansikte i Finland och Sverige*. Helsinki: Svenska social- och kommunalhögskolan.

Kroll, C.; Blomberg, H. & Svallfors, S. (2000). "Konjunkturernas offer eller godissamhällets verktyg". *Socialvetenskaplig tidskrift*, no. 3, pp. 244–266.

Kuhnle, S. (ed.) (2000). *Survival of the European Welfare State*. London: Routledge.

Kuhnle, S. (2011). "Towards a Nordic-East Asian welfare dialogue?". *Journal of Asian Public Policy*, vol. 4, no. 3, pp. 254–262.

Kuhnle, S. & Hort, S. E. O. (2005). *The Developmental Welfare State in Scandinavia: Lessons for the Developing world*. Geneva: United Nations Institute for Social Development.

Kuhnle, S. & Hort, S. E. O. (forthc.). "Velferdsbegreppet i Langtidsprogrammen/utredningarna". In: Blomberg, H. (ed.) (forthc.). Title and publisher still not decided.

Kuhnle, S. & Selle, P. (1992). "Governmental understanding of voluntary organizations: policy implications of conceptual change in post-war Norway". In: Kuhnle, S. & Selle, P. (eds.) (1992). *Government and Voluntary Organizations*. Aldershot: Avebury.

Kumlin, S. & Rothstein, B. (2005). "Making and Breaking Social Capital: The Impact of Welfare State Institutions". *Comparative Political Studies*, vol. 38, no. 4, pp. 339–365.

Kvist, J.; Fritzell, J.; Hvinden, B. & Kangas, O. (eds.) (2011). *Changing Social Equality: The Nordic welfare model in the 21st Century*. Bristol: The Policy Press.

Kvist, R. (1995). "Swedish Saami Policy 1550–1990". In: Åkerman, S. & Granatstein, J. (eds.) (1995). *Welfare States in Trouble*. Umeå: Swedish Science Press.

Kwon, H.-J. (2005). *Transforming the Developmental Welfare State in East Asia*. London: Palgrave.

Kwon, H.-J. & Kim, Y. (2012). *Making National Social Protection Strategy in Cambodia*. Global Research Network on Social Protection in East Asia, proceedings from the 6th workshop. Seoul: Asia Development Institute.

Lagergren, M. & Batljan, I. (2000). *Will there be a helping hand: Macroeconomic scenarios of future needs and costs of health and social care for the elderly in Sweden 2000–30*. Långtidsutredningen 1999/2000. Stockholm: Ministry of Health and Social Affairs.

Lappegård, T (2011). "The Columbus' egg of Norwegian family policy". *Demografia* (English Edition), vol. 54, no. 5, pp. 79–88.

Lawrence, R. (2009). *Shifting Responsibilities and Shifting Terrains: State Responsibility, Corporate Social Responsibility and Indigenous Claims*. Stockholm: Department of Sociology.

Lawson, A. (2008). *Demokrati på förortska: Storstadssatsningen i Stockholm, Haninge, Huddinge och Södertälje*. Södertörn Research Reports, 2008:2. Huddinge: Södertörn University.

Leibfried, S. & Mau, S. (eds.) (2008). *Welfare States: Construction, Deconstruction, Reconstruction*, vols. I–III. Cheltenham: Edward Elgar.

Lewis, J. (1992). "Gender and the Development of Welfare Regimes". *Journal of European Social Policy*, vol. 2, no. 3, pp. 159–173 (reprinted in Leibfried & Mau 2008).

Leira, A. (1993). "Mothers, Market and the State: A Scandinavian 'Model'?" *Journal of Social Policy*, vol. 22, no. 3, pp. 329–347.

Lindbeck, A. et al. (1994). *Turning Sweden Around*. Cambridge: MIT Press.

Lindberg, H. (2007). "The Role of Economists in Liberalising Swedish Agriculture". *Economic Journal Watch*, vol. 4, no. 2, pp. 213–229.

Lindberg, H. (2008). "Politikbyte och idéernas betydelse – reformeringen av den svenska jordbrukspolitiken". *Historisk tidskrift*, vol. 128, vol. 1, pp. 29–54.

Lindbom, A. (2007). "Obfuscating Retrenchment: Swedish Welfare Policy in the 1990s". *Journal of Public Policy*, vol. 27, no. 2, pp. 129–150.

Lindbom, A. (2011). *Systemskifte? Den nya svenska välfärdspolitiken*. Lund: Studentlitteratur.

Lindbom, A. & Rothstein, B. (2005). *The Mysterious Survival of the Swedish Welfare State*. Paper presented at the Annual Meeting of the American Political Science Association. Chicago.

Linderborg, Å. (2007). *Mig äger ingen*. Stockholm: Atlas.

Lindgren, K. O. (2010). *Is there a paradox of redistribution? Studying the redistributiveness of unemployment benefits*. Uppsala: Department of Government. (Mimeo.)

Lindh, S. (2013). "Tankar om stadsplanering i Stockholm". In: Hort, S. E. O. (ed.) (2013). *På cykeltur genom livet: En vänbok till Gunnar Wetterberg*. Stockholm: Atlantis.

Lindh, G. & Dahlin, E. (2011). "A Swedish Perspective on the Importance of Bourdieu's Theories for Career Counseling". *Journal of Employment Counseling*, vol. 37, no. 4, pp. 194–203.

Lindh, T.; Malmberg, B. & Palme, J. (2005). "Generations at War or Sustainable Social Policy in Aging Societies?" *Journal of Political Philosophy*, vol. 13, no. 4, pp. 470–489.

Lindqvist, R. & Lundälv, J. (2012). "Social Citizenship in Sweden – tensions between activation and medicalization in health insurance." Paper presented at the Seventeenth International Seminar on Issues in Social Security, 18–20th June. Sigtuna.

Lindström, J. (2006). "Skolan mitt i Ronna och Hovsjö". In: Axelsson, M. & Bunar, N. (eds.) (2006). *Skola, språk och storstad*. Stockholm: Pocky.

Lindvall, J. (2004). *The Politics of Purpose: Swedish Macroeconomic Policy after the Golden Age*. Göteborg: Department of Political Science Gothenburg University.

Lindvret, J. (2006). *Ihålig arbetsmarknadspolitik*. Umeå: Borea.

Littorin, S.-O. (2010). *Uppdrag arbete*. Stockholm: Ekerlinds.

Loberg, F. (2012). *Juholt: Utmanaren*. Stockholm: ETC.

Loxbo, K. (2007). *Bakom socialdemokraternas beslut: En studie av den politiska förändringens dilemman: Från 1950-talets ATP-strid till 1990-talets pensionsuppgörelse*. Växjö: Växjö University Press.

Lundberg, U. (2003). *Juvelen i kronan: Socialdemokraterna och den allmänna pensionen.* Stockholm: Hjalmarsson & Högberg.

Lundberg, U. & Åmark, K. (2001). "Social Rights and Social Security. The Swedish Welfare State 1900–2000". *Scandinavian Journal of History,* vol. 26, no. 3, pp. 157–176.

Lundquist, L. (2011). *Flocken i massamhället: Den politiska ordningens villkor och uttryck.* Lund: Arkiv.

Lundqvist, Å. (2001). *Bygden, bruket och samhället: Om människor och organisationer i brukssamhället.* Lund: Arkiv.

Lundqvist, Å. (2011). *Family Policy Paradoxes: Gender Equality and Labour Market Regulation in Sweden 1930–2010.* Bristol: The Policy Press.

Lödemel, I. (1997). *The Welfare Paradox: Income Maintenance and Personal Social Services in Norway and Britain 1946–1966.* Oslo: Scandinavian University Press.

Löfgren, H. (2013). *The Privatization of Public Housing in Stockholm Municipality: A Commodification of a Welfare Service.* Paper presented at the Baltic and East European Welfare State Seminar, 19 March, Södertörn University.

Mann, M. (1993). *The Sources of Social Power. Volume Two: The Rise of Classes and Nation-states 1750–1914.* Cambridge. Cambridge University Press.

Marklund, S. (1988). *Paradise Lost? The Nordic Welfare States and the Recession 1975–1985.* Lund: Arkiv.

Marshall K. & Butzbach, O. (eds.) (2003). *New Social Policy Agendas for Europe and Asia.* Washingtoin D C: The World Bank.

Martin, I. W.; Mehrotra, A. K.; & Prasad, M. (eds.) (2009). *The New Fiscal Sociology: Taxation in Comparative and Historical Perspective.* Cambridge: Cambridge University Press.

Mathieu, C. (1999). *The Moral Life of the Party: Moral argumentation and the creation of meaning in the Europe policy debates of the Christian and Left–Socialist parties in Denmark and Sweden 1990–1996.* Lund: Department of Sociology.

Mattsson, K. (2010). *Landet utanför: Ett reportage om Sverige bortom storstaden.* Stockholm: Leopard.

Meagher, G. & Szebehely, M. (eds) (2013). "Marketisation in Nordic eldercare: A research report on legislation, oversight, extent and consequences". Stockholm: Stockholm University, Department of Social Work.

Miller, K. (1991). *Denmark: A Troubled Welfare State.* Boulder: Westview Press.

Mills, C. W. (1959). *The Sociological Imagination.* New York: Preager.

Mishra, R. (1976). "Convergence Theory and Social Change: The Development of Welfare in Britain and the Soviet Union". *Comparative Studies in Society and History,* vol. 18, no. 1, pp. 28–56.

Mitchell, J. (1966). "Women: the longest revolution". *New Left Review,* First series, no. 40, pp. 11–37.

Mjøset, L. (1991). *Kontroverser i norsk sociologi.* Oslo: Gyldeldal.

Mjøset, L.; & Cappelen, Å.; Fagerberg, J. & Sofus Tranoy, B. (1994). "Norway: Changing the Model". In: Anderson, P. & Camiller, P. (eds.) (1994). *Mapping the European Left.* London: Verso.

Modéer, K. (2009). "Den svenska och nordiska samhällsreligionen". In: Mellbourn, A. (ed.) (2009). *Författningskulturer: Konstitutioner och politiska system i Europa, USA och Asien.* Lund: Sekel.

Molander, P. (1989). *En ny livsmedelspolitik.* Ds 1989:63, Jordbruksdepartementet. Stockholm: Allmänna förlaget.

Molin, J. & Ingves, S. (2008). "Can the authorities manage crisis in the financial system?" *Penning- och valutapolitik,* no. 2, pp. 5–22.

Morel, N.; Pallier, B. & Palme, J. (eds.) (2011). *Towards a Social Investment State? Ideas, policies and challenges*. Bristol: Policy Press.

Mortensen, N. (ed.) (1995). *Social Integration and marginalisation*. Frederiksberg: Samfundslitteratur.

Mulinari, D. & Neergaard, A. (2005). *Den nya svenska arbetarklassen: Rasifierade arbetares kamp inom facket*. Umeå: Borea.

Mörkenstam, U. (1999). *Om "Lapparnes Privilegier": Föreställningar om samiskhet i svensk samepolitik 1883–1997*. Stockholm: statsvetenskapliga institutionen.

Nagel, A.-H. (ed.) (1991). *Velferdskommunen: Kommunenes rolle i utviklingen av velferdsstaten*. Bergen: Alma Mater.

Nairn, T. (2003). *The Break-up of Britain*. 3rd edition. Altona: Common Ground Publishing.

Nairn, T. (2007). "The Enabling Boundary". *London Review of Books*, vol. 29, no. 20, pp. 5–7.

Nilsson, L. (2013). "Välfärdspolitik och välfärdsopinion 1986-2012: Vinster i välfärden". In: Weibull, L.; Oskarsson, M. & Bergström, A. (eds.) (2013). *Vägskäl: 43 kapitel om politik, medier och samhälle*. Gothenburg: SOM-institutet.

Nørby Johansen, L. (1986). "Denmark". In: Flora, P. (ed.) (1986). *Growth to Limits: The West European Welfare State Since World War II*, vols. I & IV. Berlin & New York: Walther de Gruyter.

Nordenmark, M. (2004). *Arbetsliv, familjeliv och kön*. Umeå: Borea.

Nordlund, A. (2003). *Resilient Welfare States: Nordic Welfare State Development in the Late 20th Century*. Umeå: Sociologiska institutionen.

Obinger, H. & Wagschal, U. (2010). "Social Expenditures and Revenues". In: Castles, F. G. et al. (eds.) (2010). *The Oxford Handbook of the Welfare State*. Oxford: Oxford University Press.

O'Brien, M. & Salonen, T. (2010). "Child Poverty and child rights meet active citizenship: A New Zealand and Sweden case study". In: *Childhood*, vol. 18, no. 2, pp. 211–226.

O'Connor, J. & Olsen, G. (eds.) (1998). *Power Resource Theory and the Welfare State: A Critical Appraisal*. Toronto: Toronto University Press.

OECD (1981). *The Crisis of the Welfare State*. Paris: OECD.

Offe, C. (1984). *Contradictions of the Welfare State*. London: Hutchinson.

Offe, C. (2009). "Epilogue". In: Cerami, A. & Vanhuysse, P. (eds.) (2009). *Post-Communist Welfare Pathways: Theorizing Social Policy Transformations in Central and Eastern Europe*. Basingstoke: Palgrave MacMillan.

Olivier, M. & Kuhnle, S. (eds.) (2008). *Norms and Institutional Design*. Stellenbosch: Sun Press.

Olofsdotter Stensöta, H. (2009). *Sjukskrivningarna och välfärdens infriare: En studie av svensk sjukvårdsbyråkrati*. Stockholm: Hjalmarsson & Högberg.

Olofsson, G. (1996). *Klass, rörelse, socialdemokrati: Essäer om arbetarrörelsens sociologi*. Lund: Arkiv.

Olofsson, G. (1999). "Norbert Elias". In: Andersen, H. & Kaspersen, L. B. (eds.) (1999). *Classical and Modern Social Theory*. Oxford: Blackwell.

Olofsson, G. (2010). "Income inequality and the service sector". In: Hort, S. E. O. (eds.) (2010). *From Linnaeus to the Future(s) – Letters from afar*. Kalmar and Växjö: Linnaeus University Press.

Olofsson, G. (2012). "Book review of Peter Baldwin: *The Narcissism of Minor Differences. How America and Europe are Alike*". *European Societies*, vol. 14, no. 2, pp. 308–311.

Olofsson, G. & Thomell, T. (2012). *Gavra*. Lund: Arkiv.

Olsen, G. (2002). *The Politics of the Welfare State*. Oxford: Oxford University Press.

Olsson Hort, S. E. (1999). "Swedische Socialpolitik unter Veränderungsdruck". In: Riegler, C. & Schneider, O. (eds.) (1999). *Sweden im Wandel: Entwicklungen, Probleme, Perspektiven*. Berlin: Arno Spitz.

Olsson Hort, S. E. (2001). "La société civile, l'État, et la sécurité sociale en Suéde: centralisation et décentralisation dans le model sociale scandinave". In: Comité d'histoire de la sécurité sociale (ed.) (2001). *Un siècle de protection sociale en Europe*. Paris: Association pour l'etude de l'histoire de la Securité sociale.

Olsson Hort, S. E. & Cohn, D. (1995). "Sweden". In: Johnson, N. (ed.) (1995). *Private Markets in Health and Welfare: An International Perspective*. Oxford: Berg.

Olsson, S. E. (1990). *Social Policy and Welfare State in Sweden*. Lund: Arkiv.

Olsson, S. E. (1991). "När makten lades till rätta". In: Olsson, S. E. & Therborn, G. (eds.) (1991). *Vision möter verklighet: Om social styrning och faktisk samhällsutveckling*. Publica. Stockholm: Allmänna Förlaget.

Olsson, S. E. (1993). "Postscript: Crisis, Crisis, Crisis – 1990–1992". In: Olsson, S. E. (1993). *Social Policy and Welfare State in Sweden*. Second, enlarged edition. Lund: Arkiv.

Olsson, S. E. & Lewis, D. (1995). "Welfare rules and Indigenous rights: the Sami people and the Nordic welfare states". In: Dixon, J. & Scheurell, R. (eds.) (1995). *Social Welfare with Indigenous Peoples*. London: Routledge.

Olsson, U. (2013). "En värdefull historia". In: Hort, S. E. O. (ed.) (2013). *På cykeltur genom livet*. Stockholm: Atlantis.

Orloff, A. (1999). "Motherhood, Work, and Welfare in the United States, Britain, Canada, and Australia". In: Steinmetz, G. (ed.) (1999) *State/Culture: State-Formation after the Cultural Turn*. Ithaka: Cornell University Press.

Orton, F. & Sundqvist, S.-I. (red.) (2011). *Sigge och hans 1000 elever*. Stockholm: SIS ägarservice.

Ostrom, E. (1990). *Governing the Commons*. Cambridge: Cambridge University Press.

Palme, J. (1999). *The Nordic model and the modernisation of social protection in Europe*. Copenhagen: Nordic Council of Ministers.

Palme, J. & Vennemo, I. (1998). *Swedish Social Security in the 1990s*. Stockholm: Ministry of Health and Social Affairs.

Palme, J. et al. (2002). "Welfare Trends in Sweden: Balancing the Books for the 1990s". *European Journal of Social Policy*, vol. 12, no. 4, pp. 329–346.

Papakostas, A. (2011). "The Rationalization of Civil Society". *Current Sociology*, vol. 59, no. 1, pp. 5–23.

Papakostas, A. (2012). *Civilizing the Public Sphere*. London: Palgrave.

Penning- och valutapolitik (2010). *Tio år med en självständig riksbank*, no. 1, special issue.

Persson, G. (1997). *Den som är satt i skuld är icke fri*. With Kask, J.-P. Stockholm: Atlas.

Petersson, O. & Wetterberg, G. (2012). "Sverige är moget för en ny övergripande skattereform". *Dagens Nyheter, Debatt*. 11 March.

Pierson, P. (1994). *Dismantling the Welfare State? Reagan, Thatcher and the Politics of Retrenchment*. Cambridge: Cambridge University Press.

Platzer, E. (2006). "From Private Solutions to Public Responsibility and Back Again: The new domestic services in Sweden". *Gender & History*, vol. 18, no. 2, pp. 211–221.

Pontusson, J. (2011). "Once again a Model: Nordic Social Democracy in a Globalized World". In: Cronin, J.; Ross, G. & James, C. (eds.) (2011). *What's Left of the Left*. Durham: Duke University Press.

Pontusson, J. & Swenson, P. (1993). "Varför har arbetsgivarna övergivit den svenska modellen?" *Arkiv för studier i arbetarrörelsens historia*, no. 53–54, pp. 37–66.

Pringle, K. (2009). "Epilogue: on developing empowering child welfare systems and the welfare research needed to create them". In: Forsberg, H. & Kröger, T. (eds.) (2009). *Social work and child welfare politics Through Nordic lenses*. Bristol: Policy Press.

Pålsson, A.-M. (2011). *Knapptryckarkompaniet: Rapport från Sveriges riksdag*. Stockholm: Atlantis.

Quadagno, J. (1994). *The Color of Welfare: How Racism undermined the War on Poverty*. Oxford: Oxford U P.

Rahe, P. (2009). *Soft Despotism, Democracy's Drift: Montensquieu, Rousseau, Torqueville and the Modern Prospect*. New Haven: Yale University Press.

Ramel, C. (1994). *The Swedish Association of Local Authorities: Corporatist, Civil Society or Welfare State Actor?* Stockholm: Stockholm University, Department of Sociology.

Regeringen (1997). *Strukturövervägningssystem for Danmark*. Copenhagen: Finansministeriet.

Reinfeldt, F. (1993). *Det sovande folket*. Stockolm: Moderata Ungdomsförbundet.

Riksdagen (2012). *Riksdagens årsbok 2011/2012*. Stockholm: Riksdagsförvaltningen.

Riksrevisionen (2011). *Miljökrav i offentlig upphandling – är styrningen mot klimatmål effektiv?* National Audit Office Report 2011:29. Stockholm: Riksrevisionen.

Ringen, S. et al. (2011). *The Korean State and Social Policy*. Oxford: Oxford University Press.

Roche, M. (2010). *Exploring the Sociology of Europe*. London: Sage.

Rokkan, S. (1999). *State Formation, Nation-Building and Mass Politics in Europe: The Theory of Stein Rokkan*. Edited by Peter Flora with Stein Kuhnle and Derek Unwin. Oxford: Oxford University Press.

Room, G. (2000). "Commodification and Decommodification: A developmental critique". *Policy and Politics*, vol. 28, no. 3, pp. 331–351.

Rothstein, B. (1992). *Den korporativa staten*. Stockholm: Norstedts.

Rothstein, B. (1996). *The Social Democratic State: The Swedish Model and the Bureaucratic Problem of Social Reform*. Pittsburgh: Pittsburgh University Press.

Rothstein, B. (2011). *The Quality of Government: Corruption, Social Trust, and Inequality in International Perspective*. Chicago: The University of Chicago Press.

Rothstein, B. & Broms, R. (forthc.). "Governing Religion: The Long-Term Effects of Sacred Financing". *Journal of Institutional Economics* (accepted for publication).

Rothstein, B. & Uslaner, E. M. (2005). "All for all: Equality, corruption, and social trust". *World Politics*, vol. 58, no. 1, pp. 41–72.

Ruin, O. (1990). *Tage Erlander: Serving the Welfare State, 1946–1969*. Pittsburgh: University of Pittsburgh Press.

Rydgren, J. (2002). "Varför inte i Sverige? Den radikala högerpopulismens relativa misslyckande". *Arkiv för studier i arbetarrörelsens historia*, no. 86–87, pp. 1–34.

Saari, J. (2001). *Reforming Social Policy: A Study of Institutional Change in Finland*. Helsinki: Social Policy Association.

Salminen, K. (1993). *Pension Schemes in the Making: A Comparative Study of the Scandinavian Countries*. Studies, 1993:2. Helsinki: The Central Pension Security Institute.

Salonen, T. (1994). *Margins of Welfare*. Torna Hällestad: Hällestad Press.

Sarstrand Marekovic, A.-M. (2010). "Swedish Education or Mother Tongue Training?". In: Hort, S. E. O. (eds.) (2010). *From Linnaeus to the Future(s) – Letters from afar*. Kalmar and Växjö: Linnaeus University Press.

Sarstrand Marekovic, A-M. (2011). *Från invandrarbyrå till flyktingmottagning: Fyrtio års arbete med invandrare och flyktingar på kommunal nivå*. Lund: Arkiv.

Sassoon, D. (1996). *One Hundred Years of Socialism*. London: I. B. Tauris.

SCB (2011). *Finansiärer och utförare inom vård, skola och omsorg 2009*. Series OE29. Stockholm: Statistics Sweden.

SCB (2012). *Population forecasts 2012–60*. Report 2012BE51. Stockholm: Statistics Sweden.

Schierenbeck, I. (2003). *Bakom välfärdstatens dörrar.* Umeå: Borea.

Schierup, C-U.; Hansen, P-O. & Castles, S. (2006). *Migration, Citizenship and the Welfare State.* Oxford: Oxford University Press.

Schierup, C-U., Ålund, A. & Kings, L. (forthc.). "Reading the Riots – Husby, Stockholm 2013, and the new movement for social justice". *Race & Class* (accepted for publication).

Schmitter, P. (2012). "Classifying an Anomaly". *New Left Review,* Second Series, no. 73, pp. 19–27.

Schubert, K.; Bazant, U. & Heberle, S. (eds.) (2009). *The Handbook of European Welfare Systems.* London: Routledge.

Schumpeter, J. (1943). *Capitalism, socialism and democracy.* London: George Allen & Unwin.

Schyman, G. (1998). *Människa kvinna mamma älskarinna partiledare.* Stockholm: Fischer & Co.

Scott, J. C. (2009). *The art of not being governed.* New Haven: Yale University Press.

Sejersted, F. (2005). *Socialdemokratins tidsålder.* Nora: Nya Doxa.

Selberg, R. (2010). "Why some nurses cry". In: Hort, S. E. O. (eds.) (2010). *From Linnaeus to the Future(s) – Letters from afar.* Kalmar and Växjö: Linnaeus University Press.

Shonfield, A. (1965). *Modern Capitalism.* Oxford: Oxford University Press.

Sipilä, J. (ed.) (1997). *Social Care Services: The key to the Scandinavian Welfare Model.* Aldershot: Ashgate.

Sjöberg, O.; Palme, J. & Carroll, E. (2010). "Unemployment Insurance". In: Castles, F. G. et al. (eds.) (2010). *The Oxford Handbook of the Welfare State.* Oxford: Oxford University Press.

Skatteverket (2011). *Statistisk årsbok.* Stockholm: National Tax Authority.

SKL (2005). *Ett granskande samhälle. Kommunerna och revisionen.* Stockholm: Sveriges Kommuner och Landsting.

Skocpol, T. (1995). *Protecting Soldiers and Mothers: The political origins of social policy in the United States.* Cambridge: Harvard University Press.

Skovedal Lindén, T. (2009). *Whose idea? Family policy in Germany and Norway and the role of international organizations.* Bergen: Universitetet i Bergen.

Slezkine, Y. (2005). *The Jewish Century.* Princeton: Princeton University Press.

Sommestad, L. (1998). "Human Reproduction and the Rise of the Welfare States". *Scandinavian Economic History Review,* vol. 46, no. 2, pp. 97–116.

Son, A. (2002). *Social Policy and Health Insurance in South Korea and Taiwan: A Comparative Historical Approach.* Uppsala: Acta Universitatis Upsaliensis.

Sparks, S. (1995). *Privatization of social services: Home-help in three Swedish municipalities.* Stockholm International Studies 95:2. Stockholm: Stockholm University.

SSA (1939–, various volumes). *Social Security Programs Throughout the World.* Washington D C: Social Security Administration (from 1939 onwards on two to three year basis).

Stark, A. (1997). "Combating the Backlash: How Swedish Women Won the War". In: Oakley, A. & Mitchell, J. (eds.) (1997). *Who's Afraid of Feminism? Seeing through the Backlash.* London: Penguin.

Statskontoret (2010). *Urban utveckling.* Stockholm: National Agency for Public Management.

Statskontoret (2011a). *Den offentliga sektorns utveckling: En samlad redovisning 2011.* Stockholm: National Agency for Public Management.

Statskontoret (2011b). *Tänk till om tillsynen: Om utformningen av statlig tillsyn.* Stockholm: National Agency for Public Management.

Statskontoret (2011c). *Fristående utvärderingsmyndigheter: En förvaltningspolitisk trend.* Stockholm: National Agency for Public Management.

Statskontoret (2012a). *Lagen om valfrihetssystem: Hur påverkar den kostnader och effektivitet i kommunerna?* Stockholm: National Agency for Public Management.

Statskontoret (2012b). *Vad händer i den offentliga sektorn: En översikt över utvecklingen 2000–2011*. Stockholm: National Agency for Public Management.

Statskontoret (2013). *Stärk kedjan! Erfarenheter från tjugo analyser av statlig styrning och organisering*. Stockholm: National Agency for Public Management.

Steinmo, S. (2010). *The Evolution of Modern States: Sweden, Japan and the United States*. Cambridge: Cambridge University Press.

Stenius, H. (1997). "The Good Life is a Life of Conformity: The Impact of Lutheran Tradition on Nordic Political Culture". In: Sørensen, Ø. & Stråth, B. (eds.) (1997). *The Cultural Construction of Norden*. Oslo: Scandinavian University Press.

Stigendal, M. (2012). "Segregation som blev utanförskap". *Invandrare och minoriteter*, no. 1, pp. 5–9.

Strand, D. (1982). *En socialdemokrats död*. Stockholm: Norstedts.

Streeck, W. & Schmitter, P. (1985). "Community, market, state - and associations? The prospective contribution of interest governance to social order". *European Sociological Review*, vol. 1, no 2, pp. 119–138.

Ström, S. (2002). *A Shared Experience: Studies on Families and Unemployment*. Stockholm: Swedish Institute for Social Research.

Ståhlberg, A.-C. (1997). "Sweden: On the way from standard to basic security?". In: Clasen, J. (ed.) (1997). *Social Insurance in Europe*. London: Policy Press.

Ståhlberg, A.-C. (2009). "Coping with Demographic Ageing in Sweden: The Role of Defined Contribution Schemes". In: Stewart, J. and Hughes, G. (eds.) (2009). *Personal Provision of Retirement Income Meeting the Needs of Older People?* Aldershot: Edward Elgar.

Stephanson, A. (2010). "The Philosopher's Island". *New Left Review*, Second Series, no. 61, pp. 197–210.

Sulkunen, P.; Tigerstedt, C.; Sutton, C. & Warenius, K. (eds.) (2000). *Broken Spirits: Power and Ideas in Nordic Alcohol Control*. Helsinki: Nordic Council for Alcohol and Drug Research.

Sundbom, L. & Sidebäck, G. (1984). *Agents of Change*. Paper presented at the ECPR, Joint session of workshops, Barcelona.

Sunesson, S. et al. (1998). "The Flight from Universalism". In: *European Journal of Social Work*, vol. 1, no. 1, pp. 19–29.

Supiot. A. (2012). "Under Eastern Eyes". *New Left Review*, Second Series, no. 73, pp. 29–36.

Sutton, C. (1996). *The Swedish Alcohol Discourse*. Stockholm International Studies 96:2. Stockholm: International Graduate School.

Svallfors, S. (ed.) (2007). *The Political Sociology of the Welfare State: Institutions, Social Cleavages, and Orientations*. Stanford: Stanford University Press.

Svallfors, S. (2011). "A Bedrock of support? Trends in welfare state attitudes in Sweden, 1981–2010". *Social Policy and Administration*, vol. 45, no. 7, pp. 806–825.

Svedberg, L.; von Essen, J. & Jernemalm, M. (2010). *Svenskarnas ideella engagemang är större än någonsin: Insatser i och utanfor föreningslivet*. Stockholm: Ersta Sköndal University College.

Svegfors, M. (2013). "Spridda anteckningar om en utredning". In: Hort, S. E. O. (ed.) (2013). *På cykeltur genom livet: En vänbok till Gunnar Wetterberg*. Stockholm: Atlantis.

Sveland, M. (2011). *Bitterbitch*. London: Corsair.

Svenning, O. (1979). *Första halvlek*. Stockholm: Tiden.

Svensson, P. (2013). "Historieätarna – Striden om den nordiska modellen". *Arena*, vol. 20, no. 1.

Swedish Church (2009). "Weddings and Marriages." Letter to the Church of England. Uppsala: Swedish Church.

Swedish government (1996). *Cutting Unemployment in Half*. Stockholm: Prime Minster's Office.

Swedish government (2006). *Statement of Government*. 6 October. Stockholm: Prime Minister's Office.

Szebehely, M. (2011). "Insatser för äldre och funktionshindrade i privat regi". In: Hartman, L. (ed.) *Konkurrensens konsekvenser: Vad händer med svensk välfärd?* Stockholm: SNS.

Sörbom, A. & Wennerhag, M. (2012). "Individualization, Life Politics and the Reformulation of Social Critique: An Analysis of the Global Justice Movement". *Current Sociology*, vol. 39 no. 3, pp. 453–478

Tarschys, D. (2010). "Policy Metrics under scrutiny: The legacy of new public management". In: Joas, H. & Klein, B. (eds.) (2010). *The Benefit of Broad Horizons: Intellectual and Institutional preconditions for a Global Social Sciences. Festschrift for Björn Wittrock on the occation of his 65ᵗʰ Birthday*. Leiden and Boston: Brill.

Therborn, G. (2004). *Between Sex and Power: Family in the World 1900-2000*. London: Routledge.

Therborn, G. (2012). "Class in the 21ˢᵗ century". *New Left Review*, no. 78, pp. 5–29.

Therborn, G. & Khondker, H. H. (eds.) (2006). *Asia and Europe in Globalization: Continents, Regions, Nations*. Leiden: Brill.

Tilly, C. (1998). *Durable Inequality*. Berkeley: University of California Press.

Tomasson, R. F. (1970). *Sweden: Prototype of Modern Society*. New York: Random House.

Tripp, A. M. (2000). "Letter from Finland". *The Nation*, vol. 270, no. 14, pp. 20–22.

Turner, D. (2010). "The Swedish module". *Financial Times*. 24 May.

Unger, R. M. (1997). *Politics: The Central Texts*. London: Verso.

Urban, S. (2005). *Att ordna staden: Den nya storstadspolitiken växer fram*. Lund Studies in Social Welfare, no. 24. Lund: Arkiv.

Uusitalo, P. (1984). "Monetarism, Keynesianism and the Institutional Status of Central Banks". *Acta Sociologica*, vol. 27, no. 1, pp. 31–50.

Wahl, F. (2011). *The Rise and Fall of the Welfare State*. London: Zed/Pluto.

Weir, M. (1991). "Book review: Social Policy and Welfare State in Sweden by Sven E. Olsson". *American Journal of Sociology*, vol. 97, no. 2, pp. 543–545.

Wennerhag, M. (2008). *Den globala rättviserörelsen och modernitetens omvandlingar*. Stockholm: Atlas.

Wetterberg, G. (1994). "Jordbrukets dyra vägval". In: Wetterberg, G. (1994). *Historien upprepar sig aldrig*. Stockholm: SNS

Wetterberg, G. (2009). *Money and Power: From Stockholm Banco 1656 to Sveriges Riksbank today*. Stockholm: Atlantis.

Wetterberg, G. (2010). *The United Nordic federation*. Tema Nord 2010:583. Copenhagen: Nordiska Ministerrådet.

Wijkström, F. & Lundström, T. (1997). *The Non-profit Sector in Sweden*. Manchester: Manchester University Press.

Wilensky, H. L. (1975). *The Welfare State and Equality*. Berkeley: University of California Press.

Wilensky, H. (2002). *Rich Democracies: Political Economy, Public Policy and Performance*. Berkeley: University of California Press.

Williams, R. (1976). *Keywords*. London: Fontana.

Wong, J. (2004). *Healthy Democracies: Welfare Politics in Taiwan and South Korea*. Ithaca: Cornell University Press.

Woo, M. (ed.) (2007). *Neoliberalism and Institutional Reform in East Asia: A Comparative Study*. London: Palgrave.

Yeung, A. B. (ed.) (2006). *Churches in Europe as Agents of Welfare: The cases of Denmark, Finland, Norway and Sweden*. Uppsala: Diakonivetenskapliga institutet.

Zakharov, N. (2013). *Attaining Whiteness: A Sociological Study of Race and Racialisation in Russia*. Uppsala: Department of Sociology.

Zetterberg, H. L. (1967). "Sweden – A Land of Tomorrow?". In: Wizelius, I. (ed.) (1967). *Sweden in the Sixties*. Stockholm: Almqvist & Wiksell.

Zetterberg, H. L. (1995). *Before and Beyond the Welfare State*. Stockolm: City University Press.

Zetterberg, H. L. (2009/10). *The Many-Splendored Society*, vols. 1 and 2. Scotts Valley: Createspace.

Žižek, S. (2011). *Living in the End Times*. London Verso.

Žižek, S. (2012). *Less than nothing: Hegel and the shadow of dialectical materialism*. London: Verso.

Åkerman, S. & Springfeldt, P. (1995). "The Modern Family and the New Baby Boom: Population Change in Sweden". In: Åkerman, S. & Granatstein, J. (eds.) (1995). *Welfare States in Trouble*. Umeå: Swedish Science Press.

Åmark, K. (2005). *Hundra år av välfärdspolitik: Välfärdsstatens framväxt i Norge och Sverige*. Umeå: Borea.

Östberg, K. (2009). *När vinden vände: Olof Palme*. Stockholm: Carlsson.

Österberg, E. (1993). "Vardagens sträva samförstånd: Bondepolitik i den svenska modellen från vasatid till frihetstid". In: Broberg, G. et al. (eds.) (1993). *Tänka, tycka, tro*. Stockholm: Carlsson.

Österlee, A. & Rothgang, H. (2010). "Long-Term Care". In: Castles, F. G. et al. (eds.) (2010). *The Oxford Handbook of the Welfare State*. Oxford: Oxford University Press.

Acknowledgements

Without Rebecca's encouragement and support, this project would still be several years from completion. Ever since her late student days, she has been my most creative, consistent and regular critic, challenging and constructive discussion partner, provider of significant information – plus much besides that has made life both enjoyable and endurable. Most crucially, she never forgot to remind me of deadlines. These and many other things were overheard by Josia and Jacob, in recent years mostly by Zackarias, which exposed them early on to the subjects of public administration, academic education, and social welfare in Sweden and elsewhere. Rich and abundant inputs from their own worlds of education, joy and practical learning are duly acknowledged.

This afterword has had a long gestation period since the second edition of *Social Policy and Welfare State in Sweden* went out of print in the late 1990s. Again, I would like to thank all those, Patrick Hort in particular, who were mentioned in the foreword to the original volume, written in February 1990, and not amended in the 1993 edition. A special thanks to Agnete, my mother-in-law, always there to give a helping hand, at the time included in the foreword's "clan" to which her great-granddaughter has now also belonged for almost a year. Over time, moreover, from our native land – former East Denmark or Scania – my sister Anna-Greta, active in civil society for many years, has been a most valuable informant.

Between these editions I had the good fortune to collaborate with Göran Therborn and his colleagues at the Department of Sociology at Göteborg University, and with Gunnar Wetterberg and his associates in the medium-term survey at the Ministry of Finance in Stockholm. Both environments were truly inspirational, and a separate "thank you" to both of them is long overdue. I have continued to work with Göran, most recently as parts of the editorial team of *European Societies* (*ES*, journal of the European Sociological Association), and his generous collaboration is much appreciated. Furthermore, for most of my life Gunnar has continuously shared his candid views on both contemporary and historical issues, which I sincerely enjoy.

There are also a number of other friends who have helped out during these decades of walking in the wilderness of social inquiry. In particular Olli Kangas and Sten-Åke Stenberg are fondly remembered from the days of coding – "quick and dirty" – at the Swedish Institute for Social Research. So too are students at IGS among them in particular Sang-Hoon Ahn, Daniel Cohn, Mike Eglinski, Dave Lewis, Susanne McMurphy, Samantha Sparks and Anette Soon. And Claes Ramel, once at the Stockholm University Department of Sociology.

Colleagues, students and friends at Lund, Stockholm, Göteborg, Berkeley, Bergen, Mälardalen, Södertörn, Uppsala and Linnaeus universities have provided substantial insights over the years, commenting diligently on nascent drafts of papers written in the small hours, and on top of the usual workload at centres of tertiary mass education (Bergen and UCB excepted, most recently SNU as well). Input has also come from a number of persons I have talked with in government – particularly at the two National Audit Offices (both the old RRV and "3R") – and civil society, above all during my nine years on the Research and Development Committee of the National Association of Local Authorities, and my six years of evaluating the Metropolitian Development Project. The evaluation team, professionally administered by Anna Ålund, and a group of doctoral students in sociology in Flemingsberg made life easier during a turbulent time when report after report had to be written, printed and communicated to the public, along with the administrative routines and academic course load at this newly established Swedish Haarvaard and the start-up of its Baltic and East European Graduate School. Recently, a new cohort of graduate students have added value to this undertaking. At Södertörn, Apostolis Papakostas as well as Jolanta Aidukaite, Peter Bötker, Lisa Kings, Zhanna Kravchenko, Jonas Lindström, Daniel Lindvall, Dominika Polanska, and Nikolay Zakharov were genuinely inspirational colleagues. Jolanta was the first to encourage me to delve into the rebuilding of the Baltic and East European welfare states, and Zhanna has persistently continued to do the same. Lisa Kings made me aware of the growing urban civil society research literature, and if this afterword in any meaning is a "defence of the local(s)" it is not least thanks to her, Apostolis, and Jessica Hansen, Linnaeus University, who showed me her Hovmantorp between Växjö and Kalmar in South-eastern Sweden.

Special thanks are overdue to everyone at Linnaeus who helped real-ize *Mellan hantverk och profession: Samhällsvetenskap på klassisk grund,* and *From Linnaeus to the Future(s) – letters from afar,* the latter book prepared for the 2010 XVII World Congress of Sociology in Göteborg (and later cited with approval by "the most dangerous philosopher in the West"; Žižek 2011:479). In Växjö, good food at PM and after work-conversations with Rolf Granér, Boel Lindberg and Svante Lundberg made the evenings all too short. From the start of the ES-team and throughout its tenure, Ola Agevall has made a difference. Furthermore, at a sociology seminar at Linnaeus, as discussant of chapter 2 above, another Rebecca, Selberg, also made a difference.

In particular, Neil Gilbert and Stein Kuhnle kept me going in this global research area, and their support is much appreciated. So also did several others who like Stein were members of Peter Flora's original north-west European welfare state team (France gone, Maurizio's Italy not forgotten), some of them joined Neil's various teams, and later many friends from East and South-East Asia. In this context of dis-tant friends, Rosmari Eliasson-Lappalainen, Ali Hajighasemi, Adolphe Lawson, and Anders Stephanson should also be mentioned as signifi-cant others and sources of inspiration.

Closer to home, AnnChristin and Bo Rothstein and, of course, Katinka Hort provided serious yet joyful company and were invaluable informants, lecturers and discussion partners whenever we met. So too Ann-Sofie Östling and Joakim Palme, Vällingby neighbours for more than a decade and, in Joakim's case, a workmate during the previous decade. The last five were truly Swedish "competence-raisers".

Three other long-time thought-provoking friends are the founding editor of Baltic Worlds, Anders Björnsson, who opened his pages for my occasional poems, and Sara Danius and Barbro Lagergren who sug-gested readings I would otherwise have most likely never digested.

Together with Rebecca, the first to visit me in Seoul were Christina and Christian Andersson, and Maria Knutsson, creating a domestic atmosphere and challenging a number of premature assumptions about imagined communities for which I thank them wholeheartedly.

In Korea and at Seoul National University there was a warm and welcoming atmosphere. SNU President Yeon-Cheon Oh generously invited me for lunch at Hoam. At the college, dean Yang Seung Mock and his associate deans kindly shared their time with the newcomer solving academic-cum-administrative hurdles. Emerita Sang-Kyun Kim and Sung-Jae Choi, as well as the current members of the social welfare department Tae-Sung Kim, Heung-Seek Cho, Hye-Lan Kim, Bong Joo Lee, Sang-Hoon Ahn, Inhoe Ku, Sang-Kyoung Kahng, Baeg Eui Hong, Yoo Joan Paek, and Jung-Hwa Ha provided stimulating, hospitable, and intellectual company. So too did Hye-Kyong Lee (Yonsei university) and Dal-joong Chang (SNU-political science), Kyung-sup Chang (SNU-sociology), Huck-ju Kwon (SNU-GSPA), Inchon Kim and Chulhee Kang (both Yonsei), Sunhyuk Kim and Young Jun Choi (both Korea University), and many others, such as Almedalen visitor and MP Young-ik Kim, and Jiyoung Kim of Seoul Welfare Foundation, who all generously invited me to their home turfs. The first semester with SNU's inquisitive and thoughtful students was another treat to a newcomer.

Bernt Kennerström, my first editor at Arkiv, did a tremendous job in 1990 and 1992–93 which I here belatedly acknowledge. In the spring of 2012, he again read the entire manuscript, came up with a number of perceptive comments, and saved me from fatal errors. This time, David Lindberg and Eva Frisendahl have shared the in-house editorial responsibility, and I am grateful for their patience.

Finally, I would like to thank Paavo Bergman and Gunnar Olofsson for the privilege of working with them for more than four decades. The latter still has to guide me through his beloved Gavra – in Greece. On Vätö in the northern Stockholm, or Roslagen, archipelago I look forward to many summers with Paavo in the vicinity.

None of the above-mentioned people bear any responsibility for the shortcomings of these afterthoughts.

Once again a big hug to Rebecca, Josia, Jacob, Zackarias and the rest of the clan including the "extended Flygars". And lots of love to R.

Seoul, December 2013

Contents of Volume I

Arkiv Academic Press

Arkiv Academic Press is an imprint of the Swedish publishing house Arkiv förlag. For up-to-date information on distribution and available titles, please visit:

www.arkivacademicpress.com

Published books

Ericka Johnson, *Situating Simulators. The Integration of Simulations in Medical Practice* (paperback 2012 [original edition by Arkiv förlag 2004])

Olof Hallonsten (ed.), *In Pursuit of a Promise. Perspectives on the Political Process to Establish the European Spallation Source (ESS) in Lund, Sweden* (paperback 2012)

Rebecca Selberg, *Femininity at Work. Gender, Labour, and Changing Relations of Power in a Swedish Hospital* (paperback 2012)

Sven E O Hort (birth name Olsson), *Social Policy, Welfare State, and Civil Society in Sweden.* Volume I: *History, Policies, and Institutions 1884–1988* (hardcover & paperback 2014, 3rd enlarged edition [1st edition by Arkiv förlag 1990])

Sven E O Hort (birth name Olsson), *Social Policy, Welfare State, and Civil Society in Sweden.* Volume II: *The Lost World of Social Democracy 1988–2015* (hardcover & paperback 2014, 3rd enlarged edition [1st edition by Arkiv förlag 1990])